The Civil Rights Movement

Other Books in the Turning Points Series:

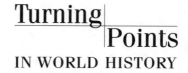

IN WORLD HISTORY

The Civil Rights Movement

Paul A. Winters, *Book Editor*

David L. Bender, *Publisher*
Bruno Leone, *Executive Editor*
Bonnie Szumski, *Editorial Director*
David M. Haugen, *Managing Editor*

Greenhaven Press, Inc., San Diego, California

Library of Congress Cataloging-in-Publication Data

The civil rights movement / Paul A. Winters, book editor.
        p.   cm. — (Turning points in world history)
    Includes bibliographical references and index.
    ISBN 0-7377-0217-6 (lib. bdg. : alk. paper). —
ISBN 0-7377-0216-8 (pbk. : alk. paper)
    1. Afro-Americans—Civil rights—History—20th century.
2. Civil rights movements—United States—History—20th century.
3. United States—Race relations. I. Winters, Paul A., 1965–   .
II. Series: Turning points in world history (Greenhaven Press)
E185.61.C612 2000
323.1'196073—dc21   99-17694
                                                                            CIP

Cover photo: Corbis/Flip Schulke

©2000 by Greenhaven Press, Inc.
P.O. Box 289009, San Diego, CA 92198-9009

Printed in the U.S.A.

Contents

Chapter 1: The Fight for Rights Begins

stead, he developed a black nationalist philosophy that stressed racial pride. His views foreshadowed the transformation of the civil rights movement into a more radical and militant black power movement.

forts failed to unite blacks on the issue and failed to make a dent in discrimination. They did, however, spawn a grassroots movement for fair housing.

The civil rights movement became linked to the anti-Vietnam War movement because the war diverted attention, activists, money, and the commitment of the federal government from the cause of equality for blacks. For these reasons, black leaders consistently spoke out against American involvement overseas.

Chapter 4: The Fight for Rights Continues

In its fight for integration during the civil rights movement, the NAACP failed to anticipate the forms that discrimination would take. It was therefore ineffective in promoting social equality for blacks. The NAACP should adopt a new strategy of litigation against discrimination.

Since the 1960s, the federal policy of affirmative action has required businesses and government agencies to increase job opportunities for minorities and women to compensate for past discrimination. Many people now want to end affirmative action. But blacks are still underrepresented in the workforce.

Thirty years after the Freedom Summer of 1964, blacks in Mississippi face unemployment and black flight from lower-middle-class neighborhoods. But blacks have been successful in securing their right to vote and in exercising their electoral power.

Foreword

Certain past events stand out as pivotal, as having effects and outcomes that change the course of history. These events are often referred to as turning points. Historian Louis L. Snyder provides this useful definition:

> A turning point in history is an event, happening, or stage which thrusts the course of historical development into a different direction. By definition a turning point is a great event, but it is even more—a great event with the explosive impact of altering the trend of man's life on the planet.

History's turning points have taken many forms. Some were single, brief, and shattering events with immediate and obvious impact. The invasion of Britain by William the Conqueror in 1066, for example, swiftly transformed that land's political and social institutions and paved the way for the rise of the modern English nation. By contrast, other single events were deemed of minor significance when they occurred, only later recognized as turning points. The assassination of a little-known European nobleman, Archduke Franz Ferdinand, on June 28, 1914, in the Bosnian town of Sarajevo was such an event; only after it touched off a chain reaction of political-military crises that escalated into the global conflict known as World War I did the murder's true significance become evident.

Other crucial turning points occurred not in terms of a few hours, days, months, or even years, but instead as evolutionary developments spanning decades or even centuries. One of the most pivotal turning points in human history, for instance—the development of agriculture, which replaced nomadic hunter-gatherer societies with more permanent settlements—occurred over the course of many generations. Still other great turning points were neither events nor developments, but rather revolutionary new inventions and innovations that significantly altered social customs and ideas, military tactics, home life, the spread of knowledge, and the human condition in general. The developments of writing, gunpowder, the printing press, antibiotics, the electric light, atomic energy, television, and the computer, the last two of which have recently ushered in the world-altering information age, represent only some of these innovative turning points.

Each anthology in the Greenhaven Turning Points in World History series presents a group of essays chosen for their accessibility. The anthology's structure also enhances this accessibility. First, an introductory essay provides a general overview of the principal events and figures involved, placing the topic in its historical context. The essays that follow explore various aspects in more detail, some targeting political trends and consequences, others social, literary, cultural, and/or technological ramifications, and still others pivotal leaders and other influential figures. To aid the reader in choosing the material of immediate interest or need, each essay is introduced by a concise summary of the contributing writer's main themes and insights.

In addition, each volume contains extensive research tools, including a collection of excerpts from primary source documents pertaining to the historical events and figures under discussion. In the anthology on the French Revolution, for example, readers can examine the works of Rousseau, Voltaire, and other writers and thinkers whose championing of human rights helped fuel the French people's growing desire for liberty; the French *Declaration of the Rights of Man and Citizen*, presented to King Louis XVI by the French National Assembly on October 2, 1789; and eyewitness accounts of the attack on the royal palace and the horrors of the Reign of Terror. To guide students interested in pursuing further research on the subject, each volume features an extensive bibliography, which for easy access has been divided into separate sections by topic. Finally, a comprehensive index allows readers to scan and locate content efficiently. Each of the anthologies in the Greenhaven Turning Points in World History series provides students with a complete, detailed, and enlightening examination of a crucial historical watershed.

Introduction

The modern civil rights movement in America dates from the 1954 Supreme Court decision in the case of *Brown v. Board of Education of Topeka, Kansas*. Prior to that, a few prominent blacks and dedicated groups had challenged discriminatory legal statutes and practices that maintained the inferior status of blacks. But a majority of blacks accommodated themselves to the laws of segregation and the codes of white supremacy that regulated not only the South but all of American society. The *Brown* decision striking down segregation in public schools, and the later success of the Montgomery bus boycott, galvanized ordinary blacks and white activists alike, and marked the end of scattered protest and the beginning of an identifiable movement.

The civil rights movement is important for the rapid advancement blacks gained during a relatively short period, but also significant are the lasting changes it effected in American political processes, legal theories, and governmental policies. Since the 1960s, the federal government and the courts have asserted their power to enforce and uphold the equal rights of all citizens, regardless of disparate state statutes.

Various groups and organizations in the civil rights movement employed different and sometimes incompatible tactics: The most successful early groups filed legal claims, befriended politicians, and lobbied governmental authorities to advance the cause of legal rights. The most vocal groups during the 1950s and 1960s marched, protested, and risked jail to win public sympathy, provoke segregationists, and prod the federal government to enforce civil rights. Some groups sought the assimilation of blacks into mainstream American society. Others sought an independent and equal position within American society for blacks. Some groups adhered to a philosophy of nonviolence. Others advocated retaliation against the racial violence inherent in the system of segregation.

Turning Points in World History: The Civil Rights Movement examines the events of the 1950s and 1960s that led to the abolition of Jim Crow laws and discriminatory practices in the South, from the *Brown* decision to the 1968 assassination of Martin Luther King Jr., as well as the enduring changes in American politics and society. The articles in this volume, selected for readability and content, analyze the historical progression, the underlying causes, and the competing strategies of the movement. They present a variety of perspectives on the leaders, groups, and milestones of this period as well as provide readers a detailed account of events.

Like other titles in the Turning Points series, this volume has many features helpful to the student of history. Each book begins with a historical overview of the subject, and each selection begins with an introduction that summarizes the arguments of the author and explains the historical context of the article. A detailed chronology lists the most significant events, and a selection of primary source documents present additional observations and relevant official excerpts.

Young readers may not be aware of the roles that many contemporary American political leaders played during the civil rights movement. The readings presented here are intended to inform and educate students about this transformative time in American history.

A Brief History of the Civil Rights Movement

Following the Civil War (1861–1865) and the destruction of the confederate South, the United States entered the era of Reconstruction (1865–1877). The country faced two tasks during these years: to reintegrate the secessionist states into the Union and to establish the status of the emancipated slaves. One condition of readmittance to the Union was a state's ratification of the Fourteenth and Fifteenth Amendments to the Constitution, which guaranteed the citizenship and rights of blacks.

The Republican Party dominated the U.S. Congress and presidency throughout this era. Radical Republicans sought to punish the southern states for seceding and starting the war. Consequently, southern whites shunned the Republican Party and the opposing Democratic Party came to dominate southern politics. As southern Democrats gained seats in Congress the radical wing of the Republican Party lost power, and Reconstruction came to an end.

Jim Crow

White supremacy in the South had not been abolished during Reconstruction. At first, vigilante groups such as the Ku Klux Klan used violence and intimidation to prevent blacks from mixing with whites socially, from voting, and from prospering financially. Later, when blacks had been squeezed out of Reconstruction-era state governments, white southerners used legal machinations to bar blacks from political participation, establishing a set of laws and social customs that came to be called Jim Crow.

The term *Jim Crow* is taken from a minstrel show song of the 1830s. It is usually associated with codes of conduct that defined segregation throughout the South. Blacks were not merely limited to living in slums, working in menial jobs, and attending inferior schools. They were not only relegated to separate railroad cars and other public facilities. They were also expected to act in a deferential manner toward whites—particularly toward white women—at all times. They might be required to step aside as whites passed on a public sidewalk, to enter a back door instead of a front entrance, or to remove their hats when speaking to a white person. Failure to observe the code might prompt insults, beatings, and even lynchings.

The Jim Crow system was also enforced by laws that effectively prohibited blacks from registering to vote. These laws included poll taxes, property ownership or residency requirements, and literacy tests. Many states also passed laws making their Democratic Parties private, "whites only" organizations. Since many blacks were poor and landless they were unable to pay the poll taxes or meet the property requirements. And since many blacks were prevented from attending school, they were unable to pass the literacy tests. Those who could manage to clear the monetary hurdles or pass the tests might still be dissuaded from voting by violence or intimidation. Poor and ill-educated whites were exempted from the laws by so-called grandfather clauses—they were allowed to register and vote because their fathers and grandfathers had been eligible to vote.

Jim Crow also permeated the economy. The sharecropping system was one of the most notorious ways in which whites, who owned most of the land, controlled the economic fortunes of blacks. In exchange for the use of farmland, black farmers might have to pay white landowners as much as half of their crop, as well as buy tools and fertilizer with another portion of the crop. And they might also be required to sell the remainder of the crop through the white landowner. The system provided white landowners many opportunities to swindle black farmers.

In addition to the violence, intimidation, and deceit used to enforce racial separation, most racial mores were enshrined in law. Southern state legislatures controlled by white supremacists passed segregation laws on everything from interracial marriages to seating on rail cars. The Supreme Court sanctioned these laws in 1883 when it struck down as unconstitutional the Civil Rights Act of 1875, which had banned discrimination in public accommodations. In little more than a decade, a landmark Supreme Court decision would further reinforce the Jim Crow system.

Plessy v. Ferguson

Homer Plessy was a shoemaker in New Orleans. Following the passage of Louisiana's Separate Car Act in 1890, Plessy and a group of politically active blacks called the Comite des Citoyens decided to test the constitutional basis of the growing number of segregation laws. In June 1892, Plessy boarded a New Orleans train bound for Covington, Louisiana, and sat down in the car designated for whites. As prearranged, he was arrested before the train left the station. His case went before local judge John Howard Ferguson.

Plessy and the Comite argued that the Separate Car Act violated the Fourteenth Amendment, which bars states from making or enforcing laws that abridge the privileges of citizens or deny citizens equal protection under the law. Ferguson ruled that the state of Louisiana had the right to regulate the railroads within its borders to prevent racial mixing. The Fourteenth Amendment guaranteed blacks legal equality, not social equality with whites, he said. Plessy appealed the decision but Louisiana's state supreme court upheld it. Four years passed before the U.S. Supreme Court took up the case.

In 1896 the Supreme Court finally ruled in the case of *Plessy v. Ferguson*, declaring that states were not required to integrate blacks and whites in order to guarantee their equality before the law, and affirming that states could establish separate public facilities for whites as long as equal accommodations were not denied to blacks. This "separate but equal" doctrine allowed segregation to prevail in the South for the next sixty years.

Early Civil Rights Organizations

With segregation firmly established as law, blacks were second-class citizens in the South. The public facilities, such as schools and hospitals, provided them were far inferior to those for whites. Limited economic and social opportunities left blacks continually at a disadvantage. And legal protection for southern blacks was nonexistent. Lynching became a frequent occurrence in the South. Each year on average fifty to sixty black men were hanged, shot, or burned to death, subject to torture and mutilation. Whites did not fear punishment for these crimes because white supremacists controlled the courts and legislatures of the South. Neither did they fear condemnation in the court of public opinion: Southern whites felt harsh punishment of a black person was justified, particularly if the black was accused of rape.

In 1909 social reformers meeting in New York City to organize a crusade against lynching founded the National Association for the Advancement of Colored People (NAACP). Its primary purpose was to provide legal assistance and representation to blacks accused of crimes in the South (though it also established scholarship funds to support the education of talented blacks and award programs to recognize the achievements of blacks). The organization's anti-lynching campaign swayed public opinion, but the NAACP could not persuade Congress to outlaw the continuing atrocities against blacks. With time, however, NAACP leaders gained experience and influence in lobbying Congress, and the organization became a formidable force in the fight against segregation.

The NAACP also fought to overturn restrictions of blacks' voting rights. NAACP lawyers argued cases all the way to the Supreme Court in order to strike down southern voter registration schemes that denied blacks the vote. The grandfather clause was abolished in 1915 in the case of *Guinn v. United States*. The white primary was declared unconstitutional in 1944 in the case of *Smith v. Allwright*. Racially discriminatory electoral districting was struck down in 1957 in the case of *Gomillion v. Lightfoot*. And the poll tax was outlawed by the Twenty-Fourth Amendment, adopted in 1964 and upheld by the Supreme Court in 1966. In addition, the NAACP sued states to force them to improve the funding and conditions of black schools.

Another influential organization was the Brotherhood of

Sleeping Car Porters. In 1925, Asa Philip Randolph breathed new life into this union, organizing black railroad workers to demand better wages and working conditions. Through labor strikes, demonstrations, marches, and court battles, Randolph won recognition of the union and concessions for black railroad workers. Randolph also merged the brotherhood into the American Federation of Labor, pushing integration of that organization and its affiliated labor unions. Blacks gained new job opportunities and increased earnings potential through the labor movement.

When the United States entered World War II in 1941, Randolph was a vocal advocate for expanding opportunities for blacks in the defense industries. He also pressured President Franklin Delano Roosevelt to begin desegregation of the armed forces. This was significant because after the war the newly enacted GI Bill allowed black soldiers to obtain college educations and better economic prospects.

Civil Rights Gains Following World War II

World War II emboldened many blacks to seek change in American race relations. Black soldiers perhaps felt the contradiction most keenly between America's condemnation of Nazism and its toleration of southern prejudice. In a few cases, black soldiers returning from the war received severe beatings at the hands of white mobs in southern cities. White supremacists thought the blacks were acting "uppity" by wearing a military uniform. Reports of violence against U.S. soldiers spurred President Harry S. Truman to take action.

Truman first formed the Committee on Civil Rights to examine race relations in America. In 1947 this committee published a report titled *To Secure These Rights*. The report echoed earlier studies of discrimination against blacks in the United States, including a landmark study of race relations, *An American Dilemma*, published in 1944 by Swedish sociologist Gunnar Myrdal. *To Secure These Rights* called for increased economic opportunities for blacks and federal enforcement of antidiscrimination measures. In 1948 Truman formed the Fair Employment Practices Commission to ensure that blacks were not discriminated against in hiring for federal jobs. He also ordered full desegregation of the armed services.

Truman, a Missouri Democrat, was expected to support a state's right to regulate segregation within its borders. Southern Democrats in Congress considered his actions a betrayal and opposed his nomination as the Democratic candidate for president in 1948. Democrats from southern states calling themselves States' Rights Democrats (nicknamed Dixiecrats) backed South Carolina governor Strom Thurmond as their presidential candidate. Truman won the nomination without southern support, however, and went on to win the presidency, but the conflict over states' rights split the Democratic Party. As this rift developed, the issue of racial discrimination took priority on the national political agenda.

Brown v. Board of Education of Topeka, Kansas

With the change in the federal government's position on race relations, civil rights organizations stepped up the fight against segregation. By the 1940s, the NAACP's Legal Defense Fund (LDF) had become a separate organization. Since the mid-1920s it had attempted to alleviate the conditions of blacks living under segregation through litigation. But in 1950 the fund decided to attack the legal foundations of segregation and challenge *Plessy* itself. The issue of segregated education became the testing ground.

In the 1930s the Legal Defense Fund helped two black men enroll in all-white law schools in states where no black law schools existed. Then in 1950, the LDF won two important cases that dismantled segregation in higher education. The University of Texas Law School had set up separate classrooms and hired teachers for its sole black student, Herman Sweatt. But NAACP lawyers argued that this scheme did not provide Sweatt equal training to become a lawyer. Likewise, in *McLaurin v. Oklahoma State Regents*, the LDF attacked segregation within the classroom. John McLaurin had been admitted to a doctoral program at the University of Oklahoma, but he was forced to sit in a special "colored" section for all of his classes. The Supreme Court ruled that this type of separation denied McLaurin an equal educational opportunity. In its ruling, the Court said the segregation of schools was unconstitutional if the quality of education was unequal.

These cases laid the groundwork to overturn the *Plessy* ruling. In 1954 the Legal Defense Fund brought before the Supreme Court the case that finally undermined the legal basis of segregation. *Brown v. Board of Education of Topeka, Kansas*, was actually a collection of cases attacking segregation in grade schools. The nominal plaintiff, Linda Brown, was a Topeka, Kansas, youngster who had been forced to ride a bus across town to attend an all-black school, even though she lived closer to a white school. Brown's co-plaintiffs included parents in Washington, D.C., including the parents of Spottswood Bolling, who protested overcrowded conditions in the capital's black schools in the case of *Bolling v. Sharpe*. In *Briggs v. Clarendon County*, Harry Briggs and other black parents sued over underfunding of black schools in their South Carolina community.

The NAACP lawyers presented evidence that the second-rate conditions of black schools fostered feelings of inferiority among the young students. They asserted that separate schools could never be equal and that the practice of racial segregation in public education was therefore unconstitutional under the Fourteenth Amendment. The Supreme Court agreed with the LDF's arguments, ruling that states must integrate their schools in order to provide equal educational opportunities to all students. The justices unanimously decided that *Plessy* contradicted the Fourteenth Amendment's guarantee of legal equality for all citizens. After hearing further arguments in the next term, in 1955 the court ordered that all states proceed to desegregate their schools "with all deliberate speed."

The Southern Manifesto

Blacks were heartened by the *Brown* ruling, but many recognized that change would come slowly. While some states and communities quietly began to comply with the Supreme Court order, staunchly segregationist states noisily denounced the ruling. Immediately after the decision was announced, white supremacists in Indianola, Mississippi, formed a so-called citizens council to resist desegregation and other civil rights measures. Similar citizens councils appeared in communities throughout the South, attempting to hold the line on separation of the races. A few southern states outlawed the National Association for the Advancement of Colored People and barred public employees (including teachers) from holding membership in the organization.

The intense anti-integrationist sentiment in the Deep South turned violent in early 1956. With a Supreme Court decision in her favor, black college student Autherine Lucy gained admittance to the all-white University of Mississippi in Jackson. Her arrival at the campus, however, precipitated riots among students and local citizens. The university quickly expelled Lucy, saying that integration was too great a threat to public order to be implemented.

Bolstered by public sentiment in their home states and stiffened in their resolve by the violence in Mississippi, segregationist southern politicians urged massive resistance to the *Brown* decision. In March 1956, representatives and senators from a number of southern states issued the Declaration of Principles—the so-called Southern Manifesto—denouncing the Supreme Court order as a breach of states' rights. The manifesto called on state officials and courts to disavow the Brown decision, stating that the high Court overreached its authority. It laid out the strategy for southern states to delay the end of Jim Crow.

In defiance of the Supreme Court order, many southern officials continued to bar blacks from white schools and other segregated facilities. They cited the likelihood of violence and their inability to prevent it as a reason to delay implementation of school integration. They allowed white students to transfer to private schools—and funded these schools with public money—to preserve all-white educational opportunities. They also attempted to allow students to "freely" choose a school to attend, believing that children of both races would elect to remain segregated. And in some cases they closed public schools to avoid integration. It would take many years and many more lengthy court battles to invalidate the schemes that southern states put in place to obstruct integration.

The Montgomery Bus Boycott

Meanwhile, growing numbers of young and middle-class blacks were losing patience with the lagging pace of civil rights progress. They were dismayed not only by southern resistance to court-ordered desegregation but also by the federal government's unwillingness to compel compliance. In December 1955, blacks in Montgomery, Alabama, seized a unique opportunity to force the issue.

On December 1, 1955, Rosa Parks was arrested on a Montgomery bus for refusing to obey an ordinance requiring blacks to sit in a designated "colored" section to the rear of the bus while whites sat in a "whites only" section at the front of the bus. The law also allowed bus drivers to expand the "whites only" section so that all whites could sit, even if blacks were forced to stand. On this occasion, Parks refused to vacate her seat when it was redesignated as a "whites only" seat, and she was promptly arrested for disturbing the peace. Because Parks was a secretary for the local NAACP office, word of her arrest spread quickly.

The Montgomery NAACP chapter had been waiting for a case to take to court to challenge the bus segregation laws. Other blacks had been arrested for defying the law, but NAACP leaders recognized that Parks would be a most sympathetic defendant. At the same time, other local activists had been looking for an occasion to stage a boycott of the city buses, where segregation was particularly rankling to many people. A few teachers quickly called for a one-day strike against the bus line, asking blacks to stay at home or find an alternate way to get to work. The success of this one-day action convinced Montgomery civil rights leaders to organize a full-scale boycott of the buses.

The organizers decided that the most effective way to gain support and spread the word in the black community was to enlist the help of local ministers and church leaders. They established the Montgomery Improvement Association (MIA) to coordinate the boycott and appointed the Reverend Martin Luther King Jr. its president. The MIA arranged a system of carpools and taxis to take blacks to their jobs and home again, and it managed to sustain the boycott for a full year.

King and the other MIA leaders attempted to negotiate with Montgomery city leaders and bus line officials to abandon the policy of forcing blacks to vacate their seats for whites. They demanded that the bus lines hire black drivers and establish more stops in black neighborhoods. The bus company protested that they were only obeying the state laws. City leaders and segregationists, for their part, tried to intimidate the taxi drivers and outlaw the carpools. They also tried to discredit King in order to split the black community. Meanwhile, the boycott continued and the buses remained largely unoccupied.

The Southern Christian Leadership Conference

Finally, in November 1956 the Supreme Court ruled in Parks's case, ordering the state of Alabama to desegregate its buses. The city of Montgomery complied with the order, and the MIA called an end to the strike. Civil rights leaders in other cities emulated the boycott tactic and scored a few comparable victories against segregation laws. In Birmingham, though, segregationists fought back by bombing the home of local minister Fred Shuttlesworth.

The momentum gained by the MIA led to the founding of the Southern Christian Leadership Conference (SCLC) in January 1957. The SCLC's mission was to rally and redirect the resources and leadership of the churches into the growing movement for civil rights. King, as the SCLC's first president, advocated the principles and tactics of nonviolent resistance to white supremacy. He believed that the suffering of blacks under Jim Crow was redemptive, that segregation was evil, and that Christian people and the churches had a duty to fight bigotry and discrimination. The philosophy of nonviolence influenced the course of protests throughout the movement.

The Federal Government Takes Action

The success of the Montgomery boycott established the course for the civil rights movement. Groups such as the

NAACP continued to fight in courts and to lobby Congress and the president to advance civil rights for blacks. But other civil rights activists began to look for ways to directly protest segregation and to force integration. Meanwhile, segregationists became more obstinate in their resistance to civil rights progress. The next clash in the growing civil rights movement occurred in Little Rock, Arkansas.

As the school year began in the fall of 1957, local NAACP activists recruited young black students to enroll in all-white Little Rock Central High School. Nine student volunteers attempted to enter the school on the first day of classes, September 4. But they found their way blocked not only by jeering white students and angry parents but also by Arkansas National Guardsmen. Governor Orval Faubus had called out the troops to keep order and to prevent the black students from entering the school grounds. When the students were finally allowed to attend classes a few days later, a riot broke out at the school. The crisis continued for nearly three weeks as the threat of violence prevented the students from going to their classes.

President Dwight D. Eisenhower pressured Faubus to stop the threats of violence and allow the young blacks to attend the high school. Eisenhower had recently won passage of the Civil Rights Act of 1957, which created the Civil Rights Commission. This was the first civil rights legislation passed since Reconstruction, and it empowered the federal government to file lawsuits against state and county officials who violated the voting rights of black citizens. Eisenhower did not want the situation in Little Rock to mar this progress. But when Faubus refused to end the crisis, Eisenhower ordered troops from the army's 101st Airborne Division to cordon off the school and escort the young black students to their classes. This was the first time since Reconstruction that federal troops had been deployed in a southern state.

Eisenhower's action reassured movement activists, who had lobbied for the federal government to actively uphold civil rights for blacks. It also angered southerners, who rallied behind segregationist politicians. But in 1960 Eisenhower won further legislation, signing the Civil Rights Act of 1960. This law authorized federal judges to appoint referees to oversee southern elections and ensure that blacks were permitted to vote. Though the law was severely limited in its scope and effect, it demonstrated the federal government's commitment to end systematic discrimination in southern political life.

The Sit-Ins

Many younger blacks, who had been inspired by the *Brown* decision and the events in Montgomery, were now frustrated by the incremental rate of progress in school desegregation and the limited scope of civil rights reforms. College students eagerly joined the movement as it gained momentum. Influenced by the philosophy of nonviolence preached by King and other leaders, they adopted a new tactic to protest segregation. As early as 1957, young blacks had staged sit-ins at segregated lunch counters, hotels, movie theaters, libraries, parks, and other public places. But in February 1960, one particular sit-in captured the nation's attention.

In Greensboro, North Carolina, four black students from nearby North Carolina A&T staged an impromptu sit-in at the "whites only" lunch counter of the Woolworth's department store. Over the course of their two-month-long protest they were joined at the lunch counter by dozens of other students, black and white. Spurred by news of the events in Greensboro, college students across the South staged similar protests. The goal of these sit-ins was to disrupt the business activities of segregated establishments and to demonstrate that such businesses profited as much from black customers as from whites.

Most of these protests were well organized, particularly those in Nashville, Tennessee, where volunteers were schooled in the tactics of nonviolent resistance by James Lawson. The sit-in participants were taught to remain calm even as crowds of angry whites taunted them with racial epithets and threw food at them or jostled them. They were also taught to remain passive when they were arrested for disturbing the peace. But the demonstrators resolutely continued the protests, and they succeeded in convincing many businesses throughout the northernmost states of the South to remove "whites only" and "colored" signs.

The success of the sit-in campaign led to the formation of the Student Nonviolent Coordinating Committee (SNCC), which reached out to students and young people across America. The energetic members of the SNCC were very active in organizing protests and demonstrations throughout the South, but they were not as skilled at fund-raising as the more established civil rights organizations. Consequently, SNCC relied on groups such as the SCLC and the NAACP to pay bail and court costs when students were arrested at the frequent protests. The arrangement caused friction between the groups, particularly since SNCC gained a great deal of press attention for its actions but SCLC and NAACP garnered most of the credit for civil rights progress.

The Freedom Rides

The Student Nonviolent Coordinating Committee was also involved in the next major protest of the movement. A December 1960 Supreme Court decision in the case of *Boynton v. Virginia*, which struck down segregation in bus and railroad terminals, provided the spark for the demonstrations. This ruling capped a series of cases dismantling segregation laws on buses and trains. The Congress on Racial Equality (CORE) initiated a series of so-called Freedom Rides in May 1961 to dramatize the continued practice of enforced discrimination in public facilities and transportation throughout the South.

CORE's idea was to send two buses with blacks and whites riding together from Washington, D.C., to New Orleans. At rest stops and restaurants along the way, the white passengers would attempt to use "colored" restrooms and lounges while the blacks would try the "whites only" facilities. The riders were met with public hostility and police harassment at every stop, even though they had informed law enforcement authorities of their plan in advance. But in Anniston, Alabama, they faced greater danger. There, one of the buses was forced off the road by a mob. The crowd set the bus on fire and beat the riders as they fled the bus.

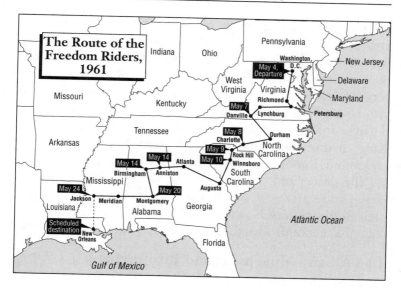

The Route of the Freedom Riders, 1961

The other bus continued on to Birmingham, where it arrived on Mothers' Day 1961. As the riders left the bus, they were violently attacked by a crowd of whites—men, women, and children. Police waited blocks away as the crowd viciously battered several of the Freedom Riders. One of the riders was beaten into a coma and left paralyzed. Stunned by the violence, CORE's leader, James Farmer, decided to call off the Freedom Rides. But SNCC volunteers then jumped in, hiring a bus in Nashville and heading for Alabama.

When the SNCC riders arrived in Birmingham, they were at once taken into police custody, ostensibly for their own protection. They were then driven back across the border to Tennessee in the middle of the night by Birmingham sheriff Eugene "Bull" Connor. Undaunted, they returned to Birmingham, but they found that they could not leave, because no bus driver could be found to continue the dangerous and controversial trip. They remained at the terminal several days, attempting to negotiate with Greyhound officials and the police to allow the continuation of the Freedom Rides. The rides finally did resume, but only when it was guaranteed that the buses would be escorted along their route by a convoy of law enforcement personnel.

Outside of Montgomery, Alabama, the state police escort abandoned the Freedom Riders' buses. When the riders debarked at the Montgomery bus terminal, they were attacked by another mob that bloodied the riders—along with an observer from the U.S. Department of Justice, Civil Rights Division—and once again, police stood by. After several days, during which the riders unsuccessfully tried to convince King to join them, the Freedom Riders continued on to Jackson, Mississippi. There, they were arrested for disturbing the peace, and many were sentenced to several months in the state prison at Parchman. The riders never reached their destination of New Orleans. But other volunteers conducted Freedom Rides throughout the South that year.

The Albany Movement and Birmingham

In November 1961, black citizens of Albany, Georgia, launched a series of demonstrations for voting rights and desegregation. In mid-December, Martin Luther King Jr. and other members of the Southern Christian Leadership Conference arrived to support the Albany movement. With SCLC aid, participants conducted marches, sit-ins, and other protests. Albany police made thousands of arrests. When Albany's jail was filled, the police shipped detainees to available jails in other cities. But when they arrested King, they faced a dilemma.

King vowed to stay in jail until the city met protesters' demands for integration. Police and white leaders knew that King could attract the attention and sympathy of the American public. And they knew he might draw support and involvement from the federal government. City leaders promised reforms and King called off his protest. But the city never carried out the reforms. The Albany movement ended in August 1962 without accomplishing many of its goals.

King and the SCLC next turned to Birmingham, Alabama. In February 1963, black citizens began a civil rights campaign that included marches, sit-ins, and voter registration efforts. Police arrested hundreds of demonstrators. In April, King was once again arrested. While in jail, he composed his famous "Letter from Birmingham Jail," chiding white church leaders for not participating in the civil rights movement and calling the nation's attention to the protests. Events in Birmingham began to gain the attention of the country. President John F. Kennedy stepped in and applied pressure to city leaders to adopt reforms.

In May, Birmingham police used firehoses and dogs to disperse blacks who had lined up to register to vote. The attack on peaceful protesters was televised nationwide on evening news programs and publicized in newspapers. Over the next few days, police arrested approximately three thousand demonstrators and again turned firehoses on marchers—this time schoolchildren. By March 10 city leaders pledged to desegregate restaurants, drinking fountains, and other public facilities. Birmingham marked a turning point in the civil rights movement: A large segment of the American public now favored measures to secure civil rights for blacks, and the federal government seemed committed to action.

The University of Alabama

Kennedy had demonstrated his firm commitment to civil rights the previous September. After a brief legal suit, black student James Meredith had secured a Supreme Court order guaranteeing his admission to the University of Mississippi Law School. The order had set off the worst white supremacist riot of the decade, killing two people. Kennedy had placed the Mississippi National Guard under federal control, ordering them to stop the violence. Mississippi's governor, Ross Barnett, had defiantly opposed this federal intervention.

In June 1963, Kennedy again faced off against a southern governor—Alabama's George Wallace—over desegregation of a state university. Rather than wait for violence to erupt, Kennedy ordered the Alabama National Guard to escort black students James Hood and Vivian Malone onto the campus of the University of Alabama. Wallace stood in the doorway of the university's admissions building and read a defiant statement to the assembled television cameras denouncing federal enforcement of desegregation and civil rights. That night, Kennedy addressed the nation with a televised speech. In the speech, he called segregation morally wrong and pledged to see it end.

The March on Washington

Kennedy introduced civil rights legislation in spring 1963. The new Civil Rights Act promised to ban discrimination in all public accommodations and to strengthen judicial enforcement of voting rights. Civil rights leaders looked for a way to secure passage of the legislation. Many groups—particularly the SCLC and SNCC—wanted to stage mass demonstrations to voice black demands for civil rights. Other more established groups, notably the NAACP, wanted to maintain their lobbying efforts to demonstrate the political strength and acumen of movement leaders. But when labor leader Asa Philip Randolph revived a long-delayed plan for a march on Washington, all the other groups fell in line behind him.

The march was held on August 28, 1963. More than 250,000 people converged on the nation's capital and gathered before the Lincoln Memorial—a symbolic act, since the march coincided with the hundredth anniversary of the Emancipation Proclamation. White church leaders and social activists joined black civil rights leaders in a day of speeches and songs. King delivered his most famous speech, in which he described his dream of an integrated America. The event clearly demonstrated popular support for the goals of the civil rights movement. Legislators felt the pressure for passage of the pending civil rights legislation.

However, less than three weeks after the march a bomb planted at the Sixteenth Street Baptist Church in Birmingham killed four young black girls. The atrocity showed that blacks still had a way to go to overcome white supremacy in the South. Then, in November 1963 the assassination of John F. Kennedy delayed passage of the Civil Rights Act.

Kennedy's successor, Lyndon B. Johnson, fought for a strengthened law that would call for equal employment opportunity as well as nondiscrimination and stronger voting rights guarantees. Johnson, a southerner from Texas, won passage of the legislation and signed it into law in July 1964. Johnson's zeal for federal enforcement of civil rights laws alienated many southern white Democrats. In 1964, George Wallace challenged Johnson for the party's presidential nomination, although he did not fare well in early caucuses. Many southern whites switched allegiance to the Republican Party. Significantly, many blacks had earlier decided that the most effective way to gain political strength in southern states was to join the Democratic Party.

Freedom Summer

With national elections coming up in 1964, civil rights groups focused on registering black voters, particularly in southern states. The Student Nonviolent Coordinating Committee had set up Freedom Schools throughout the South beginning in 1962 to teach local blacks to pass the state voter registration tests. However, southern officials administered the tests in an openly biased manner, preventing blacks from passing the tests. And white supremacists used intimidation to keep most blacks from even trying to take the test. Frustrated by slow progress in the voter registration drives, SNCC conceived a plan to create a desegregated party—the Mississippi Freedom Democratic Party—and challenge the traditional Democratic Party.

Starting in June 1964, SNCC, CORE, and other civil rights workers—under an umbrella group called the Council of Federated Organizations (COFO)—flooded into southern states to register blacks and whites in the newly established party. They recruited volunteers from northern churches and colleges for the Freedom Summer registration drive. COFO organizers gave the students and church members quick training in the philosophy of passive resistance and warned them to expect violence. But at the very start of the campaign, three workers—James Chaney, Andrew Goodman, and Michael Schwerner—were murdered near Philadelphia, Mississippi, by a lynch mob that included a local sheriff. Local officials refused to prosecute the murderers, and a local white supremacist judge—Harold Cox—dismissed federal charges of civil rights violations against the lynch mob members.

After the summer of organizing, in late July 1964 the Freedom Democratic Party challenged the seating of Mississippi delegates at the Democratic National Convention. Before the convention's rules committee it argued that the regular Mississippi delegation was not legitimate because the state Democratic Party had unlawfully excluded blacks from registering and voting. Leaders of the committee, including vice presidential candidate Hubert Humphrey, offered the Freedom Democrats a compromise of two at-large votes at the convention. The all-white Mississippi delegation walked out of the convention in protest of the deal, which the Freedom Democrats rejected as unsatisfactory. When the Freedom Democrats attempted to occupy the seats of the departed delegation, other all-white southern delegations threatened to leave. Convention leaders removed the seats in the Mississippi delegation's designated area and then ejected Freedom Democrats who tried to stand there. The Freedom Democrats succeeded in disrupting the convention, but they failed to effect any permanent voting reforms or to sustain a permanent party organization.

Selma

Many in the civil rights movement were disillusioned by the defeat at the Democratic National Convention and the deaths in Mississippi. Established civil rights groups recognized that the Civil Rights Act passed in July 1964 did not do enough to guarantee blacks the right to vote. These groups began to lobby and demonstrate for voting rights legislation. Other, more radical groups believed that it was necessary to create independent black political organizations and fight for power.

Selma, Alabama, became the focus of peaceful protests. In January 1965, blacks began conducting marches to the Dallas County Courthouse in Selma, lining up to take the voter registration test. None were allowed to take the test, but several thousand were arrested over the ensuing months by Sheriff Jim Clark, an ardent segregationist. Clark and his deputies beat peaceful demonstrators with nightsticks and committed other acts of violence during the arrests. In nearby Marion, Alabama, protesters held similar marches. There in late February a young activist, Jimmie Lee Jackson, was killed in a melee with police and white supremacists. But the federal government failed to intervene in the situation. The demonstrators became frustrated with the situation in Selma. They decided to march to Montgomery, Alabama's capital, to confront Governor Wallace and to demand to be allowed to register.

The Selma to Montgomery march was scheduled for Sunday, March 7. Participants gathered at Brown's Chapel and prepared to walk across the Edmund Pettus Bridge, which led out of town toward Montgomery. At the other end of the bridge, Alabama state troopers ordered the marchers to stop and return to the church. With little warning the troopers advanced on the marchers, shooting tear gas into the crowd and assaulting the demonstrators with nightsticks. Selma police, along with white supremacist groups, attacked the marchers from behind. The attack on the protesters came to be known as Bloody Sunday.

Undaunted by the violence, civil rights groups remained determined to continue the march. The following Tuesday, participants, whose ranks were joined by volunteers from northern churches, again gathered at Brown's Chapel and marched across the bridge. This time, however, they stopped when ordered and returned to the church. That night, one of the northern ministers, James Reeb, was beaten viciously by local white supremacists.

Days later, after Reeb died, President Johnson introduced voting rights legislation in Congress. In his speech, he characterized the violence in Selma and the resistance to civil rights for blacks as a shameful blot on America. He closed the speech by declaring, "We shall overcome"—the rallying cry of the movement.

Led by Martin Luther King Jr., civil rights activists completed the fifty-four-mile Selma to Montgomery march from March 21 to March 25. The marchers received federal protection from nearly four thousand Alabama National Guardsmen, U.S. Army troops, FBI agents, and U.S. marshals (although one participant, Viola Liuzzo, was killed afterward). They were also protected by a federal court order permitting the march to take place. The march culminated with a day of speeches in front of the Alabama capitol. The

U.S. Congress approved Johnson's legislation, the Voting Rights Act of 1965, that August.

Black Power

During the summer following the Selma to Montgomery march, SNCC workers initiated a voter registration project in Lowndes County, Alabama, and assisted local blacks in forming an independent all-black political party, the Lowndes County Freedom Organization. The new party adopted the mascot of a local college and soon came to be known as the Black Panther Party. SNCC workers in Lowndes County also began to carry weapons, betraying the nonviolent philosophy underpinning the movement up to this point. Offshoot Black Panther Parties formed across the country, including the Black Panther Party for Self-Defense in Oakland, California. This group became the most well-known Black Panther organization because it openly advocated retaliation against police violence.

Race riots had occurred in many northern and western cities throughout the 1960s. Harlem and Brooklyn experienced racial violence in July 1964, Chicago in July 1965. But the worst took place in the Watts neighborhood of Los Angeles over the course of five days in August 1965.

Civil rights protesters in the North had always preferred the black nationalist appeal of Malcolm X to the nonviolent teachings of Martin Luther King Jr. Although Malcolm X was assassinated in February 1965, his philosophy gained currency. Groups such as SNCC and the Congress of Racial Equality adopted the slogan of black power by mid-1966. Convinced that whites would never willingly allow blacks to become equal, they proposed that blacks form independent organizations and challenge the power of whites. In December 1966, SNCC excluded whites from membership. In February 1968, SNCC merged with the Black Panther Party, although the coalition did not last.

The Assassination of Martin Luther King Jr.

Racial tension and violence continued to increase across the country throughout the 1960s. Protests against the Vietnam

War contributed to the atmosphere of upheaval and turmoil. In 1968, the Democratic National Convention in Chicago became the backdrop for violent confrontations between police and antiwar and civil rights activists.

But as other groups became more radical, Martin Luther King Jr. and the SCLC maintained the course of peaceful protest and passive resistance. Mainstream civil rights organizations began to address issues of economic inequality in addition to those of social inequality. In 1966, King joined the Chicago movement, leading marches and demonstrations for fair housing. After a year of such protests, the Chicago movement failed to achieve most of its goals. But civil rights leaders successfully lobbied Congress for the Civil Rights Act of 1968, which introduced measures to end discrimination in housing.

In March 1968 King traveled to Memphis, Tennessee, to lead a strike by garbageworkers, most of whom were black, seeking better working conditions and higher wages. He was assassinated there on April 4. His death left the civil rights movement without its most visible and influential leader. But other leaders continued protests, lobbying, and voting drives, seeking equality and social justice for blacks. The civil rights movement has no identifiable endpoint: Since King's death blacks have won elected seats in local, state, and federal governing bodies, both in and outside the South. The federal government has maintained its commitment to ending illegal discriminatory practices and laws. And state and local police have shown a commitment to fighting violence and crime based on racial bias. Civil rights organizations continue to fight for the rights and social equality of blacks. And many other minorities have formed comparable rights organizations and begun similar civil rights drives.

Chapter 1

The Fight for Rights Begins

Turning | Points

IN WORLD HISTORY

Litigation and Political Lobbying

Denton L. Watson

The National Association for the Advancement of Colored People was founded in 1909 to fight discrimination, segregation, and racial violence. It is probably best known as the force behind the 1954 *Brown v. Board of Education* decision, which overturned the "separate but equal" doctrine. But the NAACP also led a successful crusade against the practice of lynching in the South. And it effectively lobbied Congress in support of civil rights legislation.

Despite its successes, the NAACP was ineffective at gaining publicity for itself, according to Denton L. Watson. In this article, Watson compares the strategy and style of Martin Luther King Jr. with that of the NAACP's leaders. King was better at arousing southern blacks and motivating them to participate in marches and demonstrations, which attracted publicity and gained the sympathy of mainstream Americans. The NAACP worked quietly but forcefully through the years to change laws and influence legislation in order to better the lives of blacks. Both strategies were important in the civil rights movement.

Watson, a former official of the NAACP, is a journalist. He is the author of *Lion in the Lobby*.

Because of the attention focused on Martin Luther King, Jr., and his nonviolent strategy, the role of the National Association for the Advancement of Colored People (NAACP) has been overshadowed and its major contributions to modern civil rights overlooked. King's ability to arouse the spirit of African Americans and give them a sense of involvement in

Excerpted from Denton L. Watson, "Assessing the Role of the NAACP in the Civil Rights Movement," *The Historian*, Spring 1993. Reprinted by permission of the author.

their own liberation was unparalleled. From the Montgomery bus boycott in 1954 to the Birmingham demonstrations in 1963, as well as in other activities, King sought to awaken the United States to the egregious wrongs done to African Americans. The NAACP's early leaders anticipated competition from King and the Southern Christian Leadership Conference (SCLC), which he headed, but NAACP leaders never had an effective public relations strategy to counter the overwhelming emotional appeal of King's oratory and the civil rights demonstrations in the South, which were tailored for the news media, especially television. Martyred in 1968, King has become so popular that the NAACP's influence and visibility have suffered. Yet, no other organization contributed more to making the U.S. Constitution responsive to the needs of all citizens.

The Founding of the NAACP

The NAACP was organized in 1909 owing to the need for an effective civil rights organization amid an explosion of racial prejudice in Springfield, Illinois. William English Walling, a white Kentuckian who was visiting nearby Chicago with his wife, voiced alarm that such violence was spreading from the South to the North. He saw an urgent "need for a nation-wide effort to combat the evil." Walling and several others joined in issuing "The Call" on 12 February 1909, which marked the founding of the NAACP. Their goal was to achieve absolute political and social equality for African Americans.

The NAACP's philosophy was linked to the same currents of eighteenth-century liberalism that had given birth to the Declaration of Independence and the Constitution. The NAACP's founders were concerned that the "republican experiment is at stake, every tolerated wrong to the Negro reacting with double force upon white citizens guilty of faithlessness to their brothers." The founders agreed to use every available means to publicize the neglected issues of civil and political equality for African Americans. By 1929 these rudimentary beginnings had become a full-scale attack on all forms of racial discrimination.

As editor of *The Crisis*, the NAACP's journal, W.E.B. Du Bois, one of the signers of the NAACP's "Call," broadened the focus of the struggle and set its tone with what he called his "stinging hammer blows" against racial injustices. In his books, pamphlets, and articles, Du Bois exposed the abysmal state of race relations in the country and defined the philosophy for the struggle.

James Weldon Johnson, who succeeded several whites to become NAACP executive secretary in 1920, is better known for creating "Lift Ev'ry Voice and Sing"—the "black national hymn"—and for his other literary accomplishments than for his effectiveness as a civil rights leader. Yet, he expanded the NAACP's membership—the base of the organization's strength—tenfold between 1916 and 1920. Johnson molded the NAACP into an effective organization by consolidating its early initiatives into full-fledged programs against disenfranchisement, peonage in the South, and U.S. atrocities in Haiti. Moreover, he expanded the NAACP's attack on lynching into a crusade that, more than any other program, defined the organization as a formidable political machine.

Johnson's indefatigable assistant, Walter White, headed one branch of the antilynching program—investigating the crime and arousing public opinion against it. In 1919, the NAACP initiated a drive in Congress for an antilynching bill, which only the House of Representatives passed in 1922. In 1930, White, who became executive secretary that year, increased respect for the organization as a political force when he teamed up with the American Federation of Labor to defeat President Herbert Hoover's appointment of Judge John J. Parker, a North Carolina racist, to the Supreme Court.

The NAACP continued to develop its humanitarian and constitutional (egalitarian) philosophy by seeking the support of the federal courts to challenge the legality of segregation laws. It sought legal redress for individual cases of injustice based on race and attacked the disenfranchisement of African Americans in the South. From its first victory in 1915 in *Guinn v. U.S.*, in which the Supreme Court ruled that the grandfather clause, which barred blacks in the South from voting, violated the Fifteenth Amendment, to others like *Nixon v. Herndon* in 1927, in which the Texas white primary was ruled unconstitutional, the NAACP began building a comprehensive legal program.

In 1935 the NAACP formalized that program when highly respected Charles Hamilton Houston, dean of Howard University Law School, joined its staff as special counsel in its newly created legal department. The same year, Houston and Thurgood Marshall, his protégé working with the Baltimore branch of the NAACP and later justice of the Supreme Court, won a case in the Baltimore City Court in which the University of Maryland Law School was ordered to admit Donald Gaines Murray, an Amherst College graduate, as its first African-American student.

The Baltimore case began the constitutional battle in which the NAACP directly challenged the practice of segregation. This resulted in the 1954 *Brown v. Board of Education* decision in which the Supreme Court reaffirmed the original purpose of the equal protection clause of the Fourteenth Amendment. In doing so, the court overturned its 1896 *Plessy v. Ferguson* decision that established the "separate but equal" doctrine. The *Brown* decision was a ringing vindication of the strategy of sociological jurisprudence that Marshall had developed and raised the civil rights struggle to a new plateau by giving it constitutional backing.

The Effect of *Brown*

Constance Baker Motley, a U.S. District Court judge in New York who was on Marshall's NAACP staff, recalled that Roy Wilkins, NAACP executive director from 1955–1976, had complained in the 1940s that no matter how hard he tried, he could not get African Americans to join the struggle. But "they knew that something had happened when the *Brown* decision came down, that the world would be changing, and they felt that they could then do something." After 1954, the speeches Wilkins and other NAACP leaders had been making and the organization's other actions began to make more sense to African Americans. In 1956, an NAACP official told the *New York Times*: "We've had a long way to go. We've had to overcome a lot of apathy built among the colored over the years." In 1961, King said that the new wave of African-American militancy had developed because "the Negro has seen the exit sign to freedom" in the school desegregation decision, adding: "The whole nation put itself on record then as saying that segregation is wrong."

Brown also undergirded the NAACP's political program. Although the NAACP was unable to get Congress to pass an antilynching law, it did attempt through a relentless publicity campaign to pressure the southern states to end the crime themselves. The campaign against lynching built on the 1929 defeat of Judge Parker's nomination and further shaped the NAACP's political program.

The New Deal was a political watershed in the civil rights struggle, since it led to the launching of a comprehensive movement by African Americans for social and economic equality. In 1937 their expectations of the federal government rose as the result of the three-day "National Conference on the Problems of the Negro and Negro Youth" in Washington. The conference was sponsored by the government to improve federal programs for African Americans. Mary McLeod Bethune, the spiritual force of the New Deal's "Black Brain Trust," noted its importance: "This is the first time in the history of our race that the Negroes of America have felt free to reduce to writing their problems and plans for meeting them with the expectancy of sympathetic understanding and interpretation." Ralph Bunche, a prominent African-American Howard University political scientist, explained that the New Deal was unprecedented because the federal government gave "broad recognition to the existence of the Negro as a national problem and undertook to give specific consideration to this fact in many ways."

World War II crystalized the political shape of those expectations. Franklin D. Roosevelt responded to the demands of A. Philip Randolph, president of the Brotherhood of Sleeping Car Porters, for an end to racial discrimination in the defense program. The president issued Executive Order 8802, which created the Fair Employment Practice Committee (FEPC). The establishment of the FEPC marked the birth of the modern civil rights movement in that it was the first time a president took action to end racial discrimination. This opened a new and critical phase in the struggle against racial oppression. From that point, the NAACP was able to convince every president through Lyndon Johnson to take decisive action against discrimination.

The creation of the NAACP's Washington bureau in 1942 was another important step. In 1946 White convinced the Senate to uphold the association's charge that Theodore "the Man" Gilmore Bilbo, an arch segregationist from Mississippi, had won renomination in a primary election by intimidating African-American voters in Jackson. The Senate barred the seating of Bilbo.

Presidential backing of the NAACP and full citizenship for African Americans continued into the administration of President Harry S Truman, when he sanctioned the formation of the President's Committee on Civil Rights in response to White's complaints about the resurgence of racial violence. The committee's landmark report, *To Secure These Rights*, clearly defined civil rights: "We can tolerate no restrictions upon the individual which depend upon irrelevant factors such as his race, his color, his religion or the social position to which he is born." Economic issues began to overshadow such earlier civil rights concerns as lynchings during and after World War II. By 1955 the United States was better positioned to match the post–World War II spirit of freedom that was rapidly spreading throughout former colonial territories. This was the time that African Americans launched the bus boycott under King's direction in Montgomery, Alabama.

Fresh from Boston University, where he had completed his doctorate, King arrived at an unprecedented moment in history when he became pastor of Montgomery's Dexter Avenue Baptist Church. As he wrote: "I had not the slightest idea that I would later become involved in a crisis in which nonviolent resistance would be applicable. I neither started the protest nor suggested it. I simply responded to the call of the people for a spokesman." In retrospect, King recognized that he had begun a "serious intellectual quest for a method to eliminate social evil" at Crozier Theological Seminary. His study of Walter Rauschenbusch's *Christianity and the Social Crisis* had indelibly influenced his thinking by giving him "a theological basis for the social concern" that he had developed from early childhood experiences in Atlanta.

Roy Wilkins and Clarence Mitchell, Jr., who was the NAACP's chief strategist in the 1960s, took a more practical approach to civil rights. When White died in 1955, Wilkins became head of the NAACP, having been groomed for the job for twenty-four years. Wilkins and Mitchell were political realists; King was a political moralist. Mitchell was a constitutional humanist; King was a moral humanist. Mitchell, like Wilkins, White, and Johnson, appealed to reason and the intellect; King appealed to the conscience. Mitchell's philosophy and training blended his strong belief in Christianity and the Constitution and the practical imperatives of the legislative process. Wilkins' philosophy was also based on the Constitution, but he encompassed a broader political scope that included intergroup relations much more than Mitchell did.

The 1955 bus boycott by King's Montgomery Improvement Association had a wide emotional appeal that the NAACP's carefully managed programs lacked. Despite King's popularity, the NAACP was highly revered by most older African Americans in the South as a beacon of hope in abysmal racial darkness—so much so that several states in the region attempted to put the NAACP out of business.

The relentless attacks on the NAACP revealed its effectiveness as much as the Montgomery bus boycott revealed the NAACP's structural handicaps. The inherent differences between the two civil rights approaches were exemplified by the sharply contrasting personalities of their leaders. Wilkins, at 54, was old enough to be King's father. His parents had fled from Mississippi to St. Louis, Missouri, where he was born in a world apart from the Jim Crow South, which shaped King's soul. King was inseparable from the people he was leading. He was of them as much as he was for them; cultural and spiritual bonds reinforced his powerful gift of oratory and training as a Baptist minister. King knew that style was much more important than substance to poor, southern African Americans as his words probed the innermost recesses of the heart with their striking cadences. He evoked emotions while Wilkins sought to foster understanding of the plight of African Americans.

The NAACP's programs reflected that intellectual approach; they were not designed to involve the masses as was the bus boycott. By its very nature the boycott was a mass movement, as were all of King's subsequent demonstrations. The live theater that the demonstrators orchestrated by confronting the southern segregationists was tailor made for media coverage. There had been no widespread cheering for the 1947 report of the President's Committee on Civil Rights. Although African Americans considered the *Brown* decision a victory, the slow enforcement of the decision led impatient young African Americans to reject the NAACP's leadership in civil rights.

Another drawback of the NAACP's legal program was that the impact of *Brown* was not as immediate as that of the bus boycott. The NAACP toiled for fourteen years to get a civil rights law passed, and even then its effect was hardly momentous. Protests such as the boycott relied on emotion, which often cannot be sustained. After nearly a year of battles by the Montgomery Improvement Association with the intransigent white City Commission of Montgomery, the bus boycott might have collapsed if the NAACP had not stepped in with its legal challenge to intra-city bus segregation. Despite the victory, the city commissioners resisted desegregation until they received the court order.

King's passing recognition of the NAACP's role in sustaining the boycott set the tone for most historical treatments of the civil rights movement. His egotistical excesses revealed in *Stride toward Freedom* were not lost on NAACP leaders, who regarded him as an upstart attracting media and competing for contributions. No matter how justified these criticisms, Wilkins, as head of the NAACP, allowed King's version of the events to go largely unchallenged.

Rosa Parks and the Montgomery Bus Boycott

Walt Harrington

On December 1, 1955, Rosa Parks was arrested on a Montgomery, Alabama, bus for refusing to give her seat to a white passenger. With Parks' arrest local civil rights leaders were able to gain the support of church leaders and organize a boycott of the buses. The legal battles that the Montgomery bus boycott provoked eventually resulted in Alabama's bus segregation laws being declared unconstitutional. More importantly, the victory inspired blacks to organize, and the boycott, with the leadership of Martin Luther King Jr., became the inspiration and blueprint for the strategy of mass political protest that characterized the civil rights movement.

In the following selection, *Washington Post* writer Walt Harrington discusses Rosa Parks and the mythology that has grown up around her decision to engage in civil disobedience. Although she has been credited with starting the bus boycott, he writes, in reality it took the participation of many civil rights workers in and around Montgomery, including Clifford Durr, Edgar D. Nixon, Rufus Lewis, and Fred Gray, as well as the thousands who boycotted the buses, to make this turning point in the civil rights movement a reality.

Rosa Parks was born in Tuskegee, Alabama, in 1913. By the time she was a toddler, the marriage of her mother and father was pretty much over and Leona had moved back to Pine Level to live with her parents. Leona wasn't your average country woman. She was a schoolteacher who had attended the private Payne University in Selma at a time when public education for most of Alabama's black children ended in the sixth grade. Unlike nearly all black families near Pine Level, Leona's family didn't crop for shares. The family owned 12 acres of land that one of Rosa's great-grandfathers, a Scotch-Irish indentured servant, had bought after the Civil War and another six acres one of her grandmothers had inherited from the family of a white girl she'd once cared for. In that time and place, the family of Rosa Parks was comfortable.

The Myth of Rosa Parks as Simple and Meek

While many blacks then felt compelled to smile and shuffle around whites, such behavior was banned in her home. Rosa's maternal grandfather, the son of a white plantation owner and a seamstress house slave, had been mistreated terribly as a boy by a plantation overseer and he hated whites. He wouldn't let Rosa and her brother, Sylvester, play with them. Rosa once stayed up late with him as he sat resolutely, shotgun at the ready, while the Ku Klux Klan rode the countryside. He told her he'd shoot the first Klansman through the door. Her grandfather was so light-skinned that he could easily pass for white, and he took joy in reaching out and shaking the hands of white strangers, calling them by their first names and introducing himself by his last name, dangerous violations of racist protocol at the time.

Young Rosa took her cues from her grandfather and stood up to white children who tried to bully her, although her grandmother warned that she'd get herself lynched someday. That Rosa had white ancestors on her mother's side and her father's side made the hard line between black and white seem even more ludicrous. As a girl, she secretly admired a dark-skinned Pine Level man who always refused to work for whites. Years later, one of the traits that attracted her to her future husband, Raymond, was that he had faced down white bullies and even helped raise money for the defense of the Scottsboro Boys, nine black Alabama youths convicted in 1931 on flimsy evidence for supposedly raping two white women. . . .

The strength and confidence of Rosa Parks and her family don't exactly jibe with the Rosa Parks myth—the myth that emerged from her refusal to move to the back of the bus in 1955, the myth that served the needs of the emergent civil rights movement and the myth that spoke so eloquently to black and white America: She was a poor, simple seamstress, Rosa Parks, humble and gentle, no rabble-rouser, a meek Negro woman, exhausted from a hard day's work, a woman who had been abused and humiliated by segregation one time too many, who without forethought chose to sit her ground. In truth, Rosa Parks was far more and far less than the mythology that engulfed her and that became the mobilizing metaphor of the Montgomery bus boycott, which lasted 381 days, raised the unknown Rev. Martin Luther King Jr. to international prominence and helped launch the modern civil rights movement.

Rosa Parks was not a simple woman. She wasn't meek. She was no more tired that day than usual. She had forethought aplenty. She didn't start the Montgomery bus boycott or the civil rights movement, neither of which burst forth from any single symbolic act. Forty years later, the defiance of Rosa Parks and the success of the boycott are enshrined in mystery and myth that obscure a deeper truth that is even richer, grander and more heroic. "I know you won't write this," says Aldon Morris, sociologist and author of *Origins of the Civil Rights Movement*, "but what Rosa Parks did is really the least significant part of the story. She refused to give up her seat and was arrested. I'm not even completely comfortable with deflating the myth. What I'm trying to say is we take that action, elevate it to epic proportions, but all the things that happened so she could become epic, we drop by the wayside. . . . That she was just a sweet lady who was tired is the myth. . . . The real story of Montgomery is that real people with frailties made change.

"That's what the magic is.". . .

Clifford Durr and E.D. Nixon

Cloverdale is a beautiful Montgomery neighborhood of landscaped yards, mature trees, flowering bushes, old, elegant homes. Cloverdale, which is integrated today, speaks to the incongruence that is the life of Virginia Durr, a 92-year-old white woman and daughter of Montgomery's gentry who, with her husband, Clifford, was one of the few whites brave or committed or foolish enough to support Rosa Parks and the bus boycott. Her husband's law practice was nearly ruined, two of her daughters had to be sent to school up North, her yard was littered with obscene leaflets. . . .

On the night Rosa Parks was arrested, Eddie Mae Pratt, now 79 and a friend of a friend of Mrs. Parks, happened to be on the crowded bus. She was standing in the rear and couldn't see the commotion up front. Word filtered back that a black woman wouldn't give up her seat to a white. Mrs. Pratt, who knew Mrs. Parks from evenings she spent sewing clothing with Bertha T. Butler, Mrs. Pratt's neighbor, finally caught a glimpse of Mrs. Parks as she was led off the bus. Suddenly, she felt weak. She wrapped her arms around her chest and when the bus lurched forward, she slipped hard enough that a black man offered her his seat and she sat down.

"Do you feel all right?" he asked.

"That's Mrs. Parks," she said, stunned.

At her stop, Mrs. Pratt ran to the nearby house of Bertha Butler, who said, "Oh, my goodness!" She called the home of E.D. Nixon, the founder and former president of the Montgomery NAACP, where Mrs. Parks had been the volunteer secretary for 12 years. Nixon called Clifford Durr, who knew Mrs. Parks because, upon Nixon's recommendation, she had been doing seamstress work for Mrs. Durr. When Nixon drove by to pick up Clifford Durr, Mrs. Durr was with him and they went and bailed out Mrs. Parks.

Forty years later, at the Sahara, where Mrs. Durr is seated in her wheelchair at the table and Mrs. Williams is helping cut her entree, an old black waiter whispers to a young black waiter: "That's Mrs. Durr, who went and got Rosa Parks out of jail."

Mrs. Durr smiles. "My claim to fame."

That's not exactly true. Clifford Durr, who grew up in Montgomery, was a Rhodes scholar with a law degree from Oxford University and a New Dealer whom Franklin Roosevelt had appointed to the Federal Communications Commission. After Clifford resigned to represent people charged as subversives in the communist witch hunts of the 1950s, the Durrs returned to their home town, where his family was the founder and owner of the prosperous Durr drugstore chain. Although politically conservative, the family supported Clifford and Virginia financially and gave him legal business. . . .

Through a New Deal acquaintance, Clifford met E.D. Nixon, who is perhaps the most unsung of Montgomery's civil rights heroes. He was a Pullman porter and the local head of A. Philip Randolph's powerful Brotherhood of Sleeping Car Porters. Nixon was close to Randolph, who in the '40s was already calling for massive grass-roots demonstrations against Southern Jim Crow laws. Nixon himself had opened the local NAACP chapter in the 1920s. In Montgomery, Nixon was "Mr. Civil Rights." He was rough-edged and poorly spoken, but he was an indefatigable man bravely willing to call public attention to the constant abuse of black people.

In those days, there was only one black lawyer in Montgomery. So when Nixon learned that Clifford Durr would take black clients, he sent them to him—no doubt also hoping to create a powerful white friend and ally. When Clifford mentioned that his wife needed a seamstress to alter the clothing their daughters received as hand-me-downs from rich relations—including Virginia's sister, the wife of former U.S. senator and then-Supreme Court Justice Hugo L. Black—Nixon sent Mrs. Parks. . . .

Getting Black Voters Registered

The east side of old black Montgomery isn't what it used to be. Alabama State still anchors the neighborhood, but many affluent blacks have migrated to the suburbs, where they now live among whites. Many doctors and lawyers, even public school teachers with two modest incomes have abandoned Montgomery's old black neighborhoods. But Rufus Lewis, 88 years old, a giant in the Montgomery civil rights movement, a man barely known outside his circle of aged contemporaries, still lives on the old black east side. . . .

Back in the '40s, Lewis became obsessed with black voting rights. Night after night, he traveled the countryside teaching blacks how to register. In Montgomery, he founded the Citizens Club, a private nightclub blacks could join only if they were registered voters. An entire generation of Montgomery blacks say Rufus Lewis is the reason they first voted. Lewis was the first to ramrod the Montgomery bus boycott's labyrinthine automobile transport system that helped get black boycotters back and forth every day for 13 months. Lewis, with Nixon's concurrence, nominated Martin Luther King Jr. to head the organization leading the boycott. . . .

"We got a lotta folks registered," he says, smiling. They mimeographed the literacy test, taught folks the answers, traveled by cover of night through the backwoods Jim Crow landscape, sent light-skinned blacks to the Montgomery registrar's office to learn if it was open that day, drove folks to the courthouse. When people failed the test—as they usually did the first time or two—Lewis and his workers did it all again, and then again. . . .

Does Mr. Lewis know that history records his achievements?

"Well, that's fine to be remembered in the books," he says, . . . "but the best part of it was being there to help the people who needed help. . . . That was our job."

Rosa Parks Was Politically Untouchable

The night Rosa Parks was arrested, E.D. Nixon and Clifford Durr recognized instinctively that Mrs. Parks was the vessel they'd been seeking to challenge the segregated bus laws. Other blacks had been arrested for defying those laws. Only months before, a 15-year-old girl, Claudette Colvin—inspired by a high school teacher's lectures on the need for equal rights, angered by the conviction of a black high school student for allegedly raping a white woman—had refused to give up her seat to a white, then resisted arrest when the police came. She kept hollering, "It's my constitutional right!" Nixon had decided against contesting her case: She had fought with police, she came from the poorer side of black Montgomery and, it was later learned, she was pregnant. He had also rejected the cases of several other women

recently arrested, waiting for just the right vessel to arrive.
Then came Mrs. Parks. "We got a lady can't nobody touch," Nixon said. There were other advantages. Rosa Parks, because of her well-mannered, serene demeanor, her proper speech, her humble, saintly way, her ascetic lifestyle—she didn't drink, smoke or curse—carried not only the image but the reality of the deserving Negro. Mrs. Parks had the qualities middle-class whites claimed in themselves and denied in blacks. Nothing about her supported the white contention that she deserved to be treated as inferior.

She had another advantage: Although whites may have viewed blacks as a single entity, the social class fissures within the black community—between educated and uneducated, affluent and poor—ran deep. Mrs. Parks bridged that gap: She was of "working-class station and middle-class demeanor," as Taylor Branch wrote in *Parting the Waters*. She came from a good family, her relatives were prominent in Montgomery's St. Paul AME Church, she was educated at Miss White's and later Alabama State's lab school, and she had the manners—as Virginia Durr said—of a "lady." In her role as NAACP secretary, she was respected by the city's educated activist community. But she was also a seamstress who earned $23 a week, whose fingers and feet were tired from honest work. She was a PR bonanza—with a bonus.

She was velvet hiding steel.

That night, after hushed conversations, Nixon and Clifford Durr asked if she would plead not guilty and fight her arrest in court. Nixon said they could take the case to the Supreme Court. Her husband, Raymond, a barber, was terrified, and Mrs. Durr later recalled in her memoir, *Outside the Magic Circle*, that he kept saying, "Rosa, the white folks will kill you! Rosa, the white folks will kill you!" Like a chant. Mrs. Parks was perfectly calm.

"I'll go along with you, Mr. Nixon."

The Rosa Parks Myth

Her decision wasn't as simple as it seems, wasn't made in that one instant, but was a long time coming. In her 1992 autobiography, *Rosa Parks: My Story*, the source for many of the details about her life and attitudes, Mrs. Parks writes that as she sat on the bus, waiting for the police to arrive, she was thinking about the night as a girl when she sat with her grandfather, shotgun at the ready, while the KKK rode the countryside. The humiliating segregation of Montgomery's buses was much on her mind. Not only had Claudette Colvin's arrest occurred last spring, but just a month earlier, a bus driver had ordered Mrs. Parks's dear friend, Bertha Butler, to move back to make room for a white man: "You sit back there with the niggers." Mrs. Butler was a woman raising two children on her own, who also worked as a seamstress, who sometimes sewed until 5 a.m. for extra income and who still found time to run voter clinics in her home two nights a week. She had befriended Mrs. Parks because she so admired her civil rights work. Mrs. Butler didn't move at the order, and the standing white man, in soldier's uniform, had intervened: "That's your seat and you sit there." Mrs. Butler, now retired at age 76 and living near Philadelphia, was glad she wasn't the one to get arrested. "God looked at me and said I wasn't strong enough," she says. "Mrs. Parks was the person.". . .

It is embedded in the American psyche that Rosa Parks acted on the spur of the moment, and her arrest is often called the "spark" that ignited the modern civil rights movement. In fact, Rosa Parks's act and the firestorm that followed were more like spontaneous combustion—a fire ignited by the buildup of heat over time in material ripe for explosion. Mrs. Parks, who wasn't afraid as she waited for her arrest, who felt oddly serene, revealed the lifetime thread of experiences that had led to her action when the police arrived and asked once more if she would move. In the way of the Bible, she answered with a question:

"Why do you all push us around?"

No moral philosopher, the cop said, "I don't know."

Then she was led away. . . .

A Unifying Indignity

On the night Rosa Parks was arrested, after she had agreed to become bus segregation's test case, 24-year-old Fred Gray, one of Montgomery's two black attorneys then, arrived home late from out of town and got the word. Gray had grown up in Montgomery, attended Alabama State and gone to Ohio for law school because Alabama didn't have a law school for blacks. When the state required five attorneys to sign character affidavits before he could practice, Gray had gone to E.D. Nixon, who helped him find the lawyers. One of them was Clifford Durr. Gray had returned home with one goal—to "destroy everything segregated." Mrs. Parks immediately offered her services. Every day, she came to his downtown office at lunch, answered his mail for free, encouraged his idealism. They talked not only about the buses, but inferior black schools, segregated parks, swimming pools and toilets. In his memoir, *Bus Ride to Justice*, Gray, now 64, later wrote, "She gave me the feeling that I was the Moses that God had sent to Pharaoh."

Fred Gray upped the ante. Late on the night Mrs. Parks was arrested, he visited Jo Ann Robinson, an Alabama State professor and president of the Women's Political Council, a group composed of female university professors, public school teachers, nurses, social workers and the wives of Montgomery's black professional men. For months, Robinson had been laying plans for a bus boycott. Although she and most of Montgomery's affluent blacks owned cars and didn't ride the buses often, she had taken a bus to the airport in 1949 and mistakenly sat in a white seat. The driver went wild, screamed, threatened. "I felt like a dog," she later said.

Every black person who rode a bus had a tale to tell: the man who paid his last coin in fare only to have the bus drive off before he could return and enter through the back door, the woman who was attacked when she stepped onto a bus to pay ahead of a white man, the pregnant woman who fell when a bus pulled away as she stepped off. In 1953 alone, the Women's Council had received 30 complaints from black bus riders.

It was a unifying indignity.

Inspired by the Supreme Court ruling that had banned "separate but equal" schools in 1954, Robinson had even written the mayor and warned that if black riders weren't treated more courteously "twenty-five or more local organizations" were planning a bus boycott. It was a hopeful time. Already, a boycott in Baton Rouge, Louisiana, organized by the Rev. T.J. Jemison, had won concessions for black riders in that city. And in Little Rock, Arkansas, officials had devised a plan to integrate its schools. But nothing had come of Robinson's demands. Then Fred Gray dropped by.

At midnight, Robinson went to Alabama State and furtively used its government-owned paper and mimeograph machines to run off 52,500 leaflets announcing a boycott of Montgomery's buses on the day of Mrs. Parks's trial. The next morning, Robinson and her Women's Council cohorts and students distributed the leaflets to black schools, stores, taverns, beauty parlors and barber shops. When Alabama State's black president, H. Councill Trenholm, who served at the pleasure of the Alabama governor, learned of her action, he called her into his office and demanded an explanation. She told him another black woman had been humiliated on a bus; she promised to pay for the mimeograph paper. He calmed down, warned her to work behind the scenes. Trenholm's wife, too, was a Women's Council member.

The rest is history. Rosa Parks was found guilty and fined $10, plus $4 in court costs. To keep the followers of Rufus Lewis and E.D. Nixon from squabbling, King became the compromise choice to lead the boycott. When black preachers cozy with Montgomery's powerful whites balked at the idea, Nixon, in his rugged way, questioned their manhood: "You ministers have lived off these wash-women for the last hundred years and ain't never done nothing for them." After Nixon's taunt, King himself said, "Brother Nixon, I'm not a coward." Nixon planted the story of the boycott with a friendly white reporter at the *Montgomery Advertiser*. It became front-page news and announced the boycott to every black in Montgomery.

There were bombings, threats, lawsuits, harassing phone calls. Victory was not preordained; it came a day at a time. The city's stubborn refusal to compromise on bus seating—other segregated Southern cities didn't have specific seats reserved only for whites—probably hardened the resolve of the boycotters. The bombings certainly turned national public opinion against the segregationists. In 1956, young Fred Gray successfully took his argument against Montgomery's bus segregation to the U.S. Supreme Court. Although many people believe it was Rosa Parks's case that went before the high court, Gray actually didn't use her as a plaintiff because of technicalities in her case that might have undermined his federal lawsuit. Instead, five women whose names are mostly lost to history filed suit: Aurelia Browder, Claudette Colvin, Susie McDonald, Jeanetta Reese and Mary Louise Smith.

Victory had a price: Jo Ann Robinson and about a dozen other activist ASU employees lost their jobs. Monroe J. Gardner, whose granddaughter is now a federal magistrate in Montgomery, used his car to transport people during the boycott. He was beaten. Samuel Patton Sr., a boycott supporter and prominent builder, lost his line of bank credit. E.L. and Dorothy Posey, who ran the only black-owned parking lot in downtown Montgomery, let their lot be used as a transit staging point. After the boycott, they lost their business. Anne Smith Pratt volunteered dispatching cars to pick up waiting riders. Her marriage ended when her husband was sent overseas and she refused to leave her post. Not to mention the hardships endured by thousands of working-class blacks who walked miles to work every day in the heat, the cold, the rain. Says sociologist Aldon Morris, "People made this happen."

A Symbol of Justice

During the boycott, Rosa Parks helped run the auto dispatch system. She wasn't a leader of the movement, and didn't try to be. She traveled the country raising money. Already, she was a symbol. When she, King and nearly 100 others were charged with conspiracy during the boycott, a photo of her being fingerprinted ran on the front page of the *New York Times*—perhaps because King was out of town and not available to be photographed during his arrest. That picture, mistakenly believed by many to have been taken the night she was first arrested, became a piece of movement iconography. . . .

The mother of the civil rights movement.

"A saint of American history," a TV reporter calls her.

"I don't consider myself a saint," says Mrs. Parks, who still wears her hair braided and rolled behind her head, still speaks so softly her voice is nearly inaudible, still is velvet hiding steel. "I'm just a person who wanted to be seated on the bus."

But again and again, Rosa Parks tells audiences she didn't remain in her seat because she was physically weary. No, she was weary of the injustice. Again and again, she mentions that she was working at the NAACP before her arrest. No, she didn't plan her arrest, but her whole life from childhood was leading up to it. Without being asked, she is responding to the mythic tale that, ironically, holds her up to worship and diminishes her: the simple seamstress, the meek Negro woman, exhausted from a day's work, who without forethought chose to sit her ground. . . .

"She remains a pure symbol," says University of Georgia sociologist Gary Fine, an expert in political symbolism. "For everyone today and in the '50s, it was a text story with only one possible reading—this poor woman who refused to move to the back of the bus. What possible explanation could you possibly have for making her move? It was so transparently egregious." But for a symbol to have 40 years of staying power, Fine says, it must carry a deeper cultural resonance about "our own self-image."

"By protecting this image we are celebrating core values for ourselves as Americans," he says. "There is a universal consensus now that integration is good. She symbolizes this now. Everybody on all sides can use her." For blacks, she is evidence that they forced change. For whites, she is evidence that they were willing to change. . . .

Ordinary People Made It Happen

"If you rode the bus, you were mistreated," [current Montgomery City Council president Joe] Dickerson says. . . . "And so the time was right. It could have been anybody . . . I guess when the time is right, it's just like Nelson Mandela. If anybody had told Mandela, 'You're gonna be free and you're gonna rule South Africa, man,' you talked like a fool. 'I'm not gonna get outta jail!' So there is a time for everything. And you have to play your role."

Rosa Parks's grandfather who refused to shuffle for whites played his role. So did the dark-skinned man in Pine Level who wouldn't work for whites. Rosa's mother, who sacrificed so Rosa could go to Miss White's school. Miss White. Julius Rosenwald. A. Philip Randolph. The NAACP lawyers who laid decades of groundwork for the 1954 Supreme Court schools decision. The Rev. T.J. Jemison, who organized the earlier Baton Rouge bus boycott. Those who took the literacy test again and again. Raymond Parks. H. Councill Trenholm, Ralph Abernathy, Eddie Mae Pratt, Anne Smith Pratt, E.L. and Dorothy Posey, Zecozy Williams, Bertha Smith, Monroe J. Gardner, Samuel Patton Sr., Johnnie Carr, Bertha T. Butler, Zynobia Tatum, Aurelia Browder, Claudette Colvin, Susie McDonald, Jeanetta Reese, Mary Louise Smith. And, of course, E.D. Nixon, Rufus Lewis, Jo Ann Robinson, Fred Gray, Clifford and Virginia Durr and Martin Luther King Jr., who transformed a demand for seats into a mission for God. And the 40,000 who refused to ride.

Strands in a thread.

Rosa Parks, too, played her role.

She still does.

"The message is ordinary people doing extraordinary things," says sociologist Aldon Morris, who fears that the simplified mythology that enshrouds Rosa Parks and the Montgomery bus boycott, the belief that it was all God-ordained, can obscure the determination, fearlessness and skilled organization of the people who made the movement. "To believe that King or Rosa Parks are heroes, it creates passivity. . . . Young people then ask, 'Where's the new Martin Luther King?' . . . People don't understand that power exists within the collectivity."

"The peoples," as E.D. Nixon said.

Nonviolence and Racial Justice

Martin Luther King Jr.

World Wars I and II gave impetus to freedom movements throughout the world, and many countries in Africa and Asia gained independence from European colonial rule. Most of these wars were fought through violent insurgencies. A few, however, followed the model of passive resistance established by Mohandas K. Gandhi in the struggle for Indian independence.

In the following selection, written in 1957, Martin Luther King Jr. advocates and defines a strategy of nonviolent resistance for the American civil rights movement. Blacks must endure violent attacks by bigots without resorting to violence in return, King states. They must demonstrate love for their fellow man even while condemning segregationists' evil acts of discrimination. In that way, they will dramatize the injustice of segregation and convince separatists of the immorality of racist views.

At the time of writing, King was pastor of the Dexter Avenue Baptist Church in Montgomery, Alabama, and president of the Southern Christian Leadership Conference.

The determination of Negro Americans to win freedom from every form of oppression springs from the same profound longing for freedom that motivates oppressed peoples all over the world. The rhythmic beat of deep discontent in Africa and Asia is at bottom a quest for freedom and human dignity on the part of people who have long been victims of colonialism. The struggle for freedom on the part of oppressed people in general and of the American Negro in particular has developed slowly and is not going to end suddenly. Privileged groups rarely give up their privileges without strong resistance. But when oppressed people rise up against oppression there is no stopping point short of full freedom. Realism compels us to admit that the struggle will continue until freedom is a reality for all the oppressed peoples of the world.

Hence the basic question which confronts the world's oppressed is: How is the struggle against the forces of injustice to be waged? There are two possible answers. One is resort to the all too prevalent method of physical violence and corroding hatred. The danger of this method is its futility. Violence solves no social problems; it merely creates new and more complicated ones. Through the vistas of time a voice still cries to every potential Peter, "Put up your sword!" The shores of history are white with the bleached bones of nations and communities that failed to follow this command. If the American Negro and other victims of oppression succumb to the temptation of using violence in the struggle for justice, unborn generations will live in a desolate night of bitterness, and their chief legacy will be an endless reign of chaos.

Alternative to Violence

The alternative to violence is nonviolent resistance. This method was made famous in our generation by Mohandas K. Gandhi, who used it to free India from the domination of the British empire. Five points can be made concerning nonviolence as a method in bringing about better racial conditions.

First, this is not a method for cowards; it *does* resist. The nonviolent resister is just as strongly opposed to the evil against which he protests as is the person who uses violence. His method is passive or nonaggressive in the sense that he is not physically aggressive toward his opponent. But his mind and emotions are always active, constantly seeking to persuade the opponent that he is mistaken. This method is passive physically but strongly active spiritually; it is nonaggressive physically but dynamically aggressive spiritually.

A second point is that nonviolent resistance does not seek to defeat or humiliate the opponent, but to win his friendship and understanding. The nonviolent resister must often express his protest through noncooperation or boycotts, but he realizes that noncooperation and boycotts are not ends themselves; they are merely means to awaken a sense of moral shame in the opponent. The end is redemption and reconciliation. The aftermath of nonviolence is the creation of the beloved community, while the aftermath of violence is tragic bitterness.

A third characteristic of this method is that the attack is directed against forces of evil rather than against persons who are caught in those forces. It is evil we are seeking to defeat, not the persons victimized by evil. Those of us who struggle against racial injustice must come to see that the basic tension is not between races. As I like to say to the people in Montgomery, Alabama: "The tension in this city is not between white people and Negro people. The tension is at bottom between justice and injustice, between the forces of light and the forces of darkness. And if there is a victory it will be a victory not merely for 50,000 Negroes, but a victory for justice and the forces of light. We are out to defeat injustice and not white persons who may happen to be unjust."

A fourth point that must be brought out concerning nonviolent resistance is that it avoids not only external physical violence but also internal violence of spirit. At the center of nonviolence stands the principle of love. In struggling for human dignity the oppressed people of the world must not allow themselves to become bitter or indulge in hate campaigns. To retaliate with hate and bitterness would do nothing but intensify the hate in the world. Along the way of life, someone must have sense enough and morality enough to cut off the chain of hate. This can be done only by projecting the ethics of love to the center of our lives.

The Meaning of "Love"

In speaking of love at this point, we are not referring to some sentimental emotion. It would be nonsense to urge men to love their oppressors in an affectionate sense. "Love" in this connection means understanding good will. There are three words for love in the Greek New Testament. First, there is *eros*. In Platonic philosophy *eros* meant the yearning of the soul for the realm of the divine. It has come now to mean a sort of aesthetic or romantic love. Second, there is *philia*. It meant intimate affectionateness between friends. *Philia* denotes a sort of reciprocal love: the person loves because he is loved. When we speak of loving those who oppose us we refer to neither *eros* nor *philia*; we speak of a love which is expressed in the Greek word *agape*. *Agape* means nothing sentimental or basically affectionate; it means understanding, redeeming good will for all men, an overflowing love which seeks nothing in return. It is the love of God working in the lives of men. When we love on the *agape* level we love men not because we like them, not because their attitudes and ways appeal to us, but because God loves them. Here we rise to the position of loving the person who does the evil deed while hating the deed he does.

Finally, the method of nonviolence is based on the conviction that the universe is on the side of justice. It is this deep faith in the future that causes the nonviolent resister to accept suffering without retaliation. He knows that in his struggle for justice he has cosmic companionship. This belief that God is on the side of truth and justice comes down to us from the long tradition of our Christian faith. There is something at the very center of our faith which reminds us that Good Friday may reign for a day, but ultimately it must give way to the triumphant beat of the Easter drums. Evil may so shape events that Caesar will occupy a palace and Christ a cross, but one day that same Christ will rise up and split history into A.D. and B.C., so that even the life of Caesar must be dated by his name. So in Montgomery we can walk and never get weary, because we know that there will be a great camp meeting in the promised land of freedom and justice.

This, in brief, is the method of nonviolent resistance. It is a method that challenges all people struggling for justice and freedom. God grant that we wage the struggle with dignity and discipline. May all who suffer oppression in this world reject the self-defeating method of retaliatory violence and choose the method that seeks to redeem. Through using this method wisely and courageously we will emerge from the bleak and desolate midnight of man's inhumanity to man into the bright daybreak of freedom and justice.

Malcolm X and Black Nationalism

James H. Cone

In the late 1950s and early 1960s, Malcolm X (born Malcolm Little) was the chief spokesman for the Nation of Islam, a religious and social movement whose adherents are called Black Muslims. Based primarily in large northern cities, the Nation encourages black separatism as a path to economic and social equality with whites. Malcolm X was a controversial figure because he spoke out against integration of blacks into American society.

In this article, James H. Cone discusses the life and the views of Malcolm X. Malcolm had a more lasting impact on black Americans than any other civil rights leader because he articulated the concept of black pride. He promoted a view of black history and self-worth that had been denied black Americans, both in the South where they endured segregation and in the North where they faced discrimination. Though these views were radical, they did not promote hatred of whites as was said during Malcolm's lifetime, according to Cone.

Cone is the Briggs Distinguished Professor at Union Theological Seminary in New York. He is the author of *Martin and Malcolm and America: A Dream or a Nightmare?*

No one had a greater impact on the cultural consciousness of African-Americans during the second half of the 20th century than Malcolm X. More than anyone else he revolutionized the black mind, transforming docile Negroes and self-effacing colored people into proud blacks and self-confident African-Americans. Civil rights activists became

Excerpted from James H. Cone, "Malcolm X: The Impact of a Cultural Revolutionary," *The Christian Century*, December 23–30, 1992. Copyright 1992 Christian Century Foundation. Reprinted by permission.

Black Power militants and declared, "It's nation time." Preachers and religious scholars created a black theology and proclaimed God as liberator and Jesus Christ as black. College and university students demanded and won black studies. Poets, playwrights, musicians, painters and other artists created a new black aesthetics and ardently proclaimed that "black is beautiful."

No area of the African-American community escaped Malcolm's influence. The mainstream black leaders who dismissed him as a rabble-rouser today embrace his cultural philosophy and urge blacks to love themselves first before they even think about loving others. No one loved blacks more than Malcolm nor taught us more about ourselves. Before Malcolm most blacks wanted nothing to do with Africa. But he taught us that "you can't hate the roots of the tree and not hate the tree; you can't hate your origin and not end up hating yourself; you can't hate Africa and not hate yourself." A simple, profound truth; one that blacks needed (and still need) to hear. And no one said it as effectively as Malcolm X.

Malcolm Little

Who was Malcolm X? He was born Malcolm Little in Omaha, Nebraska, on May 19, 1925. His father, J. Early Little, was a Baptist preacher and a dedicated organizer for Marcus Garvey's Universal Negro Improvement Association. His mother, M. Louise Norton, also a Garveyite, was a West Indian from Grenada.

The Little family was driven out of Omaha by the Ku Klux Klan before Malcolm reached his first birthday. Another white hate group, called the Black Legion, burned down the Little's house in Lansing, Michigan, during Malcolm's childhood. Malcolm described the experience as "the nightmare in 1929." Soon after, his father was killed, thrown under a street car by the Black Legionnaires, Malcolm reported in his *Autobiography*.

With no husband, without the proceeds of his life insurance policy (the company refused to pay) and faced with constant harassment by the state welfare officials, Louise Little, a very proud woman, broke down under the emotional and economic strain of caring for eight children during the Depression. The Little children became wards of the state. Six of them, including Malcolm, were placed in foster homes. Malcolm's delinquent behavior eventually landed him in a detention home in Mason, Michigan, where he was allowed to attend junior high. He was the only black in his class. Although Malcolm was an outstanding student and extremely popular among his peers, he dropped out of school when his white eighth grade English teacher discouraged him from becoming a lawyer and suggested carpentry as a more "realistic goal for a nigger."

From Michigan, Malcolm journeyed to Boston and then to New York where he became known as "Detroit Red." He was involved in a life of crime—numbers, dope, con games of many kinds and thievery of all sorts, including armed robbery. Malcolm described himself as "one of the most depraved parasitical hustlers" in New York—"nervy and cunning enough to live by my wits, exploiting any prey that presented itself." A few months before he reached his 21st birthday, Malcolm was convicted and sentenced to eight to ten years in a Massachusetts prison for burglary.

In prison Malcolm's life was transformed when he discovered (through the influence of an inmate) the liberating value of education and (through his family) the empowering message of Elijah Muhammad's Nation of Islam. Both gave him what he did not have: self-respect as a black person. For the first time since attending the Garvey meetings with his father, Malcolm was proud to be black and to learn about Africans who "built great empires and civilizations and cultures."

Prison Experiences

Discovering knowledge through reading raised Malcolm's consciousness. He found out that history had been "whitened" and blacks had been left out. "It's a crime," Malcolm said, expressing his anger, "the lie that has been told to generations of blacks and whites. Little innocent black children born of parents who believed that their race had no history. Little black children seeing, before they could talk, that their parents considered themselves inferior. Innocent little black children growing up, living out their lives, dying of old age—and all their lives ashamed of being black."

Malcolm pledged while in prison to use his intellectual resources to destroy black self-hate and to replace it with black self-esteem. He transformed his prison cell into a hall of learning where he educated himself about "the brainwashed condition of blacks" and the crimes which "the devil white man" had committed against them. He was so engrossed in his studies that he even forgot he was in prison. "In every free moment I had," Malcolm reflected, "if I was not reading in the library, I was reading on my bunk. You couldn't have gotten me out of books with a wedge."

It was also in prison that Malcolm developed his debating skills. Debating, he said, was "like being on a battlefield—with intellectual and philosophical bullets." He became so effective in public speaking that even his opponents had to acknowledge his talent. Martin Luther King, Jr., and other mainstream civil rights leaders refused to appear on the same platform with him. People who did debate him often regretted it. For Malcolm there was no place for moderation or disinterested objectivity when one's freedom is at stake. "You can't negotiate upon freedom," he said. "You either fight for it or shut up."

The Nation of Islam

After his release from prison in 1952 Malcolm became a minister in the Nation of Islam and its most effective recruiter and apologist. In June 1954 Elijah Muhammad appointed Malcolm the head minister of the influential Temple Number 7 in Harlem. Speaking regularly in the Temple and at many street-corner rallies, Malcolm told Harlemites that "we are black first and everything else second." "We are not Americans," he said. "We are Africans who happen to be in America. We didn't land on Plymouth Rock. That rock landed on us."

Malcolm's primary audience was the "little black people in the street," the ones at the "bottom of the social heap." His message was harsh and bitter, a "sharp truth" that "cuts" and "causes great pain." "But if you can take the truth," he assured Harlem blacks, "it will cure you and save you from an otherwise certain death." Malcolm told them that they were "zombies," "walking dead people," who had been cut off from any knowledge of their past history. "We have been robbed deaf, dumb and blind to the true knowledge of ourselves." We do not even know our names or our original language. We carry the slavemasters' names and speak their language. We even accepted the slavemasters' religion of Christianity, which teaches us that "black is a curse." How can a people make others treat and respect them as human beings if they are culturally and spiritually dead?

After describing their zombie-like state, Malcolm commanded blacks to "wake up" to "their humanity, to their own worth, and to their cultural heritage." He also told them to "clean up" themselves of drunkenness, profanity, drugs, crime and other moral failings. A resurrected, morally up-

---

Malcolm and the Black Muslims

Around the nation, the name Malcolm X triggers mixed emotions, but among the dispossessed masses of Harlem, it inspires devotion and hope. Since his ouster from the Black Muslim cult early this year—ostensibly for calling President Kennedy's assassination a case of "chickens coming home to roost"—he has pitted his own prestige against that of his former chief, Elijah Muhammad, in building a following of his own. In the process, he has ripped the Black Muslim movement into two hostile camps whose bloody encounters have become the order of the day. Purged from the No. 2 spot he used to occupy in the Black Muslim hierarchy, he is now reaching for higher stakes—participation in the Black revolt.

The entry of the firebrand advocate of bloody retaliation into the rights struggle which, as far as Blacks are concerned, has been largely non-violent, is viewed by many Blacks and Whites with grave concern. But in Harlem's tenements, where the pacific voice of Dr. Martin Luther King Jr. is but a whisper, the new power bid of Malcolm X is welcome news.

Hans J. Massaquoi, "Mystery of Malcolm X," *Ebony*, February 1993. Reprinted from *Ebony*, September 1964.

right black people will be able to "stand up" and "do something for themselves instead of sitting around and waiting for white people to solve our problems and tell us we are free."

Rejection of Integration

Initially, Malcolm's black nationalist message was very unpopular in the African-American community. The media (both white and black) portrayed him as a teacher of hate and a promoter of violence. It was the age of integration, and love and nonviolence were advocated as the only way to achieve it. Most blacks shared Martin Luther King, Jr.'s dream that they would soon enter the mainstream of American society. They really believed that the majority of whites were genuinely sorry for what America had done to blacks and were now ready to right the wrongs and to treat blacks as human beings.

Malcolm did not share the optimism of the civil rights movement and thus found himself speaking to many unsympathetic audiences. He did not mind speaking against the dominant mood of the time as long as he knew that he was speaking the truth. He defined the Nation of Islam as "the religion of naked, undressed truth." "You shall know the truth and the truth shall make you free" was his favorite biblical passage. "If you are afraid to tell truth," he railed at his audience, "you don't deserve freedom." With truth on his side, Malcolm relished the odds that were against him. His task was to wake up "dead Negroes" by revealing to them the truth about America and about themselves.

The enormity of this challenge motivated Malcolm to attack head on the philosophy of Martin King and the civil rights movement. He dismissed the charge that he was teaching hate: "It is the man who has made a slave out of you who is teaching hate." He rejected integration: "An integrated cup of coffee is insufficient pay for 400 years of slave labor." He denounced nonviolence as "the philosophy of a fool": "There is no philosophy more befitting to the white man's tactics for keeping his foot on the black man's neck." He ridiculed King's 1963 "I have a dream" speech: "While King was having a dream, the rest of us Negroes are having a nightmare." He also rejected as inhuman King's command to love the enemy: "It is not possible to love a man whose chief purpose in life is to humiliate you and still be considered a normal human being."

The Break with the Nation

As long as Malcolm stayed in the Black Muslim movement he was not entirely free to speak his own mind. He had to represent Elijah Muhammad, the sole and absolute authority in the Nation of Islam. But in December 1963 Malcolm disobeyed Muhammad and described President Kennedy's assassination as an instance of the "chickens coming home to roost." Muhammad rebuked him and used the incident as an opportunity to silence his star pupil—first for 90 days and then indefinitely. Malcolm soon realized that much more was involved in his silence than what he had said about the Kennedy assassination. Jealousy and envy in Muhammad's family circle were the primary motives behind his silencing, and this meant the ban would never be lifted.

For the sake of black people who needed to hear the message of black self-worth he was so adept in proclaiming, Malcolm reluctantly declared his independence in March 1964. His break with the Black Muslim movement was an important turning point. He was now free to develop his own philosophy of the black freedom struggle.

Malcolm, however, had already begun to show independent thinking in his great "Message to the Grass Roots" speech, given in Detroit three weeks before his silencing. In that speech he endorsed black nationalism as his political philosophy, thereby separating himself not only from the civil rights movement but, more important, from Muhammad, who had defined the Nation as strictly religious and apolitical. Malcolm contrasted "the black revolution" with "the Negro revolution." The black revolution, he said, is "worldwide," and it is "bloody," "hostile" and "knows no compromise." But the so-called Negro revolution is not even a revolution. Malcolm mocked it: "The only revolution in which the goal is loving your enemy is the Negro revolution. It's the only revolution in which the goal is a desegregated lunch counter, a desegregated theater, a desegregated public park, a desegregated public toilet; you can sit down next to white folks on the toilet." He smiled as the audience broke into hearty laughter at this.

Black Nationalism

After his break with Muhammad, Malcolm developed more fully his cultural and political black nationalist philosophy in a speech titled, "The Ballot or the Bullet." In urging blacks to exercise their constitutional right to vote, he made a move toward King and the civil rights movement. Later he became more explicit: "Dr. King wants the same thing I want—freedom." Malcolm wanted to join the civil rights movement in order to expand it into a human rights movement, thereby internationalizing the black freedom struggle, making it more radical and more militant.

During his period of independence from the Nation of Islam nothing influenced Malcolm more than his travels abroad. He visited countries in the Middle East, Africa and Europe, where he explained the black struggle for justice in the U.S. and linked it with liberation struggles throughout the world. "You can't understand what is going on in Mississippi if you don't know what is going on in the Congo," he told Harlem blacks. "They are both the same. The same interests are at stake."

On February 21, 1965, Malcolm X was shot down by assassins as he started to speak to a crowd of 400 blacks at the Audubon Ballroom in Harlem. He was only 39.

Although dead for nearly 27 years, Malcolm's influence in the African-American community is much greater today than during his lifetime. His most far-reaching impact was among the masses of African-Americans in the ghettos of American cities. He told them, as James Baldwin observed, that "they should be proud of being black and God knows they should be. This is a very important thing to hear in a country that assures you that you should be ashamed of it." Saying what Malcolm meant to her, a Harlemite said: "He taught me that I was more than a Little Black Sambo or kinky hair or nigger."

Southern States Sidestep Desegregation Orders

Forrest R. White

The Supreme Court decision in *Brown* v. *Board of Education of Topeka, Kansas,* in 1954 and the enforcement decree in 1955 are usually credited as decisive blows against legal segregation. But southern states openly resisted these decisions and acted to preserve their traditional racial separatism.

Local officials throughout the South—on city councils, school boards, and development boards—adopted a subtle but effective approach to preserving racial separatism, according to Forrest R. White. They redrew school districts, rezoned development plans, and redrew neighborhood and even city boundaries along racial lines. In this way, they copied the tactics used by northern cities, whose extralegal racial discrimination schemes were not affected by the Supreme Court's decrees. The economic and social costs of these hasty actions were high. Their effects remain visible throughout the South today.

White is the budget director for the Norfolk, Virginia, Public School District. He is the author of *Pride and Prejudice: School Desegregation and Urban Renewal in Norfolk, 1950–1959.*

Although the conventional view of *Oliver Brown, et al.* v. *Board of Education of Topeka, Shawnee County, Kansas, et al.,* decided by the United States Supreme Court 40 years ago last May, is that the ruling came as a bolt from the blue, only the extent of the decree actually came as a surprise to most of those who were charged with the planning and leadership of southern cities. There is now compelling evidence to sug-

Excerpted from Forrest R. White, "*Brown* Revisited," *Phi Delta Kappan*, September 1994. Reprinted with permission. (Endnotes in the original have been omitted in this reprint.)

gest that the 1954 *Brown* decision and its enforcement decree a year later were merely the keystone events in a decade-long effort to replace the South's elaborate system of legal (de jure) segregation with the type of de facto segregation found in northern, western, and midwestern cities as a result of well-defined racial barriers between neighborhoods.

The *Brown* Decision Was Anticipated

That there would be some sort of decision from the Court overruling at least a portion of the South's elaborate system of segregated education was a foregone conclusion among many southern leaders; clearly, the "separate but equal" facilities maintained by communities, particularly those in rural areas, were so far from equivalent that only the most callous Court could disregard the distinction. Moreover, the nation was already desegregating its facilities for the military, for interstate transportation, for public accommodation, and for recreation—either through administrative action or through legal intervention—and it was hard to imagine that a country that had so recently committed itself to fighting oppressors overseas would allow its own public schools to remain bastions of racial subjugation at home.

It now appears that the individuals charged with the leadership and management of southern cities had ample time, opportunity, and motivation to prepare for the legally mandated demise of segregated schools and facilities in their communities; that they started making plans in anticipation of such a ruling long before the *Brown* case was ever decided; and that their preparations grew increasingly intense as the prospect of court-ordered integration became more and more real. Furthermore, it seems that these leaders took deliberate steps to use all the powers at their disposal—both direct (those related to the control of school construction, educational administration, and student attendance) and indirect (those that fall under the headings of redevelopment, city planning, the enforcement of codes, and urban renewal)—to forestall court-ordered school desegregation in the South. The impact of their preemptive actions has been almost as profound as the *Brown* decision itself and can still be seen today in carefully contrived boundaries of school zones and neighborhoods, mis-sized and misplaced school buildings, demolished housing, redeveloped properties, and inappropriate use of municipal land.

Thus, although the decade of the 1950s was a time in which a carefully planned and executed legal assault on school desegregation finally bore fruit, it was also the era in which the impact of the High Court's ruling was largely minimized and even negated in many communities by an equally well-planned and quietly orchestrated underground resistance. Unfortunately, the traditional histories of this decade have focused almost entirely on the shouting match that was going on in the streets and in the legislative corridors and have largely ignored the far more consequential planning sessions that were taking place in the back rooms of city halls across the South. . . .

Interposition

In November 1955 James Kilpatrick, editor of the *Richmond News Leader*, began to promote the doctrine of "interposition"—a long-lost constitutional interpretation that compels states to "interpose" their own authority in order to protect their citizens from unjust actions of the federal government—as the answer to continuing segregation. The idea was an immediate hit and soon dominated the rhetoric of southern politicians, even in the border states that had already begun to desegregate. Within 18 months after Kilpatrick began to promote interposition as a valid legal doctrine, all eight of the states of the Deep South had passed formal interposition resolutions and a number of laws designed to use the police powers of their states to enforce segregation of their schools, parks, and playgrounds. Since it was the potential integration of the schools that caused the most public panic, the interposition argument was pushed to its greatest extreme in defense of segregated education. Even so, the states were not without creativity in their attempt to preserve segregation in other facilities, even going so far as to turn their state parks over to private contractors as a ruse to continue racial discrimination.

In addition to the anti-NAACP laws that were enacted in most of the states of the Deep South, eight states passed pupil placement laws designed to block transfers between white schools and black ones, six states authorized the closing of public schools under the threat of integration, four states provided financial aid to students who attended private schools to escape court-ordered desegregation, and most weakened their laws on compulsory attendance, teacher salaries, pupil transportation, the term of teacher contracts, and the like. Each of these laws was an attempt to delay desegregation by forcing the courts to peel away a layer of state government that had been interposed between the local schools and the courts. The doctrine of interposition was at the heart of the Southern Manifesto as well. Signed by 100 southern senators and congressmen, the manifesto proclaimed that integration was "contrary to established law" and professed that government officials had a duty to resist integration "with every legal means" at their disposal.

Although most of the rhetoric of interposition was emanating from state political leaders, most of the active efforts to block the federal courts were undertaken by local school officials because they possessed the most direct powers to manage public schools, assign pupils, manipulate attendance zones, build new buildings, and otherwise control the racial composition of classrooms. Soon, however, local governments found that some of the same tactics that could be used to block the desegregation of schools had wide applications in preserving segregated neighborhoods as well. Suddenly the race was on to rezone, rebuild, and redevelop the cities in an all-out effort to create well-defined color barriers between neighborhoods, to isolate black populations, to demolish mixed-race areas, to relocate integrated schools, and otherwise to create an even more segregated society than had existed before *Brown*.

Foremost among the local powers of interposition were the ability actually to assign individual students to schools and the authority to control the size and shape of school attendance zones. At least seven states relied on the creative use of pupil assignment as a way to deter integration. Several factors other than the race of the students could be used to support the creation of school attendance zones: the distance from home to school, the maximum utilization of school space, transportation considerations, topographical barriers, and the conformity of institutions (which was meant to prevent frequent transfers).

Northern and midwestern cities intent on limiting integration already relied heavily on their authority to draw boundary lines that reflected the racial characteristics of the neighborhoods rather than the locations of the schools, and it did not take long for southern school officials to become just as adept at blocking desegregation with this technique. When faced with court-ordered desegregation, the city of Charlottesville, Virginia, for instance, divided itself into six elementary school zones; the lines of one of the "black" zones were so carefully drawn that the area included almost all the black students who had applied to go to previously all-white schools.

Southern leaders also found that the federal courts would grant them broad leeway to exercise their "administrative discretion" in matters of construction and zoning—even if administrative discretion had the same effect, because of prevailing housing patterns, as designating a building as a "white" or "black" facility. Several practices related to determining the location and size of new buildings and limiting attendance zones had been used for decades in northern cities to limit integration. The careful location of schools and other public buildings for the purpose of minimizing integration was not only accepted by the courts but also strongly urged by newspaper editor Kilpatrick, who was fast becoming the chief spokesman for southern defiance. "A great part of the problem, especially in the cities, could be handled by the relocation of school buildings and the gerrymandering of enrollment lines," he counseled. The Richmond school board, under the leadership of Lewis Powell, Jr., who was later to sit on the U.S. Supreme Court, responded to Kilpatrick's advice by building several new schools in black neighborhoods. Norfolk created one new school by pushing six mobile classrooms off the back of a truck a few weeks after the federal district court released the addresses of the plaintiffs in its own school desegregation suit. The undisputed administrative authority of the local boards extended even to the assignment of a general racial designation to a facility. Norfolk and Newport News, Virginia, both turned formerly all-white elementary schools over to their black school systems in order to deter an impending desegregation ruling from the courts. Norfolk even built six minischools, with five rooms each, to ensure the single-race composition of their attendance zones.

Legal Rezoning Preserves Segregation

Thus in the period immediately following the *Brown* decision, almost every school board and governmental agency in the South was focusing on the proximity of black students to white schools. The realization was growing that school boards, city councils, and other public agencies were not powerless before the courts. Legal scholars were careful to point out that "the Constitution . . . does not require integration. It merely forbids discrimination. It does not forbid such discrimination as occurs as a result of voluntary action [such as choice of residence, neighborhood, or city]."

City councils, although generally more reluctant than their school boards to take overt actions to block the federal courts, were just as motivated to use every legal means at their disposal to delay or deter the threat of school desegregation, even going so far as to appropriate school funds on a month-to-month basis so as to intimidate black leaders and keep their school boards in check. Although most of the cities' powers were related to urban renewal—redevelopment, planning, zoning, enforcement of codes, and economic development—and not to schools, southern cities were quick to learn that they possessed a potent arsenal of tools that could be used to block integration.

Closing a threatened school was a community's most obvious defense when faced with a court order to desegregate, and school-closing powers lay at the heart of Virginia's "Massive Resistance" statutes—the governor was required to close any integrated public school—and at the heart of its more unofficial system of providing public support for segregated (white) private schools. Schools in Norfolk, Arlington, and Charlottesville were closed by the state for most of the 1958–59 school year, locking out 10,000 white students in Norfolk alone. Prince Edward County, however, provided the best example of Virginia's Massive Resistance plan: public schools there were closed for several years while a white private academy flourished with state-supported tuition grants.

Even though closing schools was thought to be the ultimate weapon in the fight against school desegregation, closing whole neighborhoods was even more destructive, and it was the application of municipal powers related to urban renewal that had the most lasting effect on the South. Robert Weaver, who was then director of the federal Housing and Home Finance Agency, has written that, "in a few southern cities . . . urban renewal too often seemed to be an instrument for wiping out racially integrated living." This was certainly the case in Norfolk, where a frantic second stage of redevelopment tore down the homes of almost 20,000 people—nearly one-tenth of the population—in little more than a year. Unlike earlier redevelopment efforts, this one did not focus on substandard multifamily structures in central city slums, although Norfolk still had plenty of those. Instead, most of the houses that were destroyed were safe, decent, and even modern homes of middle-class families living on the edge of downtown. Their sudden demolition had little to do with the quality of housing; rather, demolition was driven by the fact that the houses were located in the mixed-race neighborhoods where all the plaintiffs in the city's school desegregation suit lived.

Just as effective as tearing down all the houses in a neighborhood was the selective renewal of mixed-race areas or the resizing of neighborhoods with the careful placement of public land. Some cities—notably Mobile, Alabama—relied on their interstate highways to divide neighborhoods and school attendance zones into racially distinct areas. Others, when faced with a situation in which black students lived closer to white schools than to black ones, used their powers to acquire additional land for parks, playgrounds, state colleges, industrial parks, or other public purposes, thereby placing topographical barriers between neighborhoods and thus preserving the racial character of their schools. St. Louis and Baltimore appear to have employed a combination of natural geographic barriers and selective redevelopment to keep blacks confined to racially distinct school attendance zones.

Just as school boards could manipulate attendance zones, cities could change their own size through merger and annexation and thus alter the pattern of school attendance. When Newport News was faced with court-ordered desegregation in 1958, for instance, the city merged with Warwick County, and the resultant ripple effect on school attendance zones allowed it to delay integration successfully for another year. Richmond also used this strategy effectively, and at least one study has indicated that this city's efforts to annex surrounding counties was motivated largely by racial considerations.

All Levels of Government Seek to Preserve Segregation

Thus the local governments—even more than the states— had at their disposal a large arsenal of powers that could be "interposed" between the courts and the schools to create segregated neighborhoods, enforce well-defined color barriers, isolate black populations, relocate integrated schools, and otherwise forestall court-ordered school desegregation. This was certainly the charge by plaintiffs in a number of school desegregation suits—a claim in part supported by demographic researchers and other social scientists, but they have chosen to blame school boards rather than redevelopment authorities, planning commissions, or city councils. Most educational researchers have chosen to focus on the political implications of decisions that were made by school boards only when they actually faced a court order to desegregate. Thus they lend credence to the theory that, in most communities, the school boards were the villains.

The truth is that school boards were merely being dragged along in the planning, redevelopment, and housing activities of other local officials; that is, the placement of schools and the drawing of new attendance zones in many cities were only the last acts in a far more elaborate plot to replace de jure segregation with de facto segregation. In fact, southern cities appear to have used their powers of urban renewal to forestall school desegregation more often in the 1950s than in the 1960s, the decade for which more extensive documentation exists. Not only was the motivation perhaps stronger in the 1950s, but also community groups and the courts were less inclined to scrutinize actions that bore the imprint of racial planning—partly because up to that point all planning in the South, and in most of the rest of the nation as well, was designed to support the "separate but equal" and "neighborhoods of choice" concepts that were legally permissible for several years after Brown.

In light of the enormous controversy surrounding school desegregation, it is not hard to see how the same tools that could be used to promote new growth could just as easily be enlisted in the effort to prevent certain land uses, especially those related to integrated school districts. The building boom that was already going on in most southern communities provided ample opportunity to apply the powers of urban renewal to the preservation of segregated schools. In addition, in the older cities of the South, there was a feeling of urgency prompted by situations in which blacks lived in closer proximity to white schools than to their own. It was when these two factors—opportunity and urgency—were present to a large degree that redevelopment projects, the building of new schools and highways, and other public initiatives were undertaken, partly to achieve racially segregated school districts—that is, to move with all deliberate speed from de jure to de facto segregation.

The NAACP Did Not Anticipate Southern Schemes

Thurgood Marshall and the lawyers at Howard University who plotted the demise of school segregation laws for the NAACP knew that it would take years to overthrow the legal structure that both established separate-race schools and kept them unequal. They knew as well that it would take decades to overcome centuries of prejudice and the peculiar social and political conventions that supported segregated schools. They did not know, however, that they were up against forces in the South that were even then working just as hard to undermine and counteract their efforts. And they never contemplated that these same forces would be willing to wreak long-term havoc on their own communities—to close schools, demolish neighborhoods, artificially divide cities, and manipulate the size and location of school buildings—just to preserve an outdated social doctrine.

The school desegregation battle passed relatively quickly, leaving only a few brief, but indelible memories—federal troops in Little Rock, padlocked schools in Norfolk, George Wallace blocking the doors to Ole Miss—before de jure segregation faded forever from the national scene. Unfortunately, the scars of the effort to forestall desegregation through interposition are far more lasting and can still be seen today in mis-sized and misplaced schools, needlessly demolished homes and neighborhoods, poorly and hastily contrived urban renewal efforts, and highways created partly to divide residential zones.

Massive Resistance by Southern States

Calvin Trillin

In response to the 1955 *Brown* implementation order, many southern states adopted a policy of "massive resistance" to desegregation. These states argued that it was each state's right to determine social policy and to implement laws. The Mississippi State Sovereignty Commission was formed to prevent what was seen as federal and judicial encroachment on the authority and power of the state.

The efforts of the commission to resist integration appear nearly comic today, in Calvin Trillin's view. The investigations of suspected miscegenation and the surveillance of the comings and goings of "integrationists" seem amusing now, though they were in deadly earnest in the 1950s. The commission ruined the reputations and careers of a number of civil rights supporters. Its opposition to civil rights likely also emboldened Klan members who murdered civil rights activists. Mississippi engaged in an effort to create a closed society by controlling the media and suppressing dissenting opinions. But its adherence to a tradition of racial separatism could not withstand the national pressure for desegregation created by the civil rights movement.

Trillin was a reporter for *Time* during the 1960s and is now a regular contributor to the *New Yorker*. He is the author of many books, including *An Education in Georgia: Charlayne Hunter, Hamilton Holmes and the Integration of the University of Georgia*.

When it comes to the operations of the Mississippi State Sovereignty Commission, I have always been partial to the smaller stories. Consider, for example, the Grenada, Mississippi, baby inspection. In the early sixties, a white woman in Grenada, a county seat in the north-central part of the state, gave birth to an out-of-wedlock baby, and there were rumors around town that the baby had been fathered by a black man. The State Sovereignty Commission had been established by the legislature in 1956, in the days when the white South was erecting its defenses against the decision of the United States Supreme Court, in Brown v. Board of Education, that segregation in public education is unconstitutional. The Commission was charged to "do and perform any and all acts and things deemed necessary and proper to protect the sovereignty of the State of Mississippi, and her sister states, from encroachment thereon by the federal government." Being an agency that always interpreted that mission broadly, it dispatched one of its investigators, Tom Scarbrough, to see if Grenada had truly been the scene of what Southern politicians of that era tended to call the mongrelization of the races.

Racial Classification

After interviewing a number of Grenada residents, Scarbrough accompanied the local sheriff for an inspection of the baby under suspicion. It's easy to envision those two officials of the State of Mississippi trying to edge in close to the crib— large men, as I imagine them, with the sheriff wearing a pistol and further burdened, perhaps, by what people in regular contact with the Southern law-enforcement community come to think of as a sheriff's belly. In Scarbrough's report, which ran four or five thousand words, he wrote, "I was looking at the child's fingernails and the end of its fingers very closely." From this I assume that he believed African ancestry could be detected by the presence of distinctive half-moons at the cuticles—a theory that was an article of faith in my grade school in Missouri, during a period when I was also persuaded for a while that Japanese people had yellow blood. The baby's fingernails might have been too small for a conclusive half-moon search. Scarbrough said in his report, "We both agreed we were not qualified to say it was a part Negro

child, but we could say it was not 100 percent Caucasian."
Perhaps sensing this indecision, the mother parried shrewdly:
the baby's father, she said, was Italian.

The Commission's Files

Even as a connoisseur of the smaller stories, I acknowledge
that the big stories do carry a certain impact. Officially, the
files of the State Sovereignty Commission remain sealed
until a lawsuit to open them, which began in federal district
court in 1977, is finally resolved. But the activity surrounding the suit has already dislodged formerly secret information that has resulted in front-page headlines about stories
that made front-page headlines the first time around. It is
now known, for instance, that an early black applicant to the
University of Southern Mississippi who was convicted of
several crimes and thrown into prison was framed; an alternative plan was to murder him. It is known that during the
1964 trial of Byron De La Beckwith for the murder of
Medgar Evers the Sovereignty Commission investigated potential jurors for the defense and furnished such capsule bi-
ographies as "He is a contractor and believed to be Jewish."
It is known that the Sovereignty Commission got weekly reports from paid spies within the Council of Federated Organizations (COFO), the umbrella organization of the 1964
voter-registration effort known as the Mississippi Summer
Project, and that it distributed license-plate numbers of
COFO cars, including the one that Michael Schwerner and
James Chaney and Andrew Goodman had been riding in before they were murdered, in Neshoba County, that summer.

In 1990, such stories, based on State Sovereignty Commission documents, ran for eight pages one day in the Jackson *Clarion-Ledger*, which reported not only that a black
newspaper editor had been on the Commission's payroll—
one of his duties was to run a story, furnished by the Sovereignty Commission, that linked Martin Luther King, Jr., to
the Communist Party—but that the *Clarion-Ledger* itself had
routinely killed stories that the Sovereignty Commission
wanted killed and run stories that the Sovereignty Commission wanted run. According to a memo quoted in the *Clarion-*

Ledger in 1990 by Jerry Mitchell, the reporter who revealed many of the Sovereignty Commission documents, the Commission had even prevailed on the Jackson newspapers to drop the honorific "Rev." from the names of ministers who were civil-rights activists: "Our friends of the press could drop their titles from news articles and if queried they could say they do not consider them as ministers 'as how can a man profess to serve God when he is actually serving atheistic Communism?'"

For me, practically any document in the secret files of the State Sovereignty Commission has a certain resonance: at the beginning of the sixties, I was in and out of Mississippi, originally as a reporter for the Southern bureau of *Time*. I can now place the source, say, of a front-page Jackson *Daily News* item that I've kept all these years—an item that begins, under a four-column headline, "Mississippi authorities have learned that the apparently endless 'freedom' rides into Mississippi and the south were planned in Havana, Cuba, last winter by officials of the Soviet Union." Reading about Tom Scarbrough's fingernail inspection brings back into focus what I came to think of during my time in the South as a regional obsession with yard-sale anthropology. Any number of white people explained to me, for instance, that the brains of black people were capable of processing specific statements but not general or abstract statements. (My response was always "Give me an example.")

Life in Mississippi

But, as I go through the State Sovereignty Commission material now available, what I still find most interesting is how small a deviation from the Mississippi way of life was required to attract the attention of Scarbrough or one of his colleagues—a pastor's attendance at an interracial meeting or a professor's choice of a suspect textbook or a student's attendance at the wrong concert. That was the aspect of the Commission that had most fascinated me from the start— from the time, in 1961, when I spent a few days in the state to look into revelations that the Sovereignty Commission had tried to smear a senior at the University of Mississippi named Billy Barton, who was running for the editorship of the Ole Miss newspaper. The rumors that had been spread about Billy Barton accused him of, among other things, being a protégé of Ralph McGill—an accusation that Barton, of course, vehemently denied. He said he had never met Ralph McGill, the Atlanta newspaperman who was then widely considered by people outside the South to be the region's most distinguished journalist; and he voluntarily took a lie-detector test to confirm that statement.

Because Barton's file became public and could easily be shown to be nonsense, the case provoked some weekly newspaper editors in Mississippi into criticizing the Commission as a sort of cornpone Gestapo that had got out of hand. But in 1961 the Mississippi State Sovereignty Commission had no reason to fear grumbling from a few county weeklies. It acknowledged, in a speech given around the state, that it kept a file on "persons whose utterances or actions indicate they should be watched with suspicion on future racial attitudes." It openly contributed five thousand dollars of taxpayers' money every month to the Citizens Council—sometimes referred to as the uptown Klan—which claimed a membership of ninety thousand and was considered the most influential political force in the state. Several members of the Citizens Council's executive committee also sat on the Sovereignty Commission, and some observers considered the Commission to be basically a device for providing the Citizens Council with the resources and legitimacy of the state. Except for the smattering of editorials provoked by the Billy Barton case, there was little significant opposition to any of this. Partly through the economic intimidation that was the specialty of the Citizens Council, most of Mississippi's small store of moderate and liberal whites had been silenced or driven from the state.

The Closed Society

One of those who remained, an Ole Miss history professor named James W. Silver, wrote in the early sixties that "Mississippi is the way it is not because of its views on the Negro—here it is simply 'the South exaggerated'—but because of its closed society, its refusal to allow freedom of inquiry or to tolerate 'error of opinion.'" (Even before those words were printed in an influential book by Silver called "Mississippi: The Closed Society," the director of the State Sovereignty Commission had written to the chairman of the university's board of trustees outlining what a Commission report described as "various reasons why Dr. James Silver could be terminated from his position at the University of Mississippi without any risk of losing the University's accreditation.") Being guilty of an error of opinion did not require a drastic deviation from the Mississippi mainstream: at the time, the Citizens Council's definition of subversive organizations was broad enough to include both the Methodist Church and the United States Air Force. In other Southern states, agencies similar to the State Sovereignty Commission tended to be modest operations that left it to law-enforcement agencies to keep extensive files on people suspected of being potential "race mixers." The Mississippi State Sovereignty Commission, which had no law-enforcement duties, estimated that its files included information on ten thousand people. Mississippi was the only place where a state agency saw its duty as coördinating all aspects of the effort to maintain white supremacy, including propaganda films, thought control, and baby inspection. A completely closed society in one out of fifty states was not possible, of course, but any effort in that direction had to include the attention to minutiae which I found so fascinating.

After I began going to Mississippi, there were times when I had to remind myself that I was in one of the fifty states. In those days, a reporter from a magazine published in New York could feel like a visitor to a foreign land almost anywhere in the Deep South. White people who weren't simply hostile would often explain certain fundamental truths in the tone that a citizen of some exotic but long-established country might use to enlighten a slightly dim American tourist on rudimentary history: Northerners didn't understand Negroes the way Southerners did; local Negroes were perfectly content; race trouble was caused by outside agitators, who were mostly Communists. In almost any Southern state, there were leaders who made daily pronouncements that seemed foreign to what American children were supposedly taught in school (even the schools I went to in Missouri, which were segregated by law at the time) about equality and opportunity in the Land of the Free. But only Mississippi seemed to have come close to shutting out the rest of the country.

Mississippi Racial Attitudes

In Mississippi in 1961, there didn't seem to be any other side; it was as if a secret agreement had been made to insist that day be called night, and the entire white population of the state had been in on it. Everything appeared to be under control. The segregation of the races was complete. Voting was essentially a privilege limited to white people. Until a sit-in at the Jackson public library by students from Tougaloo, a black college on the outskirts of town, the demonstrations then sweeping other Southern cities were not seen in Jackson. Those who ran the state operated as if the Mississippi way of life were invulnerable. The State Sovereignty Commission was actually sending various prominent Mississippians to Northern service-club luncheons to talk about the tranquillity of Mississippi's race relations. The premise was not that the movement had not yet arrived in Mississippi but that it would never arrive.

In Alabama, the Freedom Riders, who came through a couple of months after the Billy Barton controversy, were attacked in Anniston and Birmingham and Montgomery; in Mississippi, residents lined the road as the bus passed, like an army under orders to stand down, and the Freedom Riders were politely arrested in the Jackson bus station for breach of peace. The next day, the governor, Ross Barnett, welcomed the reporters who were covering the Freedom Ride, and the mayor of Jackson gave each one an honorary Jackson police badge. I still have mine. (There were three black reporters on the bus, and they had not been arrested. "Professional courtesy," the police chief explained.) Among reporters in the South, Alabama was considered more dangerous then, but Mississippi, where strangers might say hello on the street and ask you how you were enjoying your visit, was somehow more ominous. Sometimes after working in Mississippi for a few days I'd drive to Memphis to write my copy and send it out. When I called my office, in Atlanta, I'd say, "I've slipped over the border."

Tales from the Files

By 1964, when Paul B. Johnson, Jr., became governor, the Mississippi monolith was beginning to show cracks. It had taken some serious hits, like the desegregation of Ole Miss, and there was enough activity by the race mixers to make Johnson's term among the busiest four years in the State Sovereignty Commission's history. Documents and reports and correspondence that the Commission routinely sent to Governor Johnson's office constitute the largest collection of Commission papers now accessible to the public. They were among the papers that the Johnson family donated to the University of Southern Mississippi, in Hattiesburg, and they were made accessible in 1989 through a state court order obtained by the *Clarion-Ledger.* The picture that emerges from the Paul Johnson papers is of a Sovereignty Commission staff, which was never very large, dashing around the state in an effort to spy on a voter-registration drive here and put an end to a boycott there. Still, as I went through the files in the W.D. McCain Library and Archives of U.S.M. one day not long ago, I found that the Commission always seemed to have time for missions of the baby-inspection variety. In 1965, for instance, Governor Johnson received a letter, written in longhand, from a couple in Biloxi. "Dear Governor Johnson," it began. "We regret to say that for the first time in our lives we need your help very badly. We are native Mississippians and are presently living in Biloxi. Our only daughter is a freshman at the University of Southern Miss. She has never before caused us any worry. However, she is in love with a Biloxi boy who looks and is said to be part Negro. . . ."

"Your recent letter and your situation fills me with great apprehension," the Governor wrote back at once. "I am having this matter investigated to the fullest." Tom Scarbrough had already been dispatched to the Gulf Coast to investigate the lineage of the suitor—presumably under orders to exercise a level of discretion that would have made a close inspection of fingernails out of the question. In a three-thousand-word report Scarbrough concluded that the young man was from a group of people in Vancleave, Mississippi, who were sometimes called "redbones" or "Vancleave Indians"—people who had always gone to white schools and churches but had always been suspected by their neighbors of being part black. (I once did a piece about a similar group, called the Turks, in South Carolina, and the standard opinion of longtime neighbors was reflected by a woman who told me, "Oh, they got some of it in 'em, all right.") The possibility of arranging to have the suitor drafted—a solution hinted at in the letter from his girlfriend's distraught parents—was looked into and dropped when it became apparent that he was too young for the draft. I couldn't find any indication in the McCain Library files that the Sovereignty Commission was able to break up the romance, but in what other state in what other period of American history could parents of no great influence write to the governor about a suitor they considered inappropriate and have the governor get right on the case? . . .

The Absence of Pressure to Change

In a way, the code phrases Mississippi used—"state sovereignty" for its system of white supremacy, "federal encroachment" for the national pressure to change—offered an accurate reflection of the situation. The Mississippi way of life was always vulnerable to contact with national institutions—the Methodist Church or the United States Air Force or the United States Court of Appeals for the Fifth Circuit. For many years, though, the pressure from Washington was not much more than nominal. Federal civil-rights legislation was bottled up by a powerful bloc of Southern senators. The Presidents in office in the decade after the Brown decision, when Mississippi was doing its best to run what James Silver called the Closed Society, did not treat the restoration of civil rights to black people in the South as a national priority. Dwight D. Eisenhower was identified with the view that you can't legislate morality. John F. Kennedy seemed to consider segregation a deplorable but essentially unalterable regional situation that was inconvenient mainly because it caused embarrassment overseas. Even Northern politicians who were particularly critical of Mississippi's single-race elections would not challenge their legitimacy, as Ed King and other delegates of the Freedom Democratic Party found out at the Democratic National Convention of 1964 when they tried to get seated in place of the all-white delegation from Mississippi. Reading through State Sovereignty Commission documents did not change my view that Mississippi had been sui generis, but it did remind me that the Closed Society had existed quite comfortably for years within the society of the United States of America. When I was in Mississippi in those days, I may have had thoughts of slipping over the border, but I was in my own country the entire time.

The Federal Government's Litigation Strategy

John Doar

In August 1957, Congress passed the first piece of civil rights legislation since Reconstruction. The Civil Rights Act of 1957 created a Civil Rights Division empowered to file federal lawsuits against state officials who violated the voting rights of American citizens. In April 1960, Congress added another statute that authorized federal judges to appoint referees to investigate voter registration irregularities.

In the following viewpoint, John Doar describes the Civil Rights Division's strategy to enforce these two acts. The division attempted to file a lawsuit against at least one registrar in every county of Louisiana, Mississippi, and Alabama. It also contested the constitutionality of those states' voter registration laws, arguing that they were engineered to keep blacks from legally registering. Though its efforts were slow to force changes in state laws, the division compiled overwhelming legal evidence that blacks were being denied the right to vote in southern states. This evidence convinced Congress of the need to pass stronger civil rights acts.

Doar was an attorney and an assistant attorney general with the Civil Rights Division from 1960 to 1967. He is now managing partner at the law firm of Doar Devorkin and Rieck in New York City.

In 1957 Congress created the Civil Rights Division (Division) as part of the Civil Rights Act of 1957. During the first two and one-half years of its life, the Division moved slowly. As late as February 1960 the Division had not yet begun to

Excerpted from John Doar, "The Work of the Civil Rights Division in Enforcing Voting Rights Under the Civil Rights Act of 1957 and 1960," *Florida State University Law Review*, Fall 1997. Copyright ©1997 by John Doar. Reprinted by permission of the author. (Footnotes in the original have been omitted in this reprint.)

act effectively to bar racial discrimination in voting.

In 1960 the Division faced extraordinary obstacles. Distinguished constitutional lawyers believed that, under the Constitution, the federal government had no power to regulate voter qualifications. According to these scholars, voter qualifications were the exclusive domain of the separate states. Each state was entitled to make an independent determination as to how literate or intelligent its citizens must be before being allowed to participate in local, state, and national elections. Because of this uncertainty, the U.S. Attorney General, William Rogers, decided that the Division should proceed cautiously until the Supreme Court decided the extent of federal authority over voting.

Differences Between State Voter Qualifications

Still, there was much that needed to be done. While Louisiana, Mississippi, and Alabama do not comprise much of the United States, the size of these states is considerable. Shreveport, at the Texas border of Louisiana, is 500 miles west of the Alabama-Georgia border. Memphis, Tennessee, is 400 miles north of New Orleans. Each of the states had its own laws respecting voter qualifications. In each state, registration procedures and practices were different. Each had peculiar application forms.

Local county or parish officials administered the state registration laws. There were some 160 counties or parishes within the states, and most needed to have their practices investigated to determine whether a pattern of racial discrimination in voting existed.

Besides the uncertain state of the law, and the size of the area where enforcement was required, there was another problem. In 1960 the Division was small—very small. It consisted of about fifteen lawyers who, as if the Division did not have enough to do, had been assigned criminal and civil jurisdiction over election fraud and federal custody matters.

Fortunately, the Division was not without resources. Among its lawyers were two remarkable men. St. John Barrett was the Division's second assistant. Harold Greene was the head of the Division's Appeals and Research Section.

Four young lawyers were apprentices to Barrett and Greene: Dave Norman, Bob Owen, Frank Dunbaugh, and Nick Flannery. Norman and Owen were among the first of the Department of Justice's honor recruits. They brought complementary abilities to the Division. A large amount of the credit for the development of the government's strategy in enforcing the Civil Rights Act of 1957 belongs to Norman, and the credit for implementing that strategy with skill, energy, and style belongs to Owen.

These lawyers quickly demonstrated their talent. In early 1961, Judge Frank Johnson of the Middle District of Alabama set the government's Macon County, Alabama, racial discrimination voting case down for trial. In a matter of days, the team of Owen, Norman, and Dunbaugh had prepared the case. Following a trial, Judge Johnson accepted the suggestion of the Division that later became known as freezing relief. He ordered the Board of Registrars to register applicants who met the qualification of the least qualified white on the voting rolls. Since the Division had proved there was universal white suffrage in Macon County, Alabama, the only qualification for voting in Macon County under Judge Johnson's order was age and residence.

Robert Kennedy Calls for Action

When Robert Kennedy arrived as the U.S. Attorney General, he was determined to make a mark for the new administration in enforcing the Civil Rights Acts. He selected Burke Marshall to head the Division. Throughout his tenure, Marshall directed and honed the Division's enforcement strategy as it was being developed by Barrett, Greene, Norman, and Owen.

Shortly thereafter, we were called to the Attorney General's office to outline the Division's strategy in enforcing the Civil Rights Acts of 1957 and 1960. Kennedy went directly to the point by asking how we were going to get something accomplished in Louisiana, Mississippi, and Alabama. We explained that there were seven judicial districts within the three states, and the Division's strategy was to develop and file a case of voter discrimination against a registrar in one county in each of the judicial districts in the three states.

We had brought a detailed map of the southern part of the United States with us. "Too slow," said the Attorney General. "It won't do. You've got to do more." He sized up the number of counties in Louisiana, Mississippi, and Alabama. He wanted pins on the map, suits filed in every county where there were under-registrations of black people, and he wanted this accomplished "the day before yesterday." Burke Marshall said, "Well, General, we're going to need more lawyers." The Attorney General asked, "How many?" Burke said, "Four." Without argument or delay, the Division got four, maybe six newly created positions. Bud Sather, Gerald Stern, John Martin, Gordon Martin, Dick Parsons, and Jim Groh were hired.

Marshall said we would need the assistance of the FBI. At the time, the FBI had 5600 agents. Theoretically, support from the FBI should have increased the Division's capability. However, before the Division could make use of the Bureau, the Division first had to learn how to carry out the assignment. Division lawyers had to master everything that goes into understanding the realities of a distant and unknown territory: the back roads; the operations of county registrar's offices; the states' registration laws; 100 years of history; the identity of the local leaders; the way the court's family in each judicial district functioned—the clerk, the judge's secretary, the marshals, the U.S. Attorney, the court reporter—you name it.

I can still recall how the Division operated during the 1961–1963 time period. On a Friday afternoon I would see a row of suitcases and briefcases lined up in the first floor corridor of the Department of Justice, alongside the offices of the Division lawyers. Whenever lawyers went south to investigate, they departed Washington on Friday night to return on the third Sunday following. This meant sixteen straight days in the field. Travel past Atlanta was on a DC-3 with local stops at Montgomery, Meridian, Jackson, Monroe, and Shreveport. At each of these airports, two or more lawyers from the Division would leave the plane and move out into the field to learn more and more about the particular counties to which they had been assigned.

Southern Strategies to Block Black Voters

As the Division lawyers criss-crossed the rural roads of Louisiana, Mississippi, and Alabama, they found a complex legal and social network designed to protect and preserve the caste system. The scheme was not haphazard. A means used was official corruption and official and unofficial intimidation in connection with voting. They also saw that Louisiana, Mississippi, and Alabama remained largely a part of the American frontier, the rural white society riddled throughout with bewildering patterns of suspicion and silence.

So the Division began, county by county, a case-by-case assault on the caste system. Suits were quickly filed in East Carroll, Ouchita, and Madison parishes in Louisiana; in Forest, Clark, Jefferson Davis, Walthall, Tallahatchee, and Panola counties in Mississippi; and in Bullock, Dallas, and Montgomery counties in Alabama.

I have often wondered how the Division could have gone about its assignment with such enthusiasm. For a long time I attributed much of it to youth, to what Joseph Conrad calls that moment of strength, of romance, of glamour—of youth. Now I think I've found the answer. The spirit of the Division lawyers assigned to enforce the Civil Rights Acts was governed by what President Havel of Czechoslovakia calls a philosophy grounded in hope. This kind of hope is not the same as optimism. It is not a willingness to invest in an enterprise that is obviously heralded for early success, but rather the ability to work hard for something because it makes sense, not because it stands a chance to succeed.

Once our suits were filed we ran into trouble. There were no District judges other than Judge Johnson on the District benches in the judicial districts of Louisiana, Mississippi, or Alabama.

The SNCC Voter Registration Drive

At the same time, other forces had begun to work. In the summer of 1961, the Student Non-Violent Coordinating Committee (SNCC) undertook a voter registration project in Mississippi. Bob Moses was placed in charge. SNCC decided to work in the counties along the Louisiana border in southwest

Mississippi. These counties, Wilkinson, Amite, Pike, and Walthall, were rural, out of the way places. To go into those counties was like going back into the nineteenth century.

As soon as Bob Moses opened his voter registration school, he began to bring black citizens to the circuit clerk and registrar's office to register. He immediately ran into serious trouble. Moses and other SNCC workers were threatened, attacked, and, after reporting their experiences to the high sheriff, arrested. Earlier, in late 1960 and early 1961, the Division had achieved some success in checking economic intimidation against sharecroppers who tried to register to vote in Haywood and Fayette counties, Tennessee, and in helping a farmer who could not get his cotton ginned in East Carroll Parish, Louisiana. But control of violence in the states of Louisiana, Mississippi, and Alabama was a different matter.

At first, the Division confronted this hostile local law enforcement in southwest Mississippi. Sather and Stern were sent to southwest Mississippi to interview witnesses. They returned with their notebooks full of information that reflected serious violations of the federal laws we were bound to enforce. The Division moved immediately before Judge Harold Cox, Chief Judge of the United States Court for the Southern District of Mississippi, to enjoin a state criminal prosecution of John Hardy, who had accompanied a young black woman, Ruby McGee, to the registrar's office to register. As he was leaving his office, the registrar hit Hardy on the head with a pistol. Hardy sought the high sheriff to complain. At the same time, the high sheriff was looking for Hardy. They met in the middle of the main street, and Hardy was immediately arrested for breach of the peace. We obtained no relief from Judge Cox, but, for the first time, Judge Richard Rives of the United States Court of Appeals for the Fifth Circuit interceded and issued an injunction pending appeal that halted the prosecution.

Murders of Black Voter Registration Workers

On Sunday, September 28, 1961, Bob Moses guided me through Amite County in order to speak with several of the local black people who had been willing to try to register. In the middle of the afternoon, we pulled up to E.W. Steptoe's house on a rural lane some miles south of Liberty. The earth was red clay, the land rolling, divided between pasture and pine trees. Mr. Steptoe said he and his friends were having trouble encouraging black citizens to register to vote. He identified the most important white person in the area—a man named Hurst, a state senator who lived on neighboring land. As boys, Steptoe and Hurst had played and fought together.

Mr. Steptoe said we should see Herbert Lee. Steptoe had not seen the white men who had been taking down license numbers of cars parked at the SNCC voter registration school, but he believed Herbert Lee had seen the white men and knew who they were. Lee lived four or five miles down a county road. We tried to see him, but he was not there and not expected back for several hours. Because I had an appointment in Hattiesburg the following morning, Mr. Lee's interview was deferred until the next trip to Mississippi. The next day I reached Meridian in time to catch the plane to Atlanta and be in my office in the Justice Department by 10:00 p.m. Monday, September 29, 1961. Upon arrival, a memo from the Bureau advised that in the morning, during an alleged dispute at the Liberty cotton gin, Hurst had shot and killed Lee. Hurst claimed that Lee had come at him with a tire iron.

Although the Division believed that the killing was unjustified, we were never able to do anything about it. Louis Allen, a local black logging trucker, saw what had happened. The next morning he testified under pressure to a coroner's jury that he saw Lee with the tire iron. At the same time he told Bob Moses he was afraid to say what really happened. Moses inquired whether under federal law there was a way Allen could be protected. We said no.

Within several days of Herbert Lee's death, suits had been prepared against the following: the sheriff of Pike County; three of his deputies; the chief of police of McComb, Mississippi; a town marshall; a state highway patrolman; the son of the sheriff; the father of the deputy sheriff; and the clerk of the Chauncey Court of Amite County for attempting to intimidate black applicants who attempted to register or persons who had encouraged white citizens to intimidate black applicants who attempted to register. But these suits were never filed. The Division decided that if local law enforcement were sued, the consequences would have been unpredictable and might have led to uncontrollable violence. It surely would have expended the Division's limited resources, and we would have had little left for the rest of Mississippi. Burke Marshall decided it was not the best way to break the caste system in Mississippi. Without reservation, I agreed with him.

Instead, the Division treated the killing of Herbert Lee as a criminal matter, but we were unable to establish the state involvement required for federal prosecution. Several years later the tragedy was made worse when Allen was murdered as he stepped out of his front door in rural Amite County to see who had come to visit him in the night. The killing of Herbert Lee and the subsequent unsolved murder of Louis Allen remain on our consciences, not because we could have done something about these terrible crimes, but because there was no federal statute at the time that permitted us to proceed with a prosecution.

Federal Lawsuits Against the States

During 1962 Division lawyers were constantly in the field. Lou Kauder, Jay Goldin, Dennis Dillon, and Frank Schwelb had signed on. The Division's voting section had grown to perhaps fifteen lawyers. With the help of research assistants, now referred to as paralegals, cases were filed on a regular basis. Hearings on preliminary injunctions were held. Although cases were lost in the district courts, we were beginning to obtain relief from the Fifth Circuit, even to the point of having Chief Judge Tuttle of the United States Court of Appeals for the Fifth Circuit assign three judges from that court (judges John Minor Wisdom, John Brown, and Griffin Bell) to hear a contempt trial against Theron Lynd, the registrar of Forest County, Mississippi, for violation of an injunction issued by that court.

While the Division pushed its county-by-county campaign, Dave Norman conceived and planned a broader attack—state-wide lawsuits. On December 28, 1961, the Division, on behalf of the United States, filed an action in the Eastern District of Louisiana against the state of Louisiana and the directors and members of the Louisiana Board of Registration. Norman's theory was that the Louisiana law was in violation of federal law and the U.S. Constitution. The Louisiana Constitution required a voter to read, understand, and give a reasonable interpretation of any section of either the U.S. or the Louisiana Constitution, the administration of which rested in the uncontrolled discretion of a parish registrar.

While proof was being developed in the Louisiana case, the Division was preparing a similar suit against the state of Mississippi. On August 29, 1962, the Division filed suit on behalf of the United States against the state of Mississippi and six county registrars throughout the state, challenging the entire system of registration in Mississippi on three grounds: Mississippi's elaborate system of registration was not being applied to most of the whites; the system vested uncontrolled discretion in the registrar; and tests of intelligence, understanding or comprehension in Mississippi were unconstitutional because black citizens had not been afforded an educational opportunity equal to that afforded white citizens.

In early September 1962 judges Wisdom, Brown, and Bell began the contempt hearing in the Federal District Court for the Southern District of Mississippi in Hattiesburg.

For several days that September, the Division tested the voting registration system by alternating between an unqualified white voter and a qualified, unregistered black applicant. By unqualified, I mean an illiterate or marginally literate applicant. At the conclusion of that trial, the Division had proven two facts about voting in Forest County, Mississippi: qualified black citizens were being kept off the rolls by a variety of illegal schemes, and there was universal white suffrage.

On July 13, 1963, the Court of Appeals judges, sitting as a

trial court in Hattiesburg, found the circuit clerk and registrar of Forest County in contempt and ordered him to immediately register forty-three black people, to agree not to use the application form as an obstacle course, and to use only fourteen sections of the Mississippi Constitution to determine an applicant's qualifications under the interpretation test.

The Division Defends SNCC Workers

During this same time the Division lawyers were involved with serious enforcement problems in the Mississippi Delta. SNCC had opened an office in Greenwood, Mississippi, and was preparing to take black applicants to the registrar's office in groups. As soon as a group effort began in late March 1963, the Greenwood police interfered. At about the same time, eight SNCC registration workers were arrested and convicted after they and about 100 local blacks walked to the city hall to protest a shooting into the house of a black registration worker. The eight SNCC workers, including Bob Moses and Jim Foreman, were sentenced to four months in jail and fined $200.

On behalf of the United States, the Division brought suit against the city of Greenwood, the mayor, fire commissioner, police chief, city prosecutor, and against LeFlore County, its county attorney, and a deputy sheriff. The Division sought a temporary restraining order. Although it was denied, we obtained agreement from the city of Greenwood and LeFlore County to release the SNCC workers pending a hearing on a preliminary injunction. In June 1963 forty-five residents of Itta Bena in LeFlore County were arrested after they marched downtown to seek police protection because an unknown person had released a noxious substance into a church where a voter registration school was being held. Within a few days of the arrest, the Division brought suit on behalf of the United States against the local enforcement officials.

The suits presented difficult assignments before a difficult federal district judge, Judge Claude Clayton of the Northern District of Mississippi. SNCC's increased pressure against the caste system caused the suits, but the suits afforded no answer.

The Division Goes to Court Against the States

On March 9, 1963, the Louisiana state-wide suit came up for trial. A massive amount of evidence was stipulated into the record and the court adjourned to reach its decision. Meanwhile, discovery was getting underway in the Mississippi state-wide suit. The state of Mississippi had served the Division with massive interrogatories that inquired into the factual underpinnings of each and every allegation of the government's complaint.

Sometime in April 1963 while Bob Owen and I were together in a motel somewhere in the Delta, we talked about how we were going to respond to those interrogatories. We decided to answer them in monumental detail, with information from most of Mississippi's eighty-two counties. We mobilized the Division's lawyers, research assistants, and secretaries, and enlisted a cadre of summer interns. We pushed them to their limits and beyond, regardless of cost, regardless of casualties. Bob Owen, however, demanded and delivered more of himself than he ever asked of anyone who worked with him.

On August 31, 1963, the Division served the United States' answers to the state of Mississippi's interrogatories. In the history of complex litigation, these interrogatory answers set a standard for responses to burdensome interrogatories calling for massive amounts of detailed information. The answers drew upon and organized the collective hard work of a small number of Division lawyers who had labored in the field for two and one-half years.

The answers covered the factual basis to support the United States' claim for relief and were contained in seven volumes. The first contained the name, race, education, and other background information of each person contacted in connection with the case. The second covered state-wide registration statistics by county and by race on six specific dates between 1890 and 1962. The third contained the factual basis showing the racially discriminatory purpose of the registration laws under attack, white primary practices in Mississippi, and the decrease in black registration since 1890. The fourth contained the facts that showed that, in

Mississippi, public education provided for black persons was inferior to public education provided for white persons. The fifth detailed how white political supremacy was established and maintained in Mississippi prior to 1955 when the constitutional interpretation test was adopted. Volumes six and seven included, by county, factual data since 1955 showing a lack of uniform administration of the voting laws, favored treatment of whites, and unlimited discretion vested in the registrars. . . .

On March 6, 1964, the court ruled in this case and the United States lost. Judge Cameron, writing for the majority, labeled the government case a frontal attack by the "'Indestructible Union' member of the partnership . . . upon the other member, the 'Indestructible State.'" The court dismissed the complaint without holding a trial. Judge Brown, in his dissent, observed that while "the tone of indestructibility is good," history teaches that no political institution is indestructible. He insisted that if a political institution were to survive, it must save itself from destruction, and that the peril of destruction was what the case was all about.

Judge Brown labeled the contest as between all citizens of the United States and the State. He clearly explained the government's theory.

> The underlying Mississippi constitutional provisions and the implementing statutory law regulating registration of voters came into being—and are currently maintained—out of a purpose by the organized State to deny Negroes the right to vote by contriving a structure having the appearance of legality, but having known, built-in devices which would, and did, effectually deny or overwhelmingly discourage the Negroes' effort toward full citizenship.

He insisted that "[t]he immediate means—the understanding test—must be judged, both in its purpose and in its effect," in light of Mississippi's policy of segregated "education and the wide disparity in the quality and quantity of education afforded by Mississippi to its white and Negro children."

On November 27, 1963, Judge Wisdom handed down the Court's opinion in United States v. Louisiana. The court declared the Louisiana statute and laws respecting its interpretation test unconstitutional, and froze the standard in those parishes where the test had been applied.

Judge Wisdom held that a wall stood in Louisiana between registered voters and unregistered eligible black voters, and that the wall must come down.

Judge Wisdom explained how the registrar selects the constitutional section and must be satisfied with the explanation. He pointed out that "[i]n many parishes the registrar is not easily satisfied with constitutional interpretation from Negro applicants." The court held that, considered in its historical setting and its actual operation and inescapable effect, this law was a sophisticated scheme to disfranchise black people. Judge Wisdom rejected apathy as a reason for the low registration of black people. Apathy is, he said, "an unctuous and self-excusing word" used to rationalize the small black registration.

Judge Wisdom's opinion and Judge Brown's dissent should be required reading in senior high school or college level American history courses in every school in the country.

Aside from these two state-wide cases, by the end of 1963 the Division had filed thirty-four suits against county registrars for discrimination in voter registration and had forty-eight other counties under investigation. It had filed twelve suits seeking injunctions against intimidation, with another eight under investigation. It had examined the voter registration records in twenty-seven counties in Alabama, fifty counties in Mississippi, and twenty-seven counties in Louisiana. In 1964 that pace continued, even though SNCC's program in Mississippi for Freedom Summer and the murders in Neshoba County in June 1964 forced the Division to revise its priorities.

The Groundwork for the Civil Rights Act of 1964

This brings me to Selma, Dallas County, Alabama, which became the turning point in the battle for voting rights. The Division had first gone to Selma in February 1961. At that time, a local organization of blacks were trying to break down the barrier to voting. Several months later Burke Marshall and Robert Kennedy authorized the Division to file its first voting case against the registrars of Dallas County. The next year SNCC opened a field office in Selma. During the next four years Division attorneys spent more time in Dallas County than in any other county in the south.

Late in 1964 Dr. King and his Southern Christian Leadership Conference organization (SCLC) came to Selma. Out of a convergence of the forces of SNCC, SCLC, and the Division, each having challenged the caste system in its own way, came a series of events that culminated at the Selma bridge where mounted state police dispersed, with clubs and tear gas, a number of blacks on their way to the state capitol in Montgomery to present their grievances to the governor. After that episode the Voting Rights Act of 1965 quickly followed.

On March 18 a bill entitled The Voting Rights Act of 1965 was introduced. On the same day Attorney General Nicholas Katzenbach appeared before the House Judiciary Committee to testify in detail about the bill. He spelled out how the registration process in the south had been perverted to test "not literacy, not ability, not understanding—but race."

Katzenbach told the Committee members that three times since 1956 Congress adopted litigation in the federal courts as the solution to this problem. He complained of the inadequacy of the judicial process and described it as "tarnished by evasion, obstruction, delay, and disrespect." He cited example after example, and he proposed a new approach to the Committee.

No one in the Division quarreled with the need for a new approach, nor with the frustrations because of judicial delay and obfuscation. But cries of frustration do not move mountains. The Division's hard work underpinned the opinions and orders of federal judges Tuttle of Georgia, Rives and Johnson of Alabama, Wisdom of Louisiana, and Brown of Texas—opinions and orders that established the freezing principal; that stayed a state criminal prosecution of an SNCC voter registration worker; that caused a real contempt trial to be held in Mississippi; and that led to Judge Wisdom's and Judge Brown's penetrating and persuasive findings as to the purpose and the effect of Louisiana's and Mississippi's constitutional and statutory requirements for voting. These decisions had an influence on individual members of the House Judiciary Committee as they decided upon the final content of the 1965 Voting Rights Bill, and on individual members of Congress to vote to pass the Voting Rights Bill.

By August 6, 1965, Congress acted, and the President signed the legislation. In acting, Congress added a very important provision to the bill. Congress provided that in every county where federal examiners had been assigned, the Attorney General might assign federal observers to any polling place within the county to see that all persons entitled to vote were permitted to vote and would have their votes properly counted. . . .

On the Monday following the passage of the Voting Rights Act, the Civil Service Commission announced that registration offices would open in nine counties in three states. On the first day of opening, these offices registered 1144 blacks. By the first of the year, federal officials operating in thirty-six counties had registered 79,815 blacks. During the same period, local officials in the five states of the deep south registered 215,000 blacks.

This compliance did not occur by chance. On the day following the passage of the Act, Attorney General Katzenbach sent letters prepared by the Division to the 650 registration officials. He explained the provisions of the statute and said he would appoint examiners when it was clear that past denials of the right to vote justified it, or where present compliance with federal law was insufficient to assure prompt registration of all eligible citizens.

Following the passage of the Act, FBI agents checked, on a weekly basis, voter registration books in every county in a five-state area. Young attorneys in the Division spent their days in rural southern counties explaining the law to local officials and to black citizens, and to bringing situations of noncompliance to the attention of the Attorney General.

On March 7, 1966, the Supreme Court upheld the validity of the Voting Rights Act.

On May 3, 1966, the first post-Voting Rights Act primary election arrived. Dallas County, Alabama, was the test county. The key race was for sheriff. The contestants were Jim Clark, the segregationist sheriff, and Wilson Baker, the sensible, moderate police chief of the city of Selma. . . .

That night the Dallas County returns came in very slowly. The largest number of citizens in Dallas County's history had appeared at the polls to vote, leading to long lines at every polling place, especially in predominantly black areas. The ballot contained seventy-three candidates competing for twenty-four different nominations. The clerks had to count each contest on each paper ballot. The race for sheriff was very close. The lead switched back and forth. First, Jim Clark was ahead, then Wilson Baker.

By three or four o'clock in the morning, six boxes containing more than 1672 black and 162 white votes remained unreported. At that time Clark held a small lead. The local probate judge sent "replacement clerks" to finish the count. These clerks were white and were part of the Clark Machine. The Justice Department immediately sent federal observers to observe the "replacement clerks." Before the count was finished, the county judge decided to impound the six boxes.

A few hours later the Dallas County Democratic Executive Committee decided to have white CPAs count the ballots in the six boxes. This went on at the county courthouse throughout the day and the next night, with federal observers in each room observing this second count. The result in the six boxes—Baker, 1412; Clark, 92—determined the result of the election. However, the Dallas County Democratic Executive Committee, consisting of forty lily-white men, immediately rejected all the votes in the six boxes.

The Division was determined that the black citizens of Dallas County not be disillusioned with their first actual participation in a local election. That afternoon the United States filed a federal court action seeking an injunction against the wholesale rejection of the ballots of registered voters. Judge Frank Johnson immediately ordered that no ballots be destroyed. From that time until the federal court decided the case twenty days later, federal observers guarded the boxes.

In preparation for the hearing, lawyers and research assistants analyzed all of the ballots for that election—17,440 ballots. Within eight days they were ready to advise the federal court about the mechanics and operation of that election, including a complete analysis of each poll list, tally sheet, certificate of result, and, where necessary, each ballot.

After hearing testimony for two days, the federal court concluded there was no evidence to indicate that votes were bought or sold, or that the boxes were stuffed. Thus, Jim Clark was defeated and Wilson Baker was elected Dallas County sheriff.

Before that time in Dallas County, Alabama, about 6500 persons usually voted in key elections. That year, 17,440 voted in the first primary and 15,717 in the November election.

On the day of that election in Selma, over 500 federal observers were in Dallas County—observers from New York, Milwaukee, Denver, and San Francisco. They were civil servants sent to the various polling places in Dallas County to observe and insure that the elections were properly held. The Division's lawyers managed the movement of federal observers.

Today my career as a lawyer is almost over. As I call upon myself to account, more and more, my memory goes back to those days and years with the Division, working for the United States, enforcing its fundamental law, and the roll call of the Division lawyers, the Civil Rights Division lawyers, keeps ringing in my ears.

Chapter 2

Peaceful Demonstrations and Radical Tactics

Turning Points
IN WORLD HISTORY

The Student Sit-In Campaign

Ronald Walters

In February 1960, four black students from North Carolina A&T State University sat down at a whites only lunch counter in a Woolworth's Department Store in Greensboro and asked to be served. They were refused service, of course, but they continued to peaceably occupy their seats, and they returned each day for more than a month to repeat their request. Over the course of the month-long protest they were joined by other students— black and white. The demonstration was the first of its kind to gain national media attention and is therefore often mistaken as the first sit-in.

In the following article, Ronald Walters describes the organization and strategy of one of the first sit-ins, conducted by students in Wichita, Kansas, in 1958. Though many of the students in this demonstration were also members of the NAACP Youth Council, the venerable civil rights organization refused to sanction it. The sit-in went forward until the lunch counter, faced with loss of revenue, agreed to voluntarily desegregate. Walters argues that although such protests gained more attention—because they met more severe resistance and violence—as they spread across the South, the sit-in campaign originated in the Midwest.

Walters is head of the department of political science at Howard University in Washington, D.C. He is the author of *We Have No Leaders: African Americans in the Post–Civil Rights Era.*

Forget the tales of John Brown and the Kansas that bled to keep slavery out of the state—that was the 1850s. In the 1950s, Wichita, Kan., was a midsize city of more than 150,000

Reprinted from Ronald Walters, "Standing Up in America's Heartland: Sitting In Before Greensboro," *American Visions*, February/March 1993, by permission of *American Visions*, 1101 Pennsylvania Ave. NW, Suite 820, Washington, DC 20004.

people, of whom only 10,000 were black. Agribusiness and defense industries were its economic base; farmers and defense workers, its social foundation. Isolated in the middle of the country, with an ascetic religious heritage and a tradition of individual farming, its people were genuinely and deeply conservative. Kansas, the family home of war hero and president Dwight Eisenhower, was the most Republican state in the nation.

Social and economic progress in these years was exceedingly difficult for Wichita's small, closely knit black community, a product of turn-of-the-century migration. We faced an implacably cold, dominant white culture. Blacks in the '50s attended segregated schools up to high school and were excluded from mixing with whites at movie theaters, restaurants, nightclubs and other places of public accommodation, except for some common sports events. Even though the signs "Black" and "White" were not publicly visible as in the South, we lived in separate worlds, just as blacks and whites did in the Southern states. Still, there was no small amount of the status that went with being "up South." We often considered ourselves better than Southerners, and the original blacks of Wichita even disdained the migration into their midst of the more Southern and country "Okies" from Oklahoma.

Segregated Lunch Counters

As a young man I worked in downtown Wichita at various jobs. Because I had the use of a car, I could eat with relatives, at home or elsewhere in the black community, while my friends and others complied with the local folkways and ate at segregated lunch counters.

In the spring of 1958, I started a new job without a car, which anchored me to the downtown area for lunch. I remember going to F.W. Woolworth one day for lunch and standing in line with other blacks behind a 2-foot board at one end of a long lunch counter. Looking at the whites seated at the counter, some staring up at us, I suddenly felt the humiliation and shame that others must have felt many, many times in this unspoken dialogue about their power and our humanity. Excluded from the simple dignity of sitting on those stools, blacks had to take their lunch out in bags and eat elsewhere. Bringing lunch from home thereafter was only quiet acquiescence to what I had faced in that line.

No flash of insight led me to confront this humiliation. It was, like other defining moments in that era, the growing political consciousness within the black community, born of discrete acts of oppression and resistance. That consciousness told me that my situation was not tolerable, that it was time at last to do something.

The Beginnings of the Movement

The Civil Rights Movement during the Eisenhower years, 1953 to 1961, was truly national—not merely in that it was an expression of African Americans, but also in its geographical breadth. However, what have emerged in popular history as the origins of the movement are the Montgomery bus boycott in 1955 and '56, which propelled Martin Luther King Jr. into prominence, and the "first" sit-in in Greensboro, N.C., in 1960, which launched the Southern student movement and the Student Nonviolent Coordinating Committee.

This Southern interpretation of our history, due in part to our image of the South, underplays its national character. The South was always regarded by everyone—black and white, North and South—as the most dangerous territory in America for blacks: Look at the lynching of Emmett Till in Mississippi in 1955, at the violent resistance by white Southerners to school integration after 1955, at the events surrounding the desegregation of Central High School in Little Rock, Ark., in 1957 and '58. Just as other mobilizations were sparked by these regional events, the Greensboro sit-in may have been, to some extent, derivative of the lunch counter sit-in, in Wichita, Kan., in 1958.

As head of the local NAACP Youth Council and a freshman college student, I knew a range of youths who might become involved in a protest against lunch counter segregation. I talked about the problem with my cousin Carol Parks, the treasurer of our youth council and the daughter of the local NAACP secretary. Carol invited me to her house to meet Frank Williams, a lawyer who was West Coast regional secretary of the NAACP. He described how a group of students at either the University of Southern California or the University of California, Los Angeles, had fought the segregation of a campus restaurant by filling it with students reading newspapers and thus occupying it that way for hours. With this information and the strong support of Chester Lewis, also a young attorney and the head of the local NAACP, we began to plan.

We targeted Dockum drugstore, part of the Rexall chain, located on Wichita's main street, Douglas Avenue. Because any action here would swiftly attract attention, we tried to anticipate what we might encounter. In the basement of the Catholic church to which Carol belonged, St. Peter Claver, we simulated the environment of the lunch counter and went through the drill of sitting and role-playing what might happen. We took turns playing the white folks with laughter, dishing out the embarrassment that might come our way. In response to their taunts, we would be well-dressed and courteous, but determined, and we would give the proprietors no reason to refuse us service, except that we were black.

We were motivated by the actions of other people in the struggle, especially by the pictures of people in Little Rock and King's Montgomery bus boycott, with which we were generally familiar. Like others who would come after us, we held a firm belief that we would be successful simply because we were right; but our confidence was devoid of both the deep religious basis of the Southern movement and the presence of a charismatic leader.

The Lack of Support

Our effort also lacked external support. We had received a telegram from Herbert Wright, national NAACP youth secretary, saying that the contemplated sit-in was not regarded as an NAACP tactic and that therefore we would not receive the benefit of legal coverage from the national office in the event of lawsuits—a strange response from someone who would later lead a team of NAACP lawyers in providing legal assistance for the wave of sit-ins in the South. Nevertheless, unknown to us, at that time the NAACP national office was ambivalent about what it called the "Montgomery model" of direct action and probably would not have become involved later on if its own youth councils had not taken action.

Although we were not daunted by the lack of support from the NAACP national office, we did not wish to act in isolation. We felt an obligation to ask not only for the permission but also for the involvement of adults, who had so much to gain from our victory. However, Lewis could not secure the backing of the adult local chapter. Faced with our boldness and the prospect that they would be vulnerable to white retaliation, the adults appeared as intimidated as our sisters and brothers in the South.

The Sit-In

Ten of us began the sit-in on Saturday morning at 10 a.m., July 19, 1958. We decided to take the vacant seats one by one, until we occupied them all, and then to just sit until whatever happened, happened. It was the prospect of being taken to jail—or worse—that led some parents to prohibit their sons and daughters from taking part in the protest.

Although we were admittedly nervous, our fears were overcome by a sense of solemnity that arose from our attempt to accomplish something outside of ourselves and our group—something historic that would benefit every black person in the community. And even though I felt the same anxiety as others, I also believed that I had to at least appear unafraid and purposeful.

The sit-in went as planned. We entered the store and took our seats. After we were settled, the waitress came over and spoke to all of us, saying, "I can't serve you here. You'll have to leave." Prepared for this response, I said that we had come to be served like everyone else and that we intended to stay until that happened. After a few hours, the waitress placed a sign on the counter that read, "This Fountain Temporarily Closed," and only opened the fountain twice to accommodate white customers. This was what we were hoping for—a shut-off of the flow of dollars into this operation.

When we showed up a few days later, filling all of the

seats, the waitress waited an hour and then made a telephone call. After a while, a white male appeared and asked, "What's the problem here? I thought she told you to leave." I repeated our position. He stared at us, confused and angry that his mild attempt at intimidation had had no effect; then he retreated to his office.

By the second week of the protest, we felt that we were winning because we were being allowed to sit on the stools for long periods. Surely the store was losing money. As we sat, we seldom spoke to each other, but many things crossed my mind. How would I react if my white classmates came in? How would they react? Would my career in college be affected, and would I be able to get another job? What did my family think about what I was doing? How would it all turn out? Were we doing the right thing after all? I am sure that the others were thinking the same things, but they never wavered. I was proud of our group.

Threats of Violence

Gradually, the word went out that there was something going on in Dockum drugstore. The store soon filled not only with shoppers but also with the curious and the hostile. The press came in, and I was interviewed by radio and newspaper reporters, but they were never to return. Then, one evening during the second week into the protest, the store began to fill up with tough young whites, members of a motorcycle gang, who were visibly disturbed and who had come to make a demonstration of their own. I remember one of them saying, "Wait until the rest of us get here. We're really going to have a party."

I had always vaguely known that the situation could become dangerous, but since none of us could anticipate what form it would take, we did not know how to prepare, except to be lawful. About 15 or 20 men gathered in the store, and the proprietor was nowhere around. I became concerned for the safety of our group, especially for the two young women, and I asked one of our young men to call the police.

When the police arrived 15 minutes later, they looked around, and an officer said, "I don't see any disturbance taking place." I replied, "OK, so you want to wait until those people over there start trying to beat us up, and then you arrest us. I understand." At that moment, the manager also begged for some intervention by the police, fearing that his store would be wrecked, but the officer said to him, in tones not meant for all of us to hear, "I have orders to keep our hands off of this." And with that the police left.

I felt that we had been abandoned to the mob, so I had to do something dramatic. I called some friends on Ninth Street, the main drag in the black community. Talking as loudly as I could, I asked them to come down quickly; we were in trouble. Then I went back to my seat, and the young whites began to threaten us. The taunting continued, getting bolder. It seemed like forever, but in only a few minutes, cars began pulling up out front. Were they ours or theirs? I didn't have to wait for the answer, because the young whites bolted toward the back exit. When they were clear, I went out front, hoping to intercept my friends before there was an excuse to put us out. As I thanked them and the three carloads of others, I noticed clubs, one pistol and some knives at the ready. It was a high-stakes gamble, even somewhat foolish, that barely paid off.

Once clear of the prospect of violence from white gangs, and despite the fact that some whites spat at us and used racist taunts, we kept the pressure on as the movement grew. It became a popular movement among youth, especially from Wichita University, and at least two white students came down to participate. What had begun as a two-day-a-week demonstration escalated into several days a week. Just as we were realizing our success in generating a mobilization, I began to worry because school was approaching, and it would be difficult to maintain the pressure with school becoming our main priority.

Success

Then suddenly, on a Saturday afternoon, into the fourth week of the protest, a man in his 30s or 40s came into the store, stopped, looked back at the manager in the rear, and said, "Serve them. I'm losing too much money." This was the conclusion of the sit-in—at once dramatic and anticlimactic.

Chester Lewis later called the vice president of the Dockum drugstore chain, Walter Heiger, to confirm the new policy and learned that Heiger had instructed all of his personnel to provide service to all people, regardless of race.

What happened in the aftermath of our sit-in was completely typical: blacks and whites were served without incident, giving the lie to the basic reason for our exclusion—that whites would cease to patronize the establishment. We also received considerable acclaim from our community. Even Herbert Wright, from the NAACP national office, who visited Wichita a few weeks later, lauded our accomplishments as he endured our criticism.

Not wanting to rest on our laurels, we targeted another drugstore lunch counter, across from East High School on Douglas Avenue, and there segregation was even more quickly ended. Other lunch counters in the city followed suit. Apparently, the owners had learned from the damage inflicted by our first sit-in. The Douglas Avenue sit-in was our last action, as school closed in quickly and our attention turned to other things.

The Dockum sit-in was followed in a few days by the beginning of a much longer campaign of sit-ins in Oklahoma City, Okla. This protest was also initiated by the NAACP Youth Council, under the leadership of the courageous 16-year-old Barbara Posey, now Barbara Jones. The Oklahoma City demonstrations were longer, beginning in September '58 and covering the greater part of 1959, and they were more violent than our comparatively brief experience in Wichita. The Oklahoma City NAACP Council was fortunate to have support from the adult chapter.

These sit-ins were followed by other protest demonstrations in the Midwest, such as the one in St. Louis, Mo., begun on February 14, 1959, by the NAACP youth group and led by William Clay, now a United States congressman. Later that year, the college chapter at the University of Chicago protested discriminatory hiring at a local restaurant; at the University of Indiana, they dealt with discrimination in barber shops; and at Ohio State University, they fought against discrimination in student housing. Then, on February 1, 1960, came the well-known sit-in in Greensboro.

The Spread of the Sit-Ins

The link between the Midwest actions and the Greensboro sit-in was more than merely sequence. Ezell Blair and Joseph McNeil, two of the four originators of the Greensboro protest, were officers in Greensboro's NAACP Youth Council. It is highly unlikely that they were unfamiliar with the sit-ins elsewhere in the country led by their organizational peers. Indeed, at the 51st Conference of the NAACP held in 1960, the national office recognized its local youth councils for the work they were doing in breaking down lunch-counter segregation.

In his speech at that conference, Robert C. Weaver, the United States' first black cabinet official, said, "NAACP youth units in Wichita, Kansas, and Oklahoma City started these demonstrations in 1958 and succeeded in desegregating scores of lunch counters in Kansas and Oklahoma." NAACP Executive Director Roy Wilkins paid tribute to the sit-in movements as "giving fresh impetus to an old struggle," and "electrif[ying] the adult Negro community, with the exception of the usual Uncle Toms and Nervous Nellies."

By summer 1960, the NAACP Youth Council–inspired protests had occurred in North Carolina, South Carolina, Virginia, Maryland, Arkansas, Florida, Louisiana, West Virginia, Tennessee, Texas, Kentucky and Mississippi. There was one ironic historical twist: On July 21, 1960, the Woolworth Company in Greensboro began to serve everyone without regard to color, nearly two years to the day after the beginning of the "first" sit-in in Wichita.

Civil Disobedience in Birmingham

David B. Oppenheimer

From February to May 1963, Martin Luther King Jr. led a campaign to register black voters in Birmingham, Alabama. King's strategy was to peacefully defy discriminatory voting laws and to dramatize the illegality of Alabama's voter registration procedures. Police Chief Eugene "Bull" Connor used police dogs and fire hoses to attack the demonstrators as he arrested hundreds, filling Birmingham's jails. The incident provoked national disgust and prompted the federal government to assert pressure on Birmingham civic leaders to voluntarily desegregate.

David B. Oppenheimer argues in the following article that although King won a major public relations victory with his strategy of civil disobedience, he lost an important judicial battle. When a southern district court imposed an injunction on the demonstrations, it foiled the Southern Christian Leadership Conference's strategy of mounting a constitutional challenge to segregation. Because they disregarded the court injunction, King and the other demonstrators were barred from disputing the justness of local laws. Though his campaign drew national attention and forced whites in Birmingham to dismantle biased practices, King lost the opportunity to strike down the legality of segregation.

Oppenheimer is an associate professor of law at Golden Gate University in San Francisco, California.

His name is rarely mentioned with the case that sent him to jail, and few associate him with the legislation that vindi-

From David B. Oppenheimer, "Martin's March," *ABA Journal*, June 1994. Copyright ©1994 American Bar Association. Reprinted by permission of the *ABA Journal*.

cated his actions. But 30 years ago this July the nation saw the dream that Martin Luther King Jr. asked it to embrace cast into law.

It was a different United States three decades ago when King went to Birmingham, Ala., to help lead a campaign to integrate downtown store facilities. Less than three months earlier the state's newly elected governor, George Wallace, had vowed in his inaugural address, "Segregation now, segregation tomorrow, segregation forever."

Laws forbade integrated restaurants, drinking fountains, rest rooms, dressing rooms, taxi cabs, ambulances, jail cells, hospitals, cemeteries, theaters or hotels. Birmingham gave up a minor-league baseball team rather than permit it to be integrated. It closed its parks, playgrounds, swimming pools and golf courses rather than comply with a federal court's desegregation order.

Any segregation that the law could not enforce, racist violence did. Bombings of homes and churches of black leaders were so common that Birmingham had been nicknamed "Bombingham." The city's best black neighborhood was known as "Dynamite Hill."

The Legacy of King's Civil Disobedience

That was the spring of 1963. By the next summer the nation was ready to respond. The message of the Civil Rights Act of 1964 was simple: segregation never.

In the years that have followed, the memory of King's victory opening Birmingham store facilities and employment to blacks, and preparing the way for introduction of the Civil Rights Act, has faded. A generation of lawyers has graduated having studied the U.S. Supreme Court decision upholding his conviction for violating a local court injunction against demonstrations and marches, but only to examine the obscure rule of law it illustrates. It is typically taught without reference to its social framework or consequences; many texts omit any reference to King.

But the legacy of the act trumpets the effectiveness of civil disobedience when practiced by a leader with the courage of a Mahatma Gandhi or Martin Luther King Jr.

King went to Birmingham at the invitation of the Rev. Fred L. Shuttlesworth, the founding leader of the Alabama Christian Movement for Human Rights, the city's major civil rights group formed in 1956 when the state of Alabama outlawed the National Association for the Advancement of Colored People.

Shuttlesworth had been the chief architect of the black boycott of Birmingham's downtown businesses during the summer of 1962. At its height, the boycott had reduced black patronage by an estimated 90 percent. It ended in a negotiated settlement to remove the "white only" signs from dressing rooms and drinking fountains. But within days, Police Commissioner Eugene "Bull" Connor gave store owners an ultimatum: Put back the signs or close the doors. The signs went back up.

King responded by sending Wyatt Tee Walker, executive director of his Southern Christian Leadership Conference, and Andrew Young, soon to be his chief aide, to meet with Shuttlesworth to begin planning a new desegregation campaign. Walker's plan was to train hundreds of black Birmingham residents in nonviolent confrontation. They would picket downtown stores, sit in at lunch counters, march on segregated city facilities, and attempt to pray at white churches.

Shuttlesworth and King would call for a boycott of downtown businesses. Mass meetings each evening in churches would rally support. The strategy was to force enough arrests so as to overwhelm the jails and focus the nation's conscience. The campaign was to continue until merchants agreed to desegregate dressing rooms and lunch counters, and to hire blacks in noncustodial positions.

On April 3, the demonstrations began. As many as 350 people had volunteered to engage in civil disobedience, but to King's disappointment, only 65 appeared and fewer than half were arrested. In the days that followed, the number arrested continued to be disappointing. By the end of the first week of the campaign, fewer than 200 demonstrators had gone to jail. Unless there was a dramatic increase in the number willing to be arrested, the strategy of commanding widespread attention by filling the jails would fail. The campaign appeared to be withering.

Disobedience of a Court Injunction

But at 9 p.m. April 10, city attorneys unwittingly changed the nation's history. Without informing King or his attorneys, they asked Alabama Circuit Court Judge William A. Jenkins Jr. for an injunction prohibiting further demonstrations. They claimed that demonstrators had violated parade-permit and trespassing laws, and were endangering peace and safety. Jenkins immediately issued a temporary injunction.

The injunction raised a special problem for King. Prior to the injunction, the demonstrators had been arrested for violating local ordinances: trespass (for sitting-in in violation of the segregation laws), vagrancy and parading without a permit. These ordinances, passed by an all-white government and never judicially reviewed, held no inherent legitimacy for King. They were unjust laws to be resisted, part of the legal structure of segregation. But in King's view an order from a judge, even a Southern judge in a segregated city, embodied greater authority than the ordinances. As a direct judicial order, it could not be ignored.

King's lawyers from the NAACP Legal Defense Fund warned him that he faced serious legal consequences if he disobeyed the injunction because of an obscure rule of law that prohibited challenging an injunction by disobeying it. The rule—the "collateral bar rule"—meant that demonstrators would not be permitted to challenge the injunction on constitutional grounds if they were arrested and charged with contempt.

On April 12, Good Friday morning, King and his closest advisers met in his hotel room to decide what to do. His father recommended that he obey the injunction and put off a planned march; another adviser agreed. Young and others said they would support whatever decision King made.

After all had spoken, he left the room and, alone, prayed for guidance. When he returned, he had changed to clothing suitable for jail.

King, Walker, Young and several other aides then went to

the Sixteenth Street Baptist Church, where a crowd of supporters had gathered.

As Shuttlesworth's lawyers described it in the U.S. Supreme Court, "at about 2:15 p.m., 52 persons emerged from the church. They formed up in pairs on the sidewalk and began to walk in a peaceful, orderly and non-obstructive way toward City Hall. They walked about 40 inches apart, carried no signs or placards and observed all traffic lights. At times they sang. . . . The walk proceeded about four blocks—to the 1700 block of Fifth Avenue—where all the participants were arrested." King, in handcuffs, was dragged by his belt to a paddy wagon and taken to solitary confinement in the Birmingham jail.

The day after his arrest, eight white Birmingham clergymen—seven ministers and a rabbi—issued a statement calling for demonstrations to end. They called the campaign "unwise and untimely."

Justifying Civil Disobedience

To write a reply—his "Letter From Birmingham Jail"—King used the edges of the newspaper in which the statement was published and paper smuggled in by his attorney. As a call for liberty, it is reminiscent of the works of Jefferson, Paine and Mill. As a defense of civil disobedience, it stands with the works of Gandhi and Thoreau.

King began the letter by answering the clergy's charge that he had no business coming to Birmingham. Invoking the apostle Paul, he explained: "I am in Birmingham because injustice is here." The clergy had deplored the sit-ins and demonstrations; King took them to task for failing to deplore the conditions that required the demonstrations—the racial violence and segregation in the city, and the unwillingness on the part of the white power structure to desegregate.

Sensitive to the criticism that by marching the demonstrators were violating the law, King turned to natural law to justify the illegal demonstrations. There are two types of laws, he argued, just and unjust. "An unjust law is no law at all." Citing Thomas Aquinas, St. Augustine and Martin Buber, he explained that a law by which a majority compels a minority to obey, without imposing the same obligation on itself, is "difference made legal," and thus unjust. In contrast, a just law—one that all must obey—is "sameness made legal."

As King sat in jail, he and 12 other ministers and one layman were charged with contempt of court for violating the injunction. The trial began April 22, in a segregated courtroom; it was over by April 26.

Pursuant to the collateral bar rule, Judge Jenkins permitted no evidence on the constitutionality of the parade ordinance. King and 10 others were convicted of criminal contempt and sentenced to five days in jail. The sentences were stayed pending appeal, and the group remained free on bail.

With the close of the trial, King knew that a dramatic new step was needed. Shuttlesworth announced that on May 2 there would be a massive march on city hall. But with an injunction prohibiting marches, and all marchers facing the threat of arrest, King wondered where the large number of demonstrators would come from. With bail coffers bare, and lengthy jail sentences a growing likelihood, few adults could afford the financial sacrifice now required.

The Rev. James Bevel, a field organizer, offered a solution. He had been running nonviolence workshops for weeks with high school students. Attendance at the meetings was growing day by day, and younger and younger students were asking to take part. The movement leaders were divided on whether to allow children younger than college-age to participate. But with few adults being arrested, King understood that here were the troops needed to fill the streets and fill the jail. King turned to the black children of Birmingham to save the campaign.

Shortly after 1 p.m. May 2, a group of 50 teen-agers stepped out of the Sixteenth Street Baptist Church, singing "We Shall Overcome." As had occurred with their adult counterparts, the Birmingham police warned them of the injunction, and then began to arrest them. But before the arrests could be completed, another 50 students marched singing from the church, and then another and another.

In wave after wave, the young marchers overwhelmed the police. Some were able to evade arrest and almost complete their planned march on city hall; others succeeded in marching to the downtown business district. Almost 1,000 were arrested. They submitted to arrest peacefully, singing and praying as they were taken to jail.

The following day 1,000 more children volunteered to march and be jailed. But Birmingham's jails were filled beyond capacity. King and Walker's strategy of filling the jails had succeeded in a single day, and Commissioner Connor knew he had to respond to the march with a new strategy of his own.

He turned to the answer the South had historically used in conjunction with the power of law to suppress blacks: the power of violence. With police dogs and water cannons, the demonstration was suppressed. But the images of the police attacks on unarmed young people were indelibly etched into the national consciousness.

As the scenes of that violence reached the American public on national television and the front pages of many newspapers, the civil rights movement entered a new era.

Demonstrations Bring National Attention

May 7 would be the final day of demonstrations. Thousands again gathered at the Baptist church. A few small groups began to march from the church. The police turned them back into the adjoining black neighborhood, informing them that they could march there without arrest; there was no more room in the jails. But these marchers were a diversion. As the police gathered at the church, about 600 teen-agers, traveling surreptitiously in small groups, converged in the downtown business section, where they picked up picket signs hidden earlier and began picketing at the segregated stores.

With hundreds of black demonstrators now behind the police lines, many police units turned and sped for downtown. As soon as they left, thousands of demonstrators emerged from the church and surged past the remaining police, heading for downtown. By early afternoon, more than 3,000 demonstrators had gathered in the business district. Unable to arrest them, police brought out water cannons, as well as a tank-like armored car. For most of the day, all commerce was paralyzed. The boycott was now a success; not only were Birmingham's black residents boycotting the downtown stores, by circumstance so were the whites.

All through the day, Burke Marshall, head of the U.S. Department of Justice's Civil Rights Division, pressured white community leaders to negotiate. President Kennedy, the attorney general and several other Cabinet members made calls to key community leaders, urging them to talk with King. Late on the night of May 7 white community leaders agreed to open negotiations and named a negotiating committee.

At midnight, they sought out King. By 4 a.m., the blueprint for a settlement had been drawn. On May 10, four weeks after King's Good Friday arrest, the settlement was announced. The fitting rooms at stores would be integrated by May 13. A biracial committee to discuss desegregation of schools, reopening parks and hiring black city employees would be appointed within 15 days. All public rest rooms and water fountains would be integrated within 30 days. Lunch counters would be integrated, and blacks would be hired as sales clerks within 60 days.

The aftermath of the settlement saw the organization of hundreds of direct action campaigns throughout the nation. On May 20, President Kennedy met with his Cabinet to determine how to reply to the growing movement. On June 11, reversing his position that he would not support a new civil rights law, Kennedy announced that he would send Congress a major civil rights bill; he directly attributed it to events in Birmingham.

In the year following Kennedy's assassination, President Johnson pushed the bill through Congress. On July 2, he signed the Civil Rights Act of 1964 into law. Title II of that act prohibits segregation or discrimination in places of public accommodation; Title VII prohibits discrimination in employment based on race, color, sex, religion or national origin. In tandem, the two sections met all of the goals of the Birmingham desegregation campaign on a national level.

The Constitution and Civil Disobedience

But the legal struggle in Birmingham and the lesson it would send into casebooks was not finished. In 1967 the appeal of the contempt of court convictions of King and the other ministers reached the U.S. Supreme Court. The case, named for King's executive assistant Walker, was *Walker v. City of Birmingham.*

The majority opinion, by Justice Potter Stewart, never mentions King, nor does it explain why the defendants were marching in Birmingham. The decision tells the story of Birmingham entirely from the view of the city's white officials:

A permit was required for marching. No permit was issued. The marchers marched anyway. They were asked to cease. They refused. An injunction was sought because violence was feared, and because the defendants were allegedly violating "numerous ordinances and statutes of the City of Birmingham."

The marchers had the right to appeal the injunction, but they chose to ignore it, the Court observed. The legal consequence was that their attempt at trial to claim that the parade ordinance was unconstitutional was barred by the collateral bar rule. The Court made no mention that a number of states, including California, had abandoned the rule as unnecessarily chilling of free speech rights.

The convictions of King and the other ministers were affirmed, and they were ordered to return to Birmingham to serve their sentences.

The *Walker* decision appears in most law school casebooks for courses on remedies and many casebooks for courses on constitutional law and civil procedure. Of the 15 casebooks in which the decision is presented for study, none mentions the "Letter From Birmingham Jail," only one refers to the 1964 Civil Rights Act, and fewer than half even identify King as a defendant in the case.

Just as the Supreme Court left King and the Birmingham story out of the case, those of us who teach and practice law have left him out of the casebooks. King has become invisible; his message from the Birmingham jail has been silenced. The Birmingham story has been silenced. The Birmingham story and the passage of the Civil Right Act is 30 years old; it is time to tell the story.

The March on Washington

Murray Kempton

The March on Washington for Jobs and Freedom Movement was initiated in the early 1940s by Asa Philip Randolph. His plan was to organize a rally of 100,000 blacks at the Lincoln Memorial as an illustration of the political power of blacks. In 1963, Randolph revived the idea in order to pressure Congress to enact civil rights legislation introduced by President John F. Kennedy. The march drew 250,000 people—black and white.

In the following selection, written in 1963, Murray Kempton argues that the march was organized to bring together feuding factions of the civil rights movement. Some groups wanted a mass public rally in support of Kennedy's legislation. But others wanted to work behind the scenes to lobby Congress for the statutes. Because the march drew national attention, the conservative organizations (including white churches) were compelled to join rather than be left out. Their presence, however, forced the radical groups to moderate the tone of their demands.

Until his death in 1997, Kempton was a journalist who wrote for the *Washington Post*, the *New York Post*, and *New York Newsday*. His books include *Part of Our Time*, *The Briar Patch*, and *Rebellions, Perversities, and Main Events*.

The most consistent quality of white America's experience with the Negro is that almost nothing happens that we—or perhaps even he—expects to have happen. Faithful to that tradition, Washington waited most of the summer for the avenging Negro army to march on Washington for Jobs and Freedom; what came was the largest religious pilgrimage of Americans that any of us is ever likely to see.

Reprinted from Murray Kempton, "A. Philip Randolph: 'The Choice, Mr. President . . . ,'" *The New Republic*, July 6, 1963, by permission of *The New Republic*.

When it was over, Malcolm X, the Muslim, was observed in the lobby of the Statler. It had, he conceded, been something of a show. "Kennedy," said Malcolm X, "should win the Academy Award—for direction." Yet while the President may have triumphed as director-manipulator, he was also deftly manipulated by those whom he strove to direct.

"When the Negro leaders announced the march, the President asked them to call it off," Bayard Rustin, its manager, remembered the next day. "When they thumbed—when they told him they wouldn't—he almost smothered us. We had to keep raising our demands . . . to keep him from getting ahead of us."

Rustin and A. Philip Randolph are men who had to learn long ago that in order to handle they must first permit themselves to be handled. The moment in that afternoon which most strained belief was near its end, when Rustin led the assemblage in a mass pledge never to cease until they had won their demands. A radical pacifist, every sentence punctuated by his upraised hand, was calling for a $2 an hour minimum wage. Every television camera at the disposal of the networks was upon him. No expression one-tenth so radical has ever been seen or heard by so many Americans.

A Painful Season of Rancor

To produce this scene had taken some delicate maneuvering. Randolph called the march last spring at a moment when the civil rights groups had fallen into a particularly painful season of personal rancor. Randolph is unique because he accepts everyone in a movement whose members do not always accept one another. His first support came from the non-violent actionists; they hoped for passionate protest. That prospect was Randolph's weapon; the moderates had to come in or be defenseless against embarrassing disorder. Randolph welcomed them not just with benevolence but with genuine gratitude. When President Kennedy expressed his doubts, Randolph answered that some demonstration was unavoidable and that what had to be done was to make it orderly.

It was the best appeal that feeling could make to calculation. The White House knew that the ordinary Negro cherishes the Kennedy brothers and that the larger the assemblage the better disposed it would be not to embarrass them. When the President finally mentioned the march in public, he issued something as close as possible to a social invitation.

No labor leader since John L. Lewis in 1933 has succeeded in employing the President of the United States as an organizer. Even Lewis only sent his organizers about the pits telling the miners that the President wanted them to join the union, and was careful never to tell Mr. Roosevelt about it. Randolph got his President live, whole and direct.

If the march was important, it was because it represented an acceptance of the Negro revolt as part of the American myth, and so an acceptance of the revolutionaries into the American establishment. That acceptance, of course, carries the hope that the Negro revolt will stop where it is. Yet that acceptance is also the most powerful incentive and assurance that the revolt will continue. The children from Wilmington, North Carolina, climbed back on their buses with the shining memory of a moment when they marched with all America—a memory to sustain them when they return to march alone. So it was, too, for all the others who came from Birmingham, Montgomery, Danville, Gadsden and Jackson—places whose very names evoke not only the cause but the way it is being won.

Gray from Jail, Haggard from Tension

The result of such support—the limits it placed on the spectacle—was illustrated by the experience of John Lewis, chairman of the Student Non-Violent Coordinating Committee. Lewis is only 25; his only credential for being there was combat experience; he has been arrested *22* times and beaten half as often. The Student Non-Violent Coordinating Committee is a tiny battalion, its members gray from jail and exhausted from tension. They have the gallant cynicism of troops of the line; they revere Martin Luther King (some of them) as a captain who has faced the dogs with them and they call him with affectionate irreverence, "De Lawd." We could hardly have had this afternoon without them.

Lewis, in their spirit, had prepared a speech full of temereties about how useless the civil rights bill is and what frauds the Democrats and Republicans are. Three of the white speakers told Randolph that they could not appear at a platform where such sedition was pronounced, and John Lewis had to soften his words in deference to elders. Equal rights for the young to say their say may, perhaps, come later.

Yet Lewis' speech, even as laundered, remained discomfiting enough to produce a significant tableau at its end. "My friends," he said, "let us not forget that we are engaged in a significant social revolution. By and large American politics is dominated by politicians who build their careers on immoral compromising and ally themselves with open forums of political, economic and social exploitation." When he had finished, every Negro on the speakers' row pumped his hand and patted his back; and every white one looked out into the distance.

So even in the middle of this ceremony of reconciliation, the void between the Negro American and a white one remained. Or rather, it did and it didn't. At one point, Martin King mentioned with gratitude the great number of white people (about 40,000 to 50,000 out of an estimated 200,000) who had joined the march. There was little response from the platform—where it must have seemed formal courtesy—but as the sound of those words moved across the great spaces between King and the visitors from the Southern towns, there was the sudden sight and sound of Negroes cheering far away. Nothing all afternoon was quite so moving as the sight of these people, whose trust has been violated so often in the particular, proclaiming it so touchingly intact in the general.

"Late We Come"

We do not move the Negro often, it would seem, and we do it only when we are silent and just standing there. On the speakers' stand there was the inevitable Protestant, Catholic and Jew without which no national ceremony can be certified. Is it hopeless to long for a day when the white brother will just once accept the duty to march, and forego the privilege to preach? Dr. Eugene Carson Blake of the National

Council of Churches told the audience that the Protestants were coming and "late we come." It was the rarest blessing— an apology. We have begun to stoop a little; and yet it is so hard for us to leave off condescending.

We cannot move the Negro by speaking, because the public white America seems to know no words except the ones worn out from having been so long unmeant. Even if they are meant now, they have been empty too long not to *sound* empty still; whatever our desires, our language calls up only the memory of the long years when just the same language served only to convey indifference.

Yet the Negro moves us most when he touches our memory, even as we chill him most when we touch his. August 28 was to many whites only a demonstration of power and importance until Mahalia Jackson arose to sing the old song about having been rebuked and scorned and going home. Then King near the end began working as country preachers do, the words for the first time not as to listeners but as to participants, the intimate private conversation of invocation and response. For just those few minutes, we were back where this movement began and has endured, older than the language of the society which was taking these pilgrims in, but still fresh where the newer language was threadbare.

The Negro comes from a time the rest of us have forgotten; he seems new and complicated only because he represents something so old and simple. He reminds us that the new, after which we have run so long, was back there all the time. Something new will some day be said, and it will be something permanent, if it starts from such a memory.

Blacks Question the Multiracial Movement

Nicolaus Mills

Though a relatively small and poorly funded organization, the Student Nonviolent Coordinating Committee was at the forefront of the civil rights movement, engaging in direct action to battle segregation in the South. Beginning in 1962, in anticipation of the 1964 presidential election, however, SNCC concentrated on registering black voters throughout the South. The voter registration drive was a huge organizational undertaking that required a massive mobilization of volunteers and money. So SNCC enrolled hundreds of students (white and black) from northern colleges and brought them to the South for the 1964 Freedom Summer project.

In the following viewpoint, Nicolaus Mills describes the debate within SNCC over bringing large numbers of whites into the movement for black civil rights. Many within SNCC felt that the movement should be led and conducted by blacks alone because it was fundamentally a fight for black dignity and worth. However, certain SNCC leaders persuasively argued that the movement could not wage a fight against the evil of segregation if it were itself segregated. (In 1966, SNCC became an all-black organization.)

Mills participated in the Freedom Summer project and was later active in the anti-Vietnam War movement. He is the author of *Like a Holy Crusade: Mississippi, 1964—The Turning of the Civil Rights Movement in America.*

In November 1963 forty members of the Student Nonviolent Coordinating Committee (SNCC) gathered in the small

Excerpted from Nicolaus Mills, "Forgotten Greenville: SNCC and the Lessons of 1963," *Dissent*, vol. 37 (Summer 1990). Reprinted by permission of *Dissent*.

131

Mississippi town of Greenville for three days of meetings. The result was a decision that would bring over one thousand volunteers—most of them white—south for the Mississippi Summer Project of 1964. Like the Students for a Democratic Society's (SDS) famous Port Huron meeting of 1962, Greenville would change the political course of the 1960s.

Greenville gets mentioned in histories of the 1960s, but unlike the Montgomery Bus Boycott or the Selma March or the murders of Schwerner, Chaney, and Goodman, Greenville has sparked little popular interest. For Greenville was talk, and in Hollywood you don't make a television docudrama, let alone a film like *Mississippi Burning*, about talk.

The talk, however, is just what makes Greenville worth turning back to. Greenville was one of the last times in the 1960s when blacks and whites in SNCC thought of themselves as a "band of brothers" yet still questioned the value of an integrated civil rights movement. As such, it speaks directly to our present situation, when integration shows signs of becoming a word we are again willing to use and civil rights heroes, like Georgia Congressman John Lewis, SNCC's chairman during its heyday, insist, "We need to talk again about building what Dr. King called a *beloved community*—a truly integrated society of blacks and whites."

To look back at Greenville is to see how even in the best of times building a multiracial civil rights movement troubled its most committed participants and, particularly if they were black, made them vulnerable to the charge that they were substituting a white agenda for authentic racial change.

Blacks and Whites in the Mississippi Movement

The steps leading to Greenville began in 1961 when Bob Moses, the man who would later head the Mississippi Summer Project of 1964, went to Mississippi to start organizing voter registration. "We are smuggling this note from the drunk tank of the county jail in Magnolia, Mississippi. Twelve of us are here, sprawled out along the concrete bunker," a 1961 Moses letter opens. "We lack eating and drinking utensils. Water comes from a faucet and goes into a hole. This is Mississippi, the middle of the iceberg. . . .

This is a tremor in the middle of the iceberg—from a stone that the builders rejected."

Two years later, the Harvard-educated Moses, who had been teaching math at the Horace Mann School in New York before going to Mississippi, was a legend in the civil rights movement. He had been threatened, beaten, shot at, but in a state where more than 90 percent of eligible black voters were kept off the rolls, he had gotten people to go to courthouses to register. And he had brought into SNCC a group of young Mississippi blacks who, like himself, were prepared to risk their lives to change the South. The inroads Moses was able to make in Mississippi were not, however, enough to spare him and SNCC from constant arrests and heavy fines. By the end of 1962 in Greenwood, where SNCC had had some of its greatest success, it was, by Moses's own admission, broke and little more than a holding operation.

Northern Students Lend a Hand

Then in 1963 a major change occurred. That fall, Moses, working with Al Lowenstein, a thirty-four-year-old liberal lawyer, brought a hundred students from Yale and Stanford to Mississippi to help in an undertaking that became known as the Freedom Vote. Its aim was to provide dramatic proof that, if given half a chance, Mississippi blacks would vote in record numbers. Polling booths were set up throughout the black community, and blacks were encouraged to cast protest ballots in the gubernatorial election for Aaron Henry, the black president of the Mississippi NAACP, and the Reverend Ed King, the white chaplain of Tougaloo College.

Two weeks before the election the SNCC staff and the students Lowenstein had recruited fanned out across the state. As expected, their efforts met with violence. Six of the Yale students were arrested within thirty-six hours of reaching Mississippi, and there were numerous beatings. But with the media on hand to report the story, the violence remained limited. On election day the precautions taken to make sure the Freedom Vote took place paid off. More than 80,000 blacks cast symbolic votes for Henry and King, and the media, intrigued by out-of-state students working in Mississippi, gave

SNCC the kind of publicity it had never received before.

This success brought SNCC new momentum. Now, instead of being limited to local campaigns, it could function on a statewide basis. But the success also meant that SNCC's heroic age of innocence was over in Mississippi. SNCC was faced with the toughest decision in its short history: Did it want to continue the kind of organizing that had gotten it through its first two years? Or did it want to switch to a political strategy that relied on the use of northern students?

The dilemma was one that success had made possible but for which there was no painless solution. The core of field secretaries on whom SNCC depended in Mississippi were, as Bob Moses put it, twenty-five or thirty young Negroes "who viewed themselves as some kind of unit." If SNCC shifted to a strategy that made white volunteers the key to its future, the influence of these field secretaries would be diminished, for they would then be forced to share control of the movement in Mississippi and to admit that by themselves blacks could not determine their own fate in the Deep South.

On the other hand, if progress continued to be as slow as it had been from 1961 to the Freedom Vote of 1963, there was a good chance that SNCC's Mississippi staff would soon become the guardians of a lost cause. "The staff was exhausted, and they were butting up against a stone wall, no breakthroughs for them," Bob Moses would later recall. "Where was help to come from? The civil rights organizations were not prepared to make Mississippi a focus."

The Arguments Against Including Whites

By middle November there was no putting off dealing with these issues. The August March on Washington (where March sponsors forced SNCC chairman John Lewis to tone down his speech) and the September bombing of the Sixteenth Street Baptist Church in Birmingham (which killed four black children) formed the backdrop for SNCC's meeting. But it was the Freedom Vote that dominated discussion.

Like those who favored a Summer Project that would make extensive use of whites, those who opposed the Project began with the lessons of the Freedom Vote. They were not at all sure that the presence of northern students had worked to SNCC's advantage. "I question the value of the publicity we gained from the Yale students," said Donna Moses, who throughout the Greenville talks clashed with her husband. She and the others opposed to the Summer Project feared that an expanded version of the Freedom Vote would leave SNCC face to face with an aroused white community but without help once August ended. "We don't have that much to gain from Negroes meeting whites," an angry MacArthur Cotton observed. "We've got too much to lose if they come down here and create a disturbance in two or three months, and they're gone."

As the debate heated up, it was its political rather than its physical dangers that its critics zeroed in on. The opponents of the Summer Project were prepared to keep working in a Mississippi in which, as one SNCC staffer put it, "with Negroes it's open season—365 days a year." But they were not prepared to support a Summer Project that, in their view, would jeopardize the gains they had made. During the Freedom Vote whites seemed to gravitate to positions of authority, and many in SNCC feared what would happen if over a whole summer the whites working in Mississippi outnumbered blacks. "Up to this point you had a minority of whites working in the movement," Charlie Cobb, a Howard University student and the future head of SNCC's Freedom Schools, observed. "Now the movement is national. So what you've got is hundreds of white people all coming South, and they can do things better than Negroes, and the question is, What do you do with them all?"

Cobb did not believe that whites came to Mississippi intending to take over SNCC, but he was convinced that tradition made it all too easy for blacks to turn over power to them. "I didn't say whites take over. I said that Negroes take whites out of the field, then put them up in leadership roles," Cobb declared. "The tendency is for the whites to articulate the demands of Negroes to the Negro person while the Negro kids stand quietly on the side. This is not done on purpose by whites, but it is done." Cobb's fears were also shared by whites in SNCC. In language almost identical to

Cobb's Mendy Samstein, a Brandeis graduate who joined SNCC after teaching at Morehouse College in Atlanta, observed, "If thousands of whites come down, there is the problem of relationships between blacks and whites. Whites convincing blacks of their rights—this entrenches the concept of white supremacy."

Cobb's opposition to a Summer Project that relied on white students did not stop with the issue of political control. He also worried about SNCC's ability to deal with white versus black values. "We've got the problem of American values in white society—values we're trying to change," he pointed out. If whites became dominant in the Summer Project, how could whites' values be challenged? Cobb wanted to know. "People can't just come down to Mississippi and say we're here to help you," Cobb insisted. "The first consciousness that Negroes have is the thing of whites, and I don't think it helps to have the whites here."

Sentiments in Favor of Black Self-Sufficiency

What Cobb and those in SNCC who believed that civil rights "should be primarily a Negro movement" came back to as an example was the postcolonial experience in Africa. They pointed out that when the colonial powers ruled, the key positions were held by whites. Afterward, the idea was to train blacks to replace them. That was the way of the future in Africa, and for SNCC, which sought to develop black political power in Mississippi, a Summer Project that relied on whites was a step backward.

As the Greenville meeting drew to a close, Ivanhoe Donaldson carried Cobb's self-sufficiency argument one step further. He raised the issue of how an SNCC that depended on whites to carry out its Summer Project would appeal to young blacks. Would they not see the black SNCC staffers they identified with put in a position of inferiority? Donaldson had become involved in SNCC when, while a Michigan State student, he helped deliver a truckload of food to blacks in Leflore County, Mississippi. His doubts about the Summer Project, in conjunction with those of Charlie Cobb, also a northerner, were revealing. Their skepticism showed that it was not just SNCC's Mississippi-born field secretaries who feared an influx of whites.

"I came to SNCC, and I saw Negroes running the movement, and I felt good. These feelings might be irrational, they might be wrong, but I have to live with them. I get the feeling the way things are going in two or three years the movement will be run by white students," Donaldson declared. Donaldson did not try to put his fears in the shape of a systematic argument. "You're fighting yourself all the way across the board. I find myself doing this all the time. I think one way and act the other," he confessed. But Donaldson's unwillingness to try to intellectualize his feelings made them all the more powerful when he concluded, "Whites are mobile, and Negroes aren't. It's all one way. . . . We're losing the one thing where Negroes can stand first."

There was, as Charlie Cobb would later acknowledge, an inherent contradiction in the stance he and the opponents of the Summer Project took at Greenville. At a time when SNCC was arguing that Mississippi should be desegregated, they were arguing that integration posed a danger for SNCC. But logic alone, as Bob Moses and those favoring the Summer Project knew, was not going to carry the day at Greenville. The feelings that Cobb and Donaldson voiced were inseparable from the pride that kept SNCC going. What was needed to move SNCC beyond such feelings was not a debater's skill but a more compelling vision of the future.

The Appeal for a Multiracial Movement

At Greenville it fell to Bob Moses to spell out that vision. In doing so, he had the support of Lawrence Guyot, who in 1964 would head the newly formed Mississippi Freedom Democratic Party. He also had the backing of Fannie Lou Hamer, a grandmother who had endured the loss of her job and a savage beating by police to become one of the most revered figures in SNCC. Moses made approval of the principles of the Summer Project a test of his leadership, and on the second day of the Greenville meeting abandoned his normally deferential style of leadership to argue for a multiracial SNCC.

Moses's starting point was the impasse that SNCC had reached in 1963. Charlie Cobb saw inviting whites to come to Mississippi for the summer of 1964 as an admission of failure. As he later put it, "You're conceding that you're not able to deal with the situation." Moses did not dispute such a reading. But for him the facts were not the whole story. SNCC bore no onus, Moses believed, for failing to cope with the racial violence of Mississippi.

Moses made a point of talking about the areas where SNCC was vulnerable. Earlier in the year he had voiced the fear that the growing automation of cotton picking, in conjunction with the efforts of the White Citizens Councils to force blacks out of Mississippi, put SNCC in a bind. Now he returned to the same subject. "If it goes like it's going, they're going to beat us back in five or six years, because the cards are stacked in their favor," he argued.

For the opponents of the Summer Project, the answer was to become a tighter, more cohesive organization. Moses, on the other hand, was convinced that SNCC should expand as it had done during the Freedom Vote, when "whites brought a searchlight from the rest of the country with them." It was a position that left Moses vulnerable to the charge of ignoring the needs of the SNCC staff and playing down the encroachments of whites. But Moses believed he had no choice. "The question of whether or not the white students coming in would take over the movement, would dominate . . . was a risk, but not as important as the risk of not being able to do anything at all," he would conclude.

Some whites, Moses readily conceded, had overstepped their bounds during the Freedom Vote. But SNCC's overall experience with whites in Mississippi was, he insisted, the opposite of what the Summer Project opponents claimed. The whites who worked for SNCC did more than pull their weight. "We almost suffocated them," Moses declared. "They had to stay in the office. They couldn't go out on the street. They couldn't go to dances. They couldn't go to this cafe or that cafe. They were in the office. They were washing dishes. They were sleeping on the floors. They really were doing all the dirty work."

The Need for Integration

The real opposition to the Summer Project stemmed, Moses believed, from a general anger toward whites, and he attacked this anger head on. "People say of white workers in the field they're more articulate and they're going to do the talking, and then if you get them in the office, they're better typists, and so they get into leadership positions," he observed. "The tone I get is that white people came in and took over, and now we're going to put them in their place." Moses understood all too well why such anger occurred. As he later put it, "It's very hard for some of the students who have been brought up in Mississippi and are the victims of this kind of race hatred not to begin to let all of that out on the white staff." But at Greenville the only concessions Moses was prepared to make were limited practical ones. "My position all along, and I think I've said this several times, you try to get as many Negroes as you can to do the job, [then] get whites to the extent that it can't do harm to the Negro community," he declared. "The type of person you have is much more important than whether he's white or not."

Beyond this point, Moses was convinced, there was no room for compromise on the race issue. "I'm not going to be part of an organization that says, 'No white people are going to be head of a project because they're white,'" he told the meeting. "My alternative is I'll gladly leave if that's the kind of organization you want to run." But having taken this stance, Moses went on to argue that SNCC's position in the civil rights movement gave it a special opportunity to show how blacks and whites should get along. Fannie Lou Hamer would later quiet the room by declaring, "If we're trying to break down this barrier of segregation, we can't segregate ourselves." This time it was Bob Moses's turn to do the same. "The one thing we can do for the country that no one else can do," he declared, "is to be above the race issue."

In an interview with Robert Penn Warren, Moses would later discuss how his reading of philosopher Albert Camus made him concerned with the ways victims are tempted to turn themselves into executioners. Moses would not quote Camus directly at Greenville, but the fears his reading of

Camus aroused were implicit in his final plea for the Summer Project. If whites were part of the Summer Project, it would, Moses argued, change the way blacks saw them. "Negroes would have to take them as people. They'd learn not to let their fears and emotions get the better of them when they talk[ed] to whites."

But most of all, Moses argued, SNCC needed whites because without them it was in danger of leading a "racist movement" in which color, not moral conduct, separated friend from foe. "The only way you can break that down," he concluded, "is to have white people working alongside you. Then it changes the whole complexion of what you're doing so it isn't any longer Negro fighting white. It's a question of rational people against irrational people."

Churches Join the Movement

James Findlay

In the summer of 1964, black civil rights organizations planned the Freedom Summer drive to educate and register black voters, primarily in Mississippi. They enlisted the help of hundreds of students from northern colleges as well as ministers from the National Council of Churches.

In the following selection, written in 1988, James Findlay relates the recollections of some of the ministers who participated in the project. Some remember the violence that southern segregationists directed at them. Others recall how their personal attitudes toward blacks were transformed by the experience. Findlay argues that these changes in individuals' outlooks were small but long-lasting successes in the effort to reconstruct race relations in America.

Findlay is a professor of history at the University of Rhode Island. He is the author of *Church People in the Struggle: The National Council of Churches and the Black Freedom Movement, 1950–1970.*

Twenty-five years ago the nation's attention was riveted on the civil rights struggle in the South. That struggle entered one of its critical stages in the summer of 1964 when young black civil rights workers in Mississippi, aided by about 800 white college students form the North, tried to bring blacks in the Magnolia state to a new level of political and social awareness. They organized voter education and voter registration drives, and Freedom Schools for the young and old. The white community met this campaign with the sternest resistance—daily harassment, the burning of black homes and churches, even murder (remember James Chaney, Andrew Goodman and Michael Schwerner?).

Reprinted, by permission, from James Findlay, "In Keeping with the Prophets: The Mississippi Summer of 1964," *The Christian Century*, June 8–15, 1988. Copyright 1988 Christian Century Foundation.

The National Council of Churches spearheaded white churches' support of the battle in Mississippi. The NCC funded and organized the intensive weeklong orientation sessions in June 1964 for nearly all the student volunteers. And in a project still little known, the NCC recruited about 300 ministers from all over the United States to go to Mississippi that summer as informal "advisers" to the students. These ministers left their jobs briefly or used their summer vacations to offer direct support to the civil rights workers. Most went for ten days or two weeks, some for longer periods. A few never returned home and are still living in Mississippi.

Recollections of White Northerners Who Went South

Recently uncovered archival data enabled me to identify and contact many of those who "went South" in 1964. I sent a brief questionnaire to them, and many responded with long and fascinating replies. They also sent newspaper clippings, sermon-reports to congregations and articles they wrote afterward for religious journals. Some produced portions of diaries, letters to families, tape recordings, even slides taken in Mississippi and at the student orientation sessions in Oxford, Ohio. One person mailed the script of a play he wrote recently based on his 1964 experiences.

Long-dormant yet sensitive nerves had been touched. One person wrote that even now he could not think about the memories without tears. Another asserted that "recalling this experience and detailing it brought back some intense feelings—anger, fright, even a brush with terror."

As "advisers" the ministers simply joined the civil rights workers in their daily routines. They picketed at courthouses, searched out potential registrants, taught in freedom schools and served as librarians and receptionists in freedom centers. As a result they, like the local people, were physically and emotionally intimidated. A few were arrested and jailed, one or two were beaten. One minister assigned to Greenwood, a very difficult town, took people to register each day. He recalled:

There was the inevitable line-up of whites yelling at us, spitting at us. One guy even urinated in my direction once. I caught a bit of it on my pants. The hardest thing for me was not to respond in some physical manner. I had fought in the Golden Gloves in high school and I usually had a very aggressive manner in my lifestyle. I can remember thinking: "You dirty S-O-B. I could take you out with one punch." Not exactly the acceptable thoughts of a clergyman, but my rage was right under the surface and I had to keep remembering the mandate of our instructor—"Don't lose your cool."

Another minister recalled walking down a road in the black community in Canton and hearing someone yell "Jump! Jump!" He tumbled into a ditch as a truck roared by, "coming down into the ditch and missing us by six inches." Later this same person hid for two hours in a bedroom of a black family's home while the deputy sheriff's car circled the neighborhood searching for him. When he left Mississippi, he remembered, "I felt that I had been in hell for three weeks. I came home with double pneumonia and total exhaustion."

Experiences of Segregation

These middle-class, idealistic church people entered a tangled world of hate and oppression most of them knew little or nothing about. Suddenly they were part of the underclass, an outcast group to be harassed and attacked if they got out of line. They found that law enforcement officials were not, as they had previously thought, dispensers of evenhanded justice but were often spearheads of a system of injustice. One Disciples of Christ participant reported that she was "amazed [after leaving Mississippi] at how long it took me to get over having my heart turn over at the sight of a police car. And I had only one week like that. Think of what it would be for persons who always fear authorities!"

In moments of fear and terror a bonding of the deepest sort occurred between blacks and whites—a fact that made a deep impression. An ironic reversal of roles took place, with northern whites feeling safe in the black community. An Episcopal laywoman recalled: "Walking down the streets of

Canton's Negro section, we were obviously of the Movement. From every porch, from every yard, came greetings.
'Hi, y'all.' To my northern accented 'Hi,' came the cheery
report, 'Fine.'" At night there were long conversations between black hosts and white visitors on porches kept un-
lighted for security purposes. The wife of a northern clergyman noted in a letter home that "we were told that Negroes
sitting on benches along the street weren't just sitting—they
were watching to see that our office [the NCC office in Hat-
tiesburg] and the COFO [Council of Federated Organiza-
tions] office across the street were safe."

One of the ministers' principal aims was to reach out to
the local white community, especially the clergy and
churches, looking for a chance to talk about the changes
whites were having to face. They hoped to create an atmosphere in which Christian reconciliation might develop.

These efforts met with little success, and most often with
vehement rebuffs. One minister who sought to attend a Sunday service at a Disciples of Christ church in McComb was
recognized as a civil rights worker and "thrown bodily out of
the building." Another Disciples minister, who remained in
Mississippi for a year, tried to join a church of his denomi-
nation in Gulfport-Biloxi. He was informed by the church's
minister that he would never be welcome in the latter's
house, nor would the minister ever visit him. Church
women's meetings were held in parishioners' homes and announced privately by phone to prevent the wife of the "out-
sider" minister from attending. Eventually the outsiders
joined a black Missionary Baptist church.

A Change in Attitudes

The attitude of white Mississippi churchpeople intensified
the northern ministers' respect for the black people they had
come to support. Despite encountering communities scarred
by poverty ("homes ranged from a few small, neat and attractive places to huts, shacks and hovels held together by
odd pieces of wood, metal and building blocks. Health and
sanitation conditions were appalling. As a result, we found a
staggering number of sick and invalid people with little hope

of regaining their health"), the ministers' remembrances were nearly all positive.

They remembered food and other essentials willingly shared ("I remember the buckets of fried chicken brought to Freedom House by neighbors. I remember the elderly people who let me live in their house even though it put their lives in jeopardy"). They remembered the courage and determination of the young civil rights workers ("The real heroes were the black 'Snick' [SNCC, or Student Nonviolent Coordinating Committee] personnel, who faced the worst dangers and took more than their share of the violence. Always they were intent on helping anyone threatened. Always they took hardship as a matter of course. These were the real leaders, and that is as it should be. It was a privilege to work with them"). They also remembered "the spiritual power of the [civil rights] meetings," especially the singing, with a passion and feeling rooted in the black church.

Above all else the ministers remembered spirited individuals who were unbroken by threats and powerfully supportive of the push toward freedom. Stories like the following were common on the questionnaires:

> There was neither gratitude nor fawning in our relationship with our hostess, but rather a fierce pride. She reigned over her house, and the six volunteers billeted with her, like an African matriarch. At six in the morning she did the daily shopping before the heat set in, yet she spent the hottest part of the day over a wood stove producing Southern fried chicken, rice, cornbread. A widow four times, but unsubdued, she answered the door concealing a long knife behind her skirts.

Some ministers later returned to Mississippi to visit their black friends, and some still correspond regularly with their hosts—small acts suggestive of the ties that were established.

The Symbolism of the Integrated Movement
One might wonder how such deep connections between people of different races and very different backgrounds could develop so quickly. Perhaps part of the answer rests in

what the northerners represented to the black people of Mississippi. As one Presbyterian minister who stayed permanently in the state explained, until the '60s white Mississippians often dubbed the few black persons who agitated for civil rights as "crazy niggers," and that perception was seldom challenged. The isolation of black activists was almost complete. In the mid-'60s, however, the white community outside Mississippi (as well as young blacks in the state) were suggesting that those "crazy niggers" were not crazy but correct in their demands.

That white churches would send ministers to Mississippi to stand with the "crazy niggers," however briefly, affirming to the world the soundness of what they were doing, was a powerful symbolic act. The ministers, as well as the black community, understood this fully. As one put it, going to Mississippi in the summer of 1964 "expressed to the blacks that there were other persons who cared and were concerned." "Here were ministers visibly giving support to the movement to change the system. To those in Mississippi working to effect change we gave encouragement, saying, 'You are not alone.'"

Most of the northern ministers did not stay long in Mississippi (something some still feel guilty about). After ten days or two weeks they were replaced. By the end of August 1964 nearly all had left. But they carried away an entirely new perception of their country and of themselves. As they testified again and again in their comments two decades later, their lives had been permanently altered.

The testimonies suggest that many had been subtly prepared for going to Mississippi. "I was reared in a Christian home where racial equality was taken for granted." "Perhaps having a black summer playmate when I was seven to ten was a memory that urged me into the 'long trip' into the South." For others the beginnings were in college or soon after: "As a student at the University of Missouri, I took home with me at Christmastime a German Catholic, a Jew, and a Chinese student who had no place to go at that time of year." A number of the ministers participating in the project had become involved before 1964 in civil rights demonstrations or interracial ministries, or had worked overseas or on Native American reservations. "At the time we were living in Horton, Kansas, in the midst of Indian reservations, and there was a strong prejudice against the Native American, which was expressed in a 'nigger' mentality. The appeal [to go to Mississippi] spoke to me, as I saw a relationship between the local Indian prejudice and the suppression of blacks."

Whites' Reasons for Going

Others could not so clearly pinpoint their reasons for going. "There was no real explanation for going to Mississippi. My decision was intuitive, emotional, nonrational. I wanted to participate. It seemed like something I could do." But the most frequently voiced feeling in the recollections was the sense that some sort of a moral demand had been placed upon the ministers: "The church had an obligation to be involved in the voter rights struggle." "I felt it was the 'right thing to do.'" One writer put it even more compellingly: "I went to Mississippi in the summer of 1964 because I felt 'called' to do so. By this I mean it was an act required by my profession of faith. The injustice inflicted on blacks I felt was so appalling that I could not in conscience do other than respond."

One of the best ways to assess the significance of the Mississippi project is to consider how the white ministers acted afterward. One wrote, "I grew up on a farm in southeastern South Dakota, and despite college and seminary was still abysmally ignorant concerning the realities of racial injustice. My involvement in this project transformed my theological understanding and shaped my ministry from that time to this day." Another minister said, "My suspicion is that the most permanent change was not in the South as such, but in the minds and hearts of us northerners, who received a mighty 'education in reality.' All of my teaching and writing about our society since those years have been deeply shaped by my experience among the black poor and oppressed of the South."

Almost all the first full-time staff members of the Delta Ministry, the NCC-sponsored civil rights group which began work in the Mississippi delta and elsewhere in the state in September 1964, had participated in the summer project. At least three of those people are still living in the state, all still engaged in race-related causes. One of them wrote in 1986: "It [the summer of 1964] transformed my life. I'm still here."

One man wrote from Zimbabwe, where as a social worker and academic he was engaged in community planning sponsored by the Disciples of Christ and a local nongovernmental agency. "My life has been dedicated to issues of justice ever since [1964]. I learned much about what faith and faithfulness mean, about what commitment entails, about how to follow, about sensitivity to others." One respondent, a campus minister in Texas in 1964, moved to Alabama a year later, where he and his wife worked at Stillman College, a predominantly black school. Several of the ministers entered interracial ministries, locally or at the national level (for example, as staff persons in denominational social-action agencies).

Some individuals were affected in very personal ways. One minister's daughter, who was also in Mississippi as a student volunteer, married a Howard University graduate and successfully integrated her immediate family. Another explained that for him Mississippi "led to the adoption of two mixed-race children." Even those few who had left the ministry sometime since 1964 had taken jobs connected in some way to their Mississippi experiences. A man living in California wrote, "Isn't it interesting that even though I am no longer doing parish ministry I am still heavily involved: this time as an elementary teacher in a racially mixed urban school."

Lasting Impacts

Relying on memories about events of almost a quarter-century ago may produce too positive a picture. The 1964 Mississippi experiences were part of the early success of the black freedom movement and reflected a brief moment when a national white-black coalition seemed to sweep everything before it. We know that the efforts of the '60s to alter race relations were followed by white backlash and a far different national mood.

But though subsequent national developments might have

embittered the churchpeople who went to Mississippi in 1964, that does not seem to have happened. The power of their experiences during that long hot summer in the Deep South reverberates across the years. One of the participants concluded: "It was the most intense moment of my life, and I felt like I was where history was, that my role as a young clergyman was much in keeping with the Old Testament prophets." Said another:

> Yes, my inner being was connected in a very powerful way to my outer behavior. That awareness has never left me. I can honestly tell people that if they care and take action, they can help change the world around them. It may be slow, but it does happen. Values can be lived, and when they are, they are life-giving. I learned to tell the truth in 1964, and have never consciously let go of that value.

The prophetic imagination truly seemed at work in these people. On a small but important stage, that band of ministers in Mississippi in 1964 represented one of mainline Protestantism's finest moments.

Freedom Summer

Mike Miller

In April 1964, Student Nonviolent Coordinating Committee (SNCC) workers formed the Mississippi Freedom Democratic Party as an alternative to the segregated Mississippi Democratic Party. They registered blacks and concerned whites in the new party, held a separate election, and chose delegates to send to the 1964 Democratic National Convention in Atlantic City. The MFDP then went before the convention's rules committee and argued that they should be considered the legitimate state delegation because the official party had unconstitutionally excluded blacks from voting in the party primary. The committee offered a compromise of two at-large seats to the MFDP. In defiance, the official delegates left the convention, and several other southern delegations threatened to do so as well. Rejecting the compromise, the MFDP also left the convention.

The convention's refusal to honestly consider the MFDP's petition produced disillusionment within SNCC, according to Mike Miller. The bitterness over the event contributed to the organization's turn toward strident black nationalism in 1966. In the following excerpt, Miller argues that SNCC's Mississippi strategy failed because the project did not spark a grassroots movement. It did not recruit and train local black leaders and organizers; it did not put in place a fundraising system; and it did not formulate any plans beyond the convention. Without those essentials, SNCC could not inspire ongoing political organizing.

Miller was an SNCC field secretary in California. He now directs a political education project in San Francisco.

Excerpted from Mike Miller, "Mississippi Musings: Freedom Summer Revisited," *Social Policy*, Fall 1994. Reprinted by permission of *Social Policy*, New York, N.Y. 10036. Copyright 1994 by Social Policy Corporation.

Too many stories of SNCC fail to acknowledge the crucial role of local Black community leaders who invited Bob Moses and SNCC to work in the state. I think I failed to realize at the time how important it was that a group of Mississippi Blacks, most of them linked to one another by their membership in local chapters of the NAACP, opened the doors for SNCC workers in the state. Many of them were veterans from World War II who had a taste of equal treatment from European whites when they were part of the army that liberated Europe. After discharge, rather than leaving the state, they stayed—determined to struggle for democracy in Mississippi as they had fought for it in Europe. Chuck McDew, an early chair of SNCC, said at the time, "We who have struggled to make the world safe for democracy must now struggle to make democracy safe for the world." These local Blacks directed Bob Moses, in his initial visits to the state, away from sit-ins or freedom rides and instead toward voter registration. It was they who were involved in early strategizing for what came to be the SNCC Mississippi Project. In contemporary organizing parlance, the local leaders were "sponsors." They played the role of legitimizing the organizing effort because they were trusted by the people the project sought to involve. You can't land in a community and expect to be welcomed. It is a mistake the northern student movement-initiated mid-'60s organizing projects made—and a lesson that any organizer needs to learn. . . .

Whites in SNCC

The Student Nonviolent Coordinating Committee went into Mississippi when almost no one else was willing to do so. For the more established national organizations, Mississippi was not a priority. It would fall last, said the leaders. Still, there were local Blacks who had bravely resisted segregation, a few publicly and many more in the small private ways that were available within (at least on the issue of race) a police state. In 1961, after visiting many of those who were leaders of local NAACP chapters or who were otherwise identified as Blacks willing to fight for equal rights, SNCC's Bob Moses started the first voter rights project in McComb.

SNCC field secretaries (joined in 1963 by CORE—the Congress of Racial Equality) worked for almost three years with the courageous few who would take the phony literacy test to register to vote. Their efforts were almost fruitless. A few thousand of the hundreds of thousands of eligible Blacks in Mississippi were registered. A high price was paid by those who sought to register: some were killed; more were beaten; many lost jobs or homes or both; churches that allowed civil rights meetings in them were bombed and burned. While a fragile movement infrastructure was slowly being built, led by local Blacks and aided by Black SNCC workers from Mississippi and elsewhere, there was little reason to think things would change. The Justice Department, FBI and the President, showed little inclination to break the massive resistance of the state's Democratic Party structure. . . .

SNCC's Mississippi Strategy in 1964 and Its Defeat

SNCC had been about "Black power" as early as 1961 when some of its field secretaries decided that integrating lunch counters and desegregating bus terminals weren't enough— that the back of the South's racism had to be broken, and a way to break it was through the vote. Nor was the vote, in and of itself, thought to be enough. SNCC's strategy was to build local Black organizations that would be able to act independently of the Democratic (or Republican) Party. In Mississippi, this independence was expressed in the Mississippi Freedom Democratic Party (MFDP). Because of their connections in the north, the volunteers helped build a national base of support for the MFDP. The SNCC-inspired strategy was brilliant in conception and sophisticated in execution. But to no avail. The Atlantic City defeat was the result of the application of political pressure on delegates by President Johnson and his agent in the matter, vice-presidential candidate Hubert Humphrey. When the screws were turned, support evaporated.

When the MFDP's challenge to the seating of the racist Democrats at the 1964 Democratic Convention was defeated, anger that had been building among many Blacks in SNCC reached new heights and created the context for the

"Black power" slogan. The slogan was both political and personal. For some, it meant various forms of Black nationalism. For others it meant repeating what history books said the Irish, Italians, Jews and other ethnic groups had done in America. For some Black power meant hostility toward all whites, including those in SNCC. The defeat was too fundamental to be dealt with easily. Some at the reunion considered MFDP's defeat an accomplishment in that it "exposed" the depth of the country's racism. But social movements demand hope for their sustenance, and exposure—however accurate—is not enough. Without hope, a vision and a believable strategy, exposure leads to despair and withdrawal or to individual and small group acts of destruction, as, for example, bombing banks—as some Movement veterans later did.

Lessons Learned

The Mississippi experience vividly teaches the limits of electoral politics. At a literature table at our conference grounds I bought the Summer 1992 *Journal of Negro History*. The issue is an historical assessment of Black mayors, and separate articles examine Mayors Hatcher (Gary), Goode (Philadelphia) and Young (Atlanta). Though not the issue's thesis, one cannot help but conclude from its evidence that in the absence of a mass movement, there is little these mayors could do to improve the quality of life of the vast majority of the Black people of their cities—nor, for that matter, of the poor and working class of whatever ethnicity or race. The same can be said of the 800-plus elected Black officials in Mississippi. In fact, it is now generally recognized that white industry will not locate in the predominantly Blackbelt counties because Blacks are too likely to unionize and Black elected officials are too sympathetic to union efforts. With capital and other resources increasingly withdrawn from Black-run cities and rural communities, Black elected officials are left to preside over the division of an evershrinking pie. It is an important lesson, one that SNCC knew in theory but was unable to implement.

Electoral politics is but one tactic of a freedom movement.

Others include negotiation, lobbying, disruption, boycotts, strikes, mutual aid (credit unions, co-ops, buying clubs, support groups), community economic development, member benefits (discount buying, health and retirement plans) and direct service. Each is a means toward solving specific problems facing people—hunger, housing, health care, child care, employment, toxic waste dumps, education and public services: each may train people to assume new positions of responsibility and offer jobs for the unemployed.

The broadly based organization is the necessary vehicle if these tactics and solutions to specific problems are to be part of building something bigger. The organization builds a sense of community and, through it, people act with power, purpose, spirit and dignity. Within such organizations education, celebration, evaluation, training and reflection take place. A freedom movement needs to become ever larger in its geographic scope, ever deeper in its levels of leadership and base of support, and ever broader in its constituency. Otherwise, the more remote centers of power (multinationals, the federal government, the International Monetary Fund and banks, to name a few examples), which must be made accountable to the interests of the poor, working and middle classes, remain untouched. Even worse, as the movement shrinks, as the face-to-face relationships that can counteract media-hype disappear, the very elected officials who emerge from the movement become increasingly dependent on wealthy individuals and big business sources of financing for their (media dominated) electoral campaigns.

Beyond Organizing

We lacked the steel discipline necessary to engage in the battle we had undertaken. The Summer Project, and the entrenched power it sought to challenge, demanded things of SNCC that went beyond its courage, dedication and brilliance. SNCC had gone into battle essentially unarmed. We were supposed to be an organization of organizers—not the grassroots organizations that, as organizers, we intended to build. SNCC lacked an effective mechanism for screening, recruiting, training, mentoring and disciplining new staff.

SNCC grew too fast—from about 20 full-time workers to over 200 in three years. There was no way for the better organizers to mentor those with the potential to learn. We had no way to fire people, thus they stayed on. The organization was too open—and some took advantage. Some Blacks who were moved aside by northern whites should have been moved long before the whites arrived. Others cracked under the stress of the continuous threat of violence. Chuck McDew called them "the walking wounded." Traumatic stress syndrome had not yet been named—but we knew it in The Movement. Jim Forman paid special attention to bringing mental health professionals into the state to help. But for some SNCC workers it was too little, too late.

We rarely asked local people for money—neither dues nor a regular mass fundraising operation were established. Many thought it wasn't possible. But at almost the same time The Movement was growing in Mississippi, Cesar Chavez was organizing the National Farm Workers Association in California—and asking its farm worker members to pay $3.50 per month in dues. When northern liberals stopped supporting The Movement through "Friends of SNCC," it was too late to develop a "bottom-up" funding strategy.

No Plan "B"

We failed to accurately assess our adversaries, and to have an alternative plan. Most of us were unprepared for the outcome of the Freedom Democratic Party's Atlantic City challenge. We had neither predicted nor developed a strategy based upon the possibility of defeat at the hands of the Democrats. People went home bitter. A subsequent January challenge to the House seating of the newly elected Mississippi Congressmen met similar defeat. Movements are not built on such defeats. The idea of "contingency planning"—having a plan "A," and a plan "B," one for the possibility of victory, the other for the possibility of defeat—was not in our lexicon.

With these failures, we were unable to sustain hope. Hope is what enlivened the '60s movement: hope for everything from paved and lighted streets and roads to an end to the plantation system that kept its Black workforce in near slavery. Hope was kept alive by the shared community of common struggle. Whatever the objective outcome of a movement's effort, as long as it keeps itself together as a community, people will fight. As The Movement song said, "Before I be a slave, I'll be buried in my grave and go home to my Lord and be free." SNCC, the "band of brothers (and sisters too), circle of trust," began to unravel after the Democratic Party Convention. SNCC could not contain its bitterness; the hope began to disintegrate.

No matter how bad the objective conditions, Nazi death-camp survivor Victor Frankl says in *Man's Search for Meaning*, we can choose our attitude toward these conditions. This is our individual freedom. But the choice is conditioned, in part, by the community of which one is part. In the death camps, people of courage inspired others—hoping, in this case, for the Allied invasion. Communists, socialists, Christian and Jewish militants organized within the camps. So, in Mississippi, SNCC organizers and student volunteers were the people of courage who inspired hope. That is why large numbers of poor Blacks in the state became involved. But hope was replaced by bitterness, the community disintegrated and little of that involvement by poor Blacks remains.

Underlying all these particular lessons was the general one. We failed to do what we said we sought to do. We didn't build lasting, democratic, autonomous grassroots organizations.

The Ineffectiveness of Nonviolence

Jan Howard

In 1963, civil rights demonstrations in Birmingham, Alabama, provoked bombings by Ku Klux Klan members and violent attacks by police. The violence outraged the nation, and the demonstrations became a catalyst of federal intervention and civil rights legislation. Earlier, in 1961, a civil rights project in Albany, Georgia, met stubborn political resistance but in a calm atmosphere. The Albany Movement was widely seen as a failure.

In the following selection, written in 1966, Jan Howard argues that, although nonviolence was the professed strategy of most civil rights groups, the provocation of violence can be seen as a secondary tactic. Civil rights leaders knew that violence by segregationists ensured public sympathy and federal support for the goals of the civil rights movement. If they could not provoke violence, then civil rights demonstrators both felt and were considered ineffective.

A participant in Freedom Summer in Mississippi, Howard is a sociologist at the Center for the Study of Law and Society in Berkeley, California. She is the coauthor of *Civil Justice and the Poor: Issues for Sociological Research.*

The civil rights movement is pledged to nonviolence. It is commonly assumed by those of us involved in it that the provocation of violence is alien to its strategy and that violence is simply a calculated risk in trying to achieve its goals. But the facts compel me to question this assumption and to

Reprinted from Jan Howard, "The Provocation of Violence: A Civil Rights Tactic?" *Dissent,* vol. 13 (January/February 1966), by permission of *Dissent.*

suggest that the provocation of violence is often used as a latent tactic.

This contention is difficult to prove. I am certain many of us working for civil rights are unconscious of the way we exploit violence. And since the whole ideology of the movement implies an abhorrence of violence, none of us wants to admit that violence is more than a calculated risk. In the South violence against civil rights workers often occurs spontaneously, without any attempt to invite it; so it is hard to know where provocation as risk leaves off and provocation as tactic begins.

Yet, the record suggests that in many situations the provocation of violence has become more than a calculated risk of the movement. It has the earmarks of a strategy.

Provoking Violence in Mississippi

Consider what happened in the 1964 Mississippi Summer Project. Its purposes were to register Negroes to vote; to teach them in Freedom Schools; and to expose white college students to the rigors of Southern poverty and repression. I understand still another goal was expressed by leaders of the project long before it actually began—getting federal troops to Mississippi to protect the voter registration drive. The fulfillment of this goal hinged on violence, and the leaders knew it. They also knew something else—that the government was reluctant to provide protection. For several years a seasoned cadre of Negro civil rights workers had been waging the voter registration drive under conditions of open brutality and terror. When they asked for federal protection, the government was uncooperative.

Leaders of the movement anticipated that bringing hundreds of outsiders to Mississippi would trigger violence, but this time the violence would be against students from white, affluent, influential families, and the federal government would be forced to protect them. The prophecy was largely correct. The project had only begun when three of the workers were murdered. This single act gave the program more publicity than any other kind of action could have. It did not bring federal troops, but it brought FBI agents and federal marshals in large numbers, and by their presence they reduced the likelihood of violence against the civil rights workers.*

The chain of events in this and similar situations forces us to consider this question: when is the provocation of violence more than a calculated risk of the movement? I suggest an answer: when the movement adopts a goal which it believes can be fulfilled only through violence. It is then, in effect, relying on violence to achieve some end. Violence is not simply a calculated risk; it is part of an over-all plan. And the instrumental value of violence is a built-in impetus for actions that will provide it.

Because the Summer Project had so many goals, one can always argue that the goal of getting federal troops had no special effect on the actions of the movement. It would have brought the students South anyway. This argument begs the question. With respect to achieving one goal, the provocation of violence can be merely a calculated risk; but with respect to achieving another, it can be a latent tactic.

Selma

Selma, Alabama, provides another illustration of what I have in mind. In discussing the rationale behind the Selma protest, Dr. Martin Luther King clearly suggests that the movement in Selma, like the movement in Mississippi, was relying on violence to achieve some goal.**

> The goal of the demonstrations in Selma, as elsewhere, is to dramatize the existence of injustice and to bring about the presence of justice. . . . Long years of experience indicate to us that Negroes can achieve this goal when four things occur:
>
> 1. Nonviolent demonstrators go into the streets to exercise their constitutional rights.

---

*Federal agents did not define their role as protective, but as "investigative." Still their presence served as a deterrent to violence.

**King, of course, turned the second march around but not until we went to the brink and in his words "made our point, revealing the continued presence of violence, and showing clearly who are the oppressed and who the oppressors."[1]

2. *Racists resist by unleashing violence against them.*

3. Americans of conscience in the name of decency demand federal intervention and legislation.

4. The Administration, under mass pressure, initiates measures of immediate intervention and remedial legislation.[2]

When nonviolent protest does provoke violent retaliation, civil rights leaders know how to capitalize on the situation and turn it to our advantage. But when nonviolence begets nonviolent opposition, this can really frustrate the movement, as I learned firsthand at Selma in the days immediately following the march that turned around. The police then blocked us from marching to the county courthouse. And King's aides followed his example, leading us to the barricades but no further.

Frustration During the First March

We were gripped by a tremendous sense of frustration and futility. I believe this reaction was caused in large part by the failure of the nonviolent technique to provoke violence. Safety Director Baker headed the police, and they were on their best behavior. They refused to be provoked into violence even when a group of Negro youths broke ranks and charged their line, and Baker readily approved all forms of nonviolent protest such as speeches and prayers. Thus, demonstrators found it impossible to make the police initiate action that the movement could capitalize on. We were forced either to be violent ourselves or to bear the burden of seemingly ineffective nonviolence. And for many this burden was shame—shame because we were just standing there, not getting through, not pushing through, not being beaten, not being arrested, just standing there.

The obvious sign of failure was that we were not getting through to the courthouse. But I think participants also sensed a more subtle sign of failure: the lack of violence. When you turn the other cheek and nobody bothers to slap it, it's hard to believe you are a threat to anyone. Both kinds of failure were articulated by spokesmen for the movement when they announced on the evening of the all-night vigil: "We will tell the police: You must let us through, or you must beat us, tear gas us, or jail us." In essence they were imploring: "You must let nonviolence work, or you must be violent. Give us some sense of effectiveness."

I am not suggesting participants in the movement are attracted to violence for its own sake. But I am suggesting we are consciously and unconsciously drawn toward violence because violence pays dividends for the movement.

First and foremost, it is a powerful catalyst to arouse public opinion. If the 600 Negroes who were tear gassed and beaten in Selma had walked all the way to Montgomery without a violent incident, we would still be awaiting a voting bill. Nor is Selma an isolated case. It was the bombings in Birmingham that forced President Kennedy to submit the historic Civil Rights Bill. The bared fangs of Bull Connor's police dogs—the burning bus of the Freedom Riders—the tear-stained face of Medgar Evers' widow: these are the alarms that awaken the conscience of America.

The Drama of Violence

When bigotry erupts into violence, this dramatizes the everyday plight of the Negro and shows the righteousness of the movement's cause. In the words of Dr. King, the murder of the three civil rights workers was "a grisly and eloquent demonstration to the whole nation of the moral degeneracy upon which segregation rests."[3] Can nonviolence pay such "eloquent" dividends?

Violence is dramatic, and Americans like the dramatic. Mass media will give extensive coverage to violence and threats of violence while they ignore more subtle injustices against the Negro and more subtle attempts to remedy injustice. And the federal government can be forced to intervene in situations of violence while it turns its back on less inflammatory brutality.

But there is more to the attraction of violence than its power to arouse the public at large. Civil rights leaders have other audiences in mind when they march into battle. They are trying to arouse the apathetic Negro by showing him that other Negroes would rather stand up in battle than be bent by the yoke of submission. And they are trying to bolster the nerve of the active Negro as well. To quote Dr. King:

> Those who have lived under the corrosive humiliation of daily intimidation are imbued by demonstrations with a sense of courage and dignity that strengthens their personalities. Through demonstrations, Negroes learn that unity and militance have more force than bullets. They find that the bruises of clubs, electric cattle prods and fists hurt less than the scars of submission.[4]

The enemy constitutes still another audience. According to King, "segregationists learn from demonstrations that Negroes who have been taught to fear can also be taught to be fearless."[5]

The Moral High Ground

A further attraction of violence for participants in a nonviolent movement inheres in the fact that violence is the antithesis of nonviolence. Thus, the moral superiority of nonviolence is most graphically displayed in a violent setting.* Nonviolence reaches the height of its legitimacy when it is counterposed with the illegitimacy of naked violence.

Finally, we should recognize that not all participants in the movement are philosophically committed to nonviolence. There is division in the ranks, and this is another pressure toward violence. A sizable number scattered throughout the movement do not believe in nonviolence, either as a principle or a tactic. Even the group that subscribes to nonviolence is divided. Some are committed to it as an end in itself; others view it simply as an expedient tactic. Since the latter have no philosophical attachment to nonviolence, they

---

*Some participants in the movement may be drawn into battle for more personal reasons: to prove to themselves and others that they are pacifists out of principle rather than fear or to prove they are truly committed to nonviolence. Thus, Charles Mauldin, a teen-age leader, wants a chance to be tested. He says, "It's easy to talk about non-violence, but in a lot of cases you've got to be tested, and reinspire yourself."[6]

The movement actually increases the attraction of violence by reserving the greatest acclaim for those who have braved it.

are more vulnerable to the appeal of violence as a strategy than the committed are. This group and the nonbelievers are constantly pressuring the committed to prove that nonviolence works. Sometimes this pressure forces the committed to exploit violence as a means of gaining symbolic victories for nonviolence. They may hastily involve the movement in a dramatic protest because they know drama has a quick payoff. Or they may try other means of winning laurels for nonviolence even if they have to throw caution and some principles to the winds. As they are forced to take more and more chances, violence as risk becomes violence as certainty.

I felt the pressure on the leaders in Selma when nonviolence appeared to be ineffective. The situation was so tense and the youngsters were so eager to take on the police that King's aides had to respond to the dissatisfaction. They made several frantic attempts to show that nonviolence works. On at least two occasions they sent small groups to the courthouse by evasive routes to stage a demonstration. One venture came within a hair of triggering mob violence. But the leaders could say to their critics that they had succeeded in getting past the police nonviolently.

Violence and Public Opinion

I am not suggesting that the violence of white segregationists always pays dividends for the movement. The impact on the public at large depends in part on the character of the victim. The brutalizing of whites arouses much more attention and anger than the brutalizing of Negroes. Violence which rallies national sentiment behind the movement can tear a local community apart and freeze positions, so that it becomes more difficult to win localized demands. Even on a national level, a given type of violence seems to pay diminishing returns. Tear gas in Selma outraged the nation, but only three weeks later smoke bombs in Camden went practically unnoticed. Does the American public have a rising degree of tolerance for violence? If so, there must be an escalation of violence to get the same effect. This may be an unforeseen consequence of using the dramatic protest to arouse public opinion.

The Limits of Nonviolence

After studying events in Birmingham and Gadsden and Danville and Americus, after interviewing staff workers of the Student Nonviolent Coordinating Committee just out of jail in Greenwood, Mississippi, watching state troopers in action in Selma, Alabama, and talking at length to voter registration workers in Greenville, Mississippi, I am rethinking some of my old views. Albany, it seems to me, was the first dramatic evidence of a phenomenon which now has been seen often enough to be believed: that there is a part of the South impermeable by the ordinary activities of nonviolent direct action, a monolithic South completely controlled by politicians, police, dogs, and prod sticks. And for this South, special tactics are required.

Howard Zinn, "The Limits of Nonviolence," *Freedomways*, vol. 4, no. 1, Winter 1964.

The strategy of the movement in this country raises a very important question: Does a movement which is dedicated to nonviolence as *the* means of action and reaction inherently need violence to sustain it? The evidence suggests that it does. I remember what Reverend Andrew Young, one of King's top aides, said in Browns Chapel as he reflected on the fact that Safety Director Baker was a nonviolent police chief. He said that the Bakers really thwart the movement but that the Bull Connors and Jim Clarks play into its hands and give it momentum.

The philosophy of nonviolent struggle seems in part to be predicated on the idea that there will be violence against the movement. The success of nonviolent struggle may require that this prophecy be fulfilled. Thus, we who are involved may be captives of a social dynamic, without necessarily being aware of the forces acting upon us. I still hear the words of the parade captain I spoke to in the march that turned around. As we followed the leaders back to Selma, he vociferously declared:

"We should have kept marching right through the troopers!"

"And what price are you willing to pay to keep marching?" I asked. "One life? Ten lives? A hundred?"

"No lives," he replied. "No lives."

Did he really mean "no lives"? Or was he refusing to admit even to himself that the nonviolent movement often thrives on violence? Perhaps he was refusing to admit something even more important—that he is disillusioned with the nonviolent approach to winning battles.

The violence of white segregationists may be necessary to sustain the nonviolent movement, but it may not be sufficient. If the public and the government do not respond to that violence, and what it represents, with enough indignation and power to change the Negro's inhuman condition to a human one–then the Negro and his white allies will totally abandon nonviolence as a principle and strategy. Already we see the emergence of the Deacons, an armed league of Negroes pledged to using violence in self-defense. And we see the nonviolent movement wrestling with its conscience and struggling to cope with the attitudes represented by the Deacons. Pressured by the reality of life, the movement has already embraced the tactic of capitalizing on violence and the tactic of provoking it. To sustain itself, will it now be forced to sanction the use of violence in self-defense? What is the next step?

Notes

1. King, Martin Luther, Jr. "Behind the Selma March," *Saturday Review*, April 3, 1965, p. 17.

2. *Ibid.*, p. 16. (Italics added)

3. King, Martin Luther, Jr. "Let Justice Roll Down," *The Nation*, March 15, 1965, p. 271.

4. *Ibid.*, p. 270.

5. *Ibid.*

6. Adler, Renata. "Letter From Selma," *The New Yorker*, April 10, 1965, p. 138.

Chapter 3

From Protest to Politics

Turning | Points
IN WORLD HISTORY

The Civil Rights Act of 1964

Alan Greenblatt

By 1963 the pace of events in the civil rights movement had quickened considerably. In Birmingham, Alabama, four young girls were killed when the Sixteenth Street Baptist Church was bombed. Medgar Evers, an NAACP field secretary, was murdered in Jackson, Mississippi. Riots occurred in Harlem. And George Wallace of Alabama became one of the last southern governors to take a defiant stand against court-ordered integration.

These dramas of protest and violence—played out on television—brought the issue of civil rights to the forefront of the national agenda, Alan Greenblatt argues in the following selection. Continued southern resistance to the *Brown* decision on one side and demands from civil rights leaders on the other forced President Kennedy to take action. He and his successor Lyndon B. Johnson forged a coalition between Republicans and liberal Democrats to pass the Civil Rights Act of 1964. The protests and violence put overwhelming pressure on Congress to adopt the legislation.

Greenblatt is a writer and contributing editor for the *Congressional Quarterly Weekly Report* and the *Washington Monthly*.

At his inauguration as Alabama governor in 1963, George C. Wallace renewed a popular campaign pledge: "I draw the line in the dust and toss the gauntlet before the feet of tyranny, and I say: Segregation now! Segregation tomorrow! Segregation forever!" Less than six months later, on June 11, the feisty Democratic politician moved to make good his vow by standing in a schoolhouse door to block the entrance

Reprinted from Alan Greenblatt, "Crossing the Line in the Dust," *Congressional Quarterly Weekly Report*, May 13, 1995, by permission of Scripps Howard News Service, a division of United Media.

of two black students, Vivian Malone and James Hood, into the University of Alabama.

Wallace knew he was playing on a national stage, the latest Southern authority to resist the Supreme Court's ruling in *Brown v. Board of Education* that desegregation should proceed "with all deliberate speed." The bantam governor had directed aides to paint a literal "line in the dust" in the doorway, along with two semicircles that marked where the governor should stand for the television cameras.

Playing to the Cameras

Squared up against Deputy Attorney General Nicholas Katzenbach, President John F. Kennedy's representative, Wallace read a proclamation denouncing "Central Government." By confronting a white bureaucrat in place of the black students, the governor was able to make government the issue rather than race. "Standing in the doorway made Wallace a star," Richard Reeves notes in his biography "President Kennedy." "On television he was the same size as the president."

Meanwhile, away from the cameras, Malone and Hood quietly reported to their dorms. Bowing to pressure off-camera, Wallace kept his campus from exploding as the University of Mississippi had the year before (when anti-integration rioters killed two men).

Kennedy also appeared on television June 11, prompted by events in Alabama to make a prime-time address on civil rights. In 1960, Kennedy had run on a civil rights platform, but as president he had sought to avoid the issue. He was mindful that his other legislation was in the hands of the Southerners who chaired two dozen of the 38 congressional committees. "If we go into a long fight in Congress," Kennedy warned the Rev. Dr. Martin Luther King Jr., "it will bottleneck everything else and still get no bill."

But by 1963, the television images could no longer be ignored. "For the horrors of the American Negro's life," novelist James Baldwin wrote, "there has been almost no language." Television lent blacks its powerful voice and access to America's homes. Pictures of white lawmen turning dogs and fire hoses on non-violent protest marchers in Birmingham, Ala., won sympathy for blacks worldwide.

During a presidential visit to Rome in 1963, Pope Paul VI embarrassed Kennedy by telling reporters he prayed for the success of American blacks in their struggle.

On May 2, 1963, during the long campaign for civil rights in Birmingham, King choreographed a visual appeal to conscience. Although jailed for his role in the protests, King still organized a march of more than 1,000 schoolchildren through streets lined with police. The pictures of snarling police dogs biting into children as young as 5 years old touched off riots in dozens of cities, as well as peaceful demonstrations in hundreds more. "Legislation was not possible until the dogs lunged at the peaceful marchers in Birmingham in 1963," historian Arthur Schlesinger Jr. would later recall.

Attorney General Robert F. Kennedy hoped to persuade his brother to act, warning that the nation might soon be engulfed in violence. The younger Kennedy acknowledged that before the election "we didn't lie awake nights worrying" about civil rights. But the issue had risen on the administration's agenda with the unfolding of events in Alabama (including the May 1962 beating of Justice Department official John Seigenthaler, who was left unconscious by a white mob in Montgomery).

Violence Necessitates Legislation

Robert Kennedy finally won his brother over on the night of the Wallace showdown. "There comes a time when a man has to take a stand," the president said, and the White House staff rushed the unexpected speech to him minutes before airtime. Casting racial justice as a moral issue and a top priority, Kennedy announced he would send comprehensive civil rights legislation to Congress.

"The events in Birmingham and elsewhere have so increased the cries for equality that no city or state or legislative body can prudently choose to ignore them," the president told the nation. "It is a time to act in Congress."

Kennedy formally submitted his brother's draft legislation

June 19, 1963, but its prognosis was not good. The young president, who had spent his 14 years in the House and Senate in near-constant pursuit of higher office, was not popular on Capitol Hill. In his first two years in office he had shown little leverage with the conservative coalition of Republicans and Southern Democrats, and a weak Kennedy bill to ban literacy tests, used to bar blacks at some polling places, had been killed by a Southern filibuster in 1962. "I can't get a Mother's Day resolution through that goddamn Congress," the president complained.

Six years before, Kennedy's vice president, Lyndon B. Johnson, had earned credit as Senate majority leader by pushing through the first civil rights legislation since 1875. Earlier in his 20-year congressional career, Johnson had opposed anti-discrimination bills. But by 1957, Johnson had hopes of winning over a national constituency, and he refused to sign the Southern Manifesto, with its call for massive resistance to the Brown decision.

Johnson twisted arms and cut deals to ensure the votes for cloture in 1957. By the time he was through amending the House bill, though, it was said to resemble the soup that Abraham Lincoln described as made from the shadow of a pigeon that had starved to death. Johnson aide Harry McPherson might have felt the 1957 debate "persuaded many Southern Negroes that at last Congress intended to do them justice," but Sen. Richard B. Russell, D-Ga., who was the leader of the Southern bloc (as well as Johnson's mentor), looked on passage of the weakened bill as "the sweetest victory of my 25 years as a senator."

With this history in mind, civil rights activists in 1963 pushed for as strong a bill as possible, so that something substantial would be left after all the congressional deal-making. "When we ask for one-half of a loaf, we get one-quarter of a loaf. We ought to ask for what we want and fight for it," argued James Farmer, leader of the Congress of Racial Equality. But the Kennedys realized that the activists could not deliver the Republican votes necessary for passage, so they immediately sought to compromise with the GOP.

Robert Kennedy nearly managed to drive away the Republicans before the game started. Testifying June 26 at the first subcommittee hearing on the 1963 bill, which aimed to ban discrimination in public accommodations and employment, the attorney general insulted House Judiciary Republicans by telling them he had not read or taken seriously their own civil rights bills, which were in some cases stronger than the administration's.

"Why should the GOP bail out the administration?" asked exasperated House Minority Leader Charles A. Halleck of Indiana. Yet Halleck knew that many Republicans supported the bill on principle. Civil rights supporters in the GOP feared that the administration would let the Senate gut the bill again. The chastened Kennedys let Judiciary's ranking Republican, William McCulloch of Ohio, rewrite the bill to his party's satisfaction over the last weekend of October 1963 and promised him veto power over any prospective Senate amendments. The deep moral conviction of this fiscal conservative swayed fence-sitting Republicans as no liberal argument could have. But as the rank and file grew aware of Halleck's and McCulloch's cooperation, someone put an umbrella, symbolizing British Prime Minister Neville Chamberlain and appeasement, on the Republican leadership desk on the House floor.

The major remaining obstacle in the House was Democrat Howard W. Smith of Virginia, chairman of the Rules Committee and long the chief undertaker for progressive legislation. Although enough Rules Committee members were in open revolt to force Smith's hand eventually, the old chairman succeeded in delaying the bill's progress long enough to open fissures in the fragile Kennedy-Halleck alliance.

After being criticized by the president and the press for the slow pace at which Congress was handling the bill, Halleck complained at a Nov. 21 news conference that the president, "who had promised major civil rights legislation in 1961," had been dragging his feet and planning to blame Congress. Liberal Democrats such as Don Edwards of California began to worry that "it was kind of running out of gas again."

But as Halleck spoke in Washington, Kennedy was in Texas on a political mission that would end abruptly and tragically with his death from an assassin's bullet on Nov. 22, 1963.

Johnson Becomes President

After assuming the presidency, Johnson looked first to passing the martyred president's priority legislation. Addressing a joint session of Congress on Nov. 27, Johnson solemnly told the nation, "No memorial oration or eulogy could more eloquently honor President Kennedy's memory than the earliest passage of the civil rights bill for which he fought so long."

The public responded with mounting support. The House acted fairly quickly, passing the bill with strong bipartisan support, 290–130, after nine days of debate in February 1964 notable for discipline and restraint. *Newsweek* reported that "what emerged was a stronger bill than Kennedy administration officials had thought feasible." The real challenge was still the Senate, where Russell and the other Southerners were waiting.

"I had to produce a civil rights bill that was even stronger than the one they'd have gotten if Kennedy had lived," Johnson later said. Johnson told the Senate that no other legislation should be considered, even in committee, until civil rights was voted on. Putting his own ambitious agenda on hold essentially undercut the deadly delaying effect of any filibuster before it could begin.

The Senate began its deliberations Feb. 17. The protests and riots that had roiled and embarrassed the South for a decade had spread north by 1964, increasing the calls for action, and for the first time civil rights supporters, including labor unions, launched an organized lobbying campaign in Congress.

Perhaps most importantly, the Leadership Conference on Civil Rights persuaded religious groups to lobby senators from Western states where blacks and organized labor were not a presence, helping to frame the issue in starkly moral terms. "There has never been as effective a lobby maintained in the city of Washington as there is today," groused Sen. Russell.

Catholic, Jewish and Protestant seminarians began a round-the-clock vigil at the Lincoln Memorial in behalf of the bill April 19, 1964, when the filibuster was already two months old. Roger Mudd of CBS began a vigil of his own the day after Easter, broadcasting nine reports daily from the Capitol steps while the Senate lurched on.

The Senate Filibuster

Appearing on "Face the Nation," Russell conceded that "any possible compromise" had been made more difficult by Kennedy's "tragic fate." In contrast to 1957, when Russell had said, "My intention is to amend this bill if possible, but to defeat it in any event," his strategy in 1964 was not to compromise at all. He dared supporters to find the 67 votes necessary to break the filibuster—something that had never been achieved on a civil rights bill.

The key, once again, was winning GOP support. Minority Leader Everett M. Dirksen of Illinois had reservations about the bill's strong fair employment provisions, but he knew the time for horse-trading on civil rights was past.

Dirksen aimed to amend the bill just enough to answer conservative GOP concerns. Steve Horn, an aide to liberal Republican Thomas H. Kuchel of California, said, "Dirksen will go through his public acting process, take a licking, and then be with us." Dirksen quietly negotiated with the Justice Department for weeks, settling on a handful of amendments that softened some of the bill's language and allowed states and localities to comply voluntarily with public accommodations requirements before the power of the federal government was brought into play, undermining the South's appeal to states' rights.

The former actor withheld his public support until May 19, during the filibuster's 12th week, when it would have maximum impact among Republicans who were eager to recess in time for the national GOP convention. "No army is stronger than an idea whose time has come," Dirksen said, quoting French novelist Victor Hugo.

Russell allowed privately that "the jig is up." The last gasp of the filibuster was heard June 9, when Robert C. Byrd, D-

W.Va., began to read an 800-page speech arguing against cloture. His 14-hour marathon address was the longest speech of the longest filibuster in Senate history. But cloture was invoked, finally, June 10 by a vote of 71-29, with 27 Republicans joining 44 Democrats. The Senate passed the bill June 19, 1964, one year to the day after John F. Kennedy had introduced it.

The Fallout

Civil rights supporters had been worn out. During his floor speech June 10, Dirksen twice swallowed ulcer pills handed to him by a page. Clair Engle, D-Calif., fatally ill and unable to speak, was wheeled onto the Senate floor to cast the last votes of his career in favor of civil rights, pointing to his eye to signify "aye."

The celebration was cut short for several of the principals, including the Kennedys. Sen. Edward M. Kennedy, D-Mass., was nearly killed June 19 in a plane crash. Senate Majority Whip Hubert H. Humphrey, who had been the floor manager for the bill, had to rush back to Minnesota where a son was about to undergo surgery for cancer.

The Republicans, too, were soon robbed of their sense of achievement because the man who would lead them in the next presidential election voted against the bill. "If my vote is misconstrued," said Sen. Barry M. Goldwater, R-Ariz., "let me suffer its consequences."

The Voting Rights Act of 1965

David J. Garrow

Beginning early in the twentieth century, civil rights organizations filed court cases on behalf of individual blacks who had been barred from registering or voting in southern states. These cases struck down some racially discriminatory voting laws but failed to end segregation practices. Eventually the federal government acted, empowering the Department of Justice to investigate and litigate patterns of bias in southern election laws.

The Voting Rights Act of 1965 represented a significant break from the strategy of litigation, according to David J. Garrow in the following article. Litigation was ineffective because it relied on judicial decisions to strike down specific discriminatory practices on a case-by-case basis. The Voting Rights Act committed the federal government to end patterns of discrimination in southern counties where black registration and participation fell below acceptable levels. Federal enforcement of the Voting Rights Act enabled thousands of blacks to register and vote.

Garrow is the Pulitzer Prize–winning author of *Bearing the Cross: Martin Luther King, Jr., and the Southern Christian Leadership Conference.*

Although the clear beginnings of [black] disfranchisement occurred between 1877 and 1890, it was the period from 1890 through 1910 that witnessed the all-but-total exclusion of African-Americans from meaningful electoral participation across the South. Although two notable Supreme Court challenges to "grandfather clause" discriminatory registration schemes in the state of Oklahoma both proved successful, in 1915 and 1939,[1] in most southern states prior to the

Reprinted from David J. Garrow, "The Voting Rights Act in Historical Perspective," *The Georgia Historical Quarterly*, vol. 74, no. 3 (Fall 1990), by permission of the Georgia Historical Society.

late 1940s the most favored and the most effective mechanism for excluding black citizens from meaningful use of the vote was the white primary: whites-only party primaries conducted by each state's Democratic party.

The NAACP Challenges the White Primary

The most prominent litigation challenges to the white primary schemes emerged from the state of Texas, but more than fifteen years of legal struggle, including four trips to the Supreme Court, were required before the white primary was finally eliminated. From the outset in the first of those cases, *Nixon v. Herndon*, the essence of the black struggle was targeted against the political fiction, supported both by the state of Texas and the Texas Democratic party, that a political party was a purely private association and that any enterprise it sponsored, including a whites-only primary that almost always determined the nominee who would later win the "public" but little-contested general election, was wholly distinct and separable from discriminatory *state* action that was prohibited by the Fourteenth Amendment.

In 1927, in its decision in *Herndon*, a unanimous Supreme Court easily concluded that where a state statute—as in Texas—expressly barred African-Americans from voting in any Democratic party primary, the notion that the Democratic primary was somehow "private" and not publicly state sponsored was a wholly implausible and unpersuasive fiction. White Democrats in Texas, however, refused to accept the conclusion that black citizens ought to be able to participate in electoral decision making, and the state legislature quickly passed a successor statute decreeing that any political party's State Executive Committee could wholly determine who could and who could not vote in a party primary. Once again lawyers representing the National Association for the Advancement of Colored People challenged the statutory scheme as state encouragement of racial discrimination and exclusion, but this time they prevailed in the Supreme Court only by the slim majority of five to four, and only with a majority opinion that all but explicitly volunteered that party membership limitations mandated by a party state *convention*, and not a committee, would not be vulnerable to successful constitutional challenge as "state action" violative of the Fourteenth Amendment.

Within weeks of that 1932 Supreme Court ruling in *Nixon v. Condon* the Texas Democratic party convention adopted whites-only primary voting rules. Although a local 1933 challenge produced limited, pro-forma success, national NAACP leaders found no support when they approached the Roosevelt administration Justice Department seeking assistance in a challenge to the widespread black Democratic disfranchisement that still prevailed all across Texas and other southern states. Local black activists in Houston, however, refused to tolerate their ongoing exclusion and initiated another federal court challenge. When it reached the Supreme Court, however, the outcome—a unanimous defeat—seemingly enshrined the political fiction that citizens should not connect or confuse the "privilege of membership in a party with the right to vote for one who is to hold public office."

Throughout the ensuing eight years NAACP lawyers and activists sought a way to erase this erroneous but controlling precedent. In 1941 a Supreme Court decision in a ballot fraud case originating in a Louisiana Democratic primary opened wide the door, as six justices, in seeming contradiction of the 1935 holding, ruled that the Fifteenth Amendment's guarantee of the right to vote covered party primaries "where the state law has made the primary an integral part of the procedure of choice, or where in fact the primary effectively controls the choice."

That last phrase effectively sounded the death knell for the whites-only, Democratic party primaries across the South, and within less than three years' time, in yet again an NAACP-initiated case out of Texas, the Supreme Court made it official and effective, ruling clearly and explicitly that "state delegation to a party of power to fix the qualifications of primary elections is delegation of a state function that may make the party's action the action of the state." That decision in *Smith* v. *Allwright*, even in the face of continuing Justice Department disinterest in any enforcement actions that might offend white southern Democrats, quickly led to lower federal court rulings in additional states such as Georgia and South Carolina that implemented the final demise of the white primary all across the region.

Just as with *Brown* v. *Board of Education of Topeka* ten years later, which similarly represented the judicial culmination of several earlier, precursor cases, *Smith* too can be viewed in historical retrospect as a significant, landmark victory in the litigative effort to win black equality and freedom. But just as *Brown*, by any tangible, quantitative measure, did little in its first years of life to bring about desegregated public schooling in the face of widespread white resistance, *Smith* also represented only one successful and modestly-sized battle because the demise of the white primary marked not an end to white efforts to disfranchise blacks, but only a change in the predominant disfranchisement strategy that whites employed.

Other Strategies to Suppress Black Voting

The years after 1944, and even more so after 1954, witnessed energetic white attempts in literally hundreds of southern counties to block black enfranchisement at an even *earlier* stage in the electoral process, namely at the initial level of a citizen's registering to vote. In locale after locale, white efforts to limit, and in some instances to prohibit entirely, black voter registration capitalized upon two distinct but compatible forms of action: racially discriminatory application of registration tests and requirements by voter registrars themselves, and extra-legal—but similarly illegal—efforts at economic and physical intimidation of prospective black registrants by white private citizens and/or public officials.

Particularly in the rural counties and parishes of Deep South states such as Mississippi, Alabama, Georgia, and Louisiana, these white efforts were as persistent as they were effective. In Mississippi the state legislature took a significant step toward aiding local registrars' easily-abusable discretion by adding a literacy requirement to the already-existing provision that allowed registrars to require an applicant to interpret, to the registrar's idiosyncratic satisfaction, any section of the state constitution which the registrar might happen to choose. Just as registrars often seemed to have sharper eyes for spelling errors or omitted items when the applicant was black rather than white, so too did black applicants always seem to be confronted with particularly obscure and convoluted sections of the state constitution when it came to the interpretation test.

For black applicants who were already on the voting rolls, for those local activists who encouraged others to register, and for those who managed to overcome discriminatory registration standards, whites in many Mississippi counties and Louisiana parishes had other tactics to apply. Especially in rural areas where black registrants were more likely to be sharecroppers than independent farmers, whites could make—and easily follow through on—threats of eviction if a voter did not remove his or her name from the rolls. Even with black landowners or small businessmen, economic harassment and intimidation—refusal to furnish services or supplies or to extend credit—could take a quick and heavy toll, forcing many people to draw back. In Mississippi's Sunflower County, for example, black registration went from 114 to 0 within several months after local whites began applying such economic intimidation tactics. For some indigenous black activists in Mississippi who nonetheless persisted, like the Reverend George Lee of Belzoni and Lamar Smith of Brookhaven, the end result was death at the hands of white gunmen.

Civil Rights Acts and Federal Litigation

The first notable federal interest in aiding prospective southern black voters was reflected in the Civil Rights Act of 1957, which, in addition to creating an independent Civil Rights Commission as well as a new Civil Rights Division within the Department of Justice, authorized the attorney general to file federal civil suits against both public officials and private citizens who for racially discriminatory reasons sought to hinder either registration and/or voting. Although many commentators realized even at the time of its enactment what a modest initiative the 1957 act was, it nonetheless heralded a significant stage in the voting rights struggle, for it committed the federal government to at least *some* enforcement of the guarantees of the Fourteenth and Fifteenth Amendments. However, the essence of its importance was that the enforcement for which it provided was through the *judicial*, and only the judicial, process. Such a course would require specific suits—and specific, documented evidence—against registrar after registrar on a county-by-county basis: a potentially immense if not supra-human task given the extent of discriminatory registration and the multiplicity of counties—82 in Mississippi, 67 in Alabama, and 159 in Georgia—all across the South.

The judicial enforcement route might well have proved inadequate in any event, but throughout the late 1950s the Eisenhower Justice Department made almost minimal use of the act, filing only a small handful of suits, none of which succeeded in adding any black registrants to voting rolls. In the spring of 1960 the United States Congress, largely at the behest of Senate Majority Leader—and Democratic presidential contender—Lyndon B. Johnson, passed a supplemental statute, the Civil Rights Act of 1960, which, among a number of modest provisions, mandated that local registration records be available for Justice Department review and allowed for the appointment of a voting "referee" to review rejected registration applicants if a local federal district judge held that county registrars were discriminating and that a referee was desirable. Many observers correctly realized that the 1960 act did little to improve federal enforcement options, but once the Kennedy Administration took office in January of 1961, its Justice Department officials moved quickly to make much more use of those modest judicial options than had their Republican predecessors.

Increased commitment did not result in any detectable impact on southern voter registration, for delays in winning access to registrars' records, difficulties in proving that economic harms inflicted upon black activists were retaliation for registration efforts, and white creativity in applying registration standards all put a damper on Justice Department efforts to enfranchise southern blacks. By mid-1962, as more and more suits against specific county registrars were prepared and filed, the Justice Department was also forced to confront another equally if not more serious obstacle to judicial enforcement: the all-but-open hesitance and resistance of many southern federal district court judges, including several new Kennedy appointees, to handle voting rights suits either expeditiously or fair-mindedly. Too often, it seemed, openly or quasi-segregationist district judges allowed Justice Department voting rights actions to sit forlornly on their dockets without action for months at a time. The excesses of the worst such offender, Judge William Harold Cox of the Southern District of Mississippi, became so pronounced as to draw critical commentary in both the national press and in prominent legal publications. . . .

The Ineffectiveness of Litigation and the Judicial Strategy

Even though the Justice Department made several efforts to challenge at a statewide level those statutory provisions that opened the door to widespread discriminatory behavior by local registrars, and even though in two particular cases Justice eventually succeeded in obtaining appellate rulings voiding those statutes, state legislatures could easily stay one step ahead by passing new statutes which would then have to be challenged all over again. Although the legislation which the Kennedy administration introduced in 1963, and which, in amended form, emerged from the Congress as the Civil Rights Act of 1964, did include one title mandating several provisions aimed at expediting voting suits and ensuring that local literacy tests be applied fairly, the voting parts of that landmark bill did very little to alter or fundamentally improve the judicial enforcement approach that the federal government had followed ever since the initial Civil Rights Act of 1957.

Those years from 1957 through 1964 reflected a far greater active federal interest in enforcing southern blacks' right to vote than had ever been the case in the seven decades preceding 1957, but the fundamental ineffectiveness of those early 1960s efforts has been agreed upon by almost every legal or scholarly commentator who has reviewed that historical record. As one law journal author correctly observed,

"Eight years of litigation provided the most persuasive argument that adjudication and court-ordered enforcement tools could not ensure extensive registration." Indeed, by March of 1965 even the attorney general, Nicholas deB. Katzenbach, was explicitly acknowledging "the inadequacy of the judicial process" and willingly admitted that the "three present statutes have had only minimal effect." Of course that willingness on the part of the attorney general had been undeniably influenced by events in the state of Alabama over the preceding several weeks, but even before "the patience of the nation with the judicial process ran out in Selma, Alabama," on March 7, 1965, some people in the Justice Department and some people in the White House, just like others in the Congress and many in the movement, had resolved that a new approach to voting rights protection and enforcement would have to be enacted into law in calendar 1965.

It bears some emphasis and acknowledgment that Johnson administration efforts to draft and introduce into Congress the legislation that in August of 1965 formally became the Voting Rights Act were well under way prior to March 7, when Selma became a national and even international name that forever thereafter would always be associated with law enforcement violence against defenseless, peaceful marchers. Furthermore, the historical record is also clear that even before the end of 1964, Johnson administration officials had resolved to offer a voting bill and that initial drafting efforts were under way. Such an acknowledgment in no way undercuts or reduces the tremendous importance of the February and March events in Selma, and the significant impact they had on mobilizing support for and speeding work on that nascent voting rights legislation, but it does underline how the futility of relying solely on the federal courts for voting rights protection had come to be appreciated, even within the White House and the Justice Department, prior to the courageous initiatives made by local and national activists in those early months of 1965 in Selma and its surrounding counties. Additionally, it also assists in understanding and explaining why the central provisions of the Johnson voting rights bill diverged so radically and so extensively from everything that had gone before with regard to federal enforcement.

The Voting Rights Act of 1965

In its essence, the bill that was drafted within the Justice Department in early 1965 and then modestly amended by the Congress before its final passage contained three principal provisions and initiatives, all of which represented a dramatic change from the efforts of the preceding years. First and foremost, it presented a "trigger formula" whereby any state or county which had had less than 50 percent of its voting age population registered to vote *or* actually turn out to vote in the 1964 presidential election would be required to suspend the use of any and all literacy tests and other, similarly abusable registration devices. Second, the attorney general, at his discretion, could assign federal personnel as "examiners" or registrars to enroll unregistered citizens in any county or parish covered by the 50 percent trigger requirement. Third, any jurisdiction subject to the trigger formula would not be able to implement any changes in its electoral practices without submitting each change for "pre-clearance" by either the Justice Department or the federal district court in the District of Columbia.

What bears emphasis here is neither the specific details nor the technical application of these or other provisions contained in the final language of the act, but the simple and inescapable fact that none of these major enforcement mechanisms relied in any way upon either locale-by-locale requirements of proving discriminatory practices in potentially time-consuming court suits or on *judicial* enforcement of the right to register and vote. Instead, the Congress in a direct and extremely efficient declaration simply mandated, pursuant to its constitutionally-granted power to enforce the guarantees of the Fifteenth Amendment by "appropriate legislation," that no registration test obstacles could be placed in front of voter applicants in locales that had unusually low levels of electoral participation by voting-age citizens. If that was not enough to open a county's rolls to meaningful access by unregistered citizens, then the federal executive branch, acting unilaterally and directly, could assign its own personnel to do the job, and, if need be, also monitor elections to be sure that those and other registrants were allowed to cast free and secret ballots. Lastly, should state or local officials attempt to come up with new tactics or provisions that could be used for racially discriminatory ends, the mandatory "pre-clearance" requirement for such changes could be used to block and void them.

Although any detailed analysis of the implementation and impact of those provisions lies outside the ambit of this paper, the importance—indeed, almost revolutionary importance—of those statutory reforms has been appreciated ever since their initial introduction in the Congress. House Judiciary Committee Chairman Emanuel Celler termed the Johnson administration measure "a bill that would have been inconceivable a year ago," and President Johnson himself, when signing the bill in August, termed it "one of the most monumental laws in the entire history of American freedom." By many standards of measurement, with southern black registration gains being only the first and most immediate yardstick, a characterization such as Johnson's is indubitably correct. Although initial implementation of the act was slightly marred by disputes over the limited number of federal examiners immediately assigned to hardcore southern counties by the Justice Department, more than three hundred thousand new black voters were added to registration rolls in areas covered by the act in the first six months of its existence.

Perhaps more tangibly and significantly, the act also led to a gradual and in time phenomenal increase in the number of black elected officials in the thirteen states of the traditional South. At the time of the act's passage that figure stood at 72, region-wide; by 1970 it had climbed to 711, and at the latest count, in 1989, it had increased to 4,265—59 percent of *all* black elected officials all across the United States and an almost sixty-fold rise from the 1965 figure.

Notes

1. *Guinn* v. *United States*, 238 U.S. 347 (1915), and *Lane* v. *Wilson*, 307 U.S. 268 (1939).

Johnson and the White Backlash

William E. Leuchtenburg

Lyndon B. Johnson, a senator from Texas, became majority leader in 1955. In that role, he shaped and guided passage of the Civil Rights Acts of 1957 and 1960. John F. Kennedy chose Johnson as his running mate because the Texan could win votes in the South. As president following Kennedy's assassination, Johnson passed the Civil Rights Act of 1964 and the Voting Rights Act of 1965.

In the following article, William E. Leuchtenburg argues that Johnson's advocacy of civil rights prompted many white southerners—staunch Democrats by tradition—to switch allegiance to the Republican party. In the 1964 election, Johnson tried to rise above the race issue dividing his party. However, although he won the election, he lost half of the traditionally Democratic southern states. By 1968, the South was solidly Republican.

Leuchtenburg is the William Rand Kenan Professor of History at the University of North Carolina, Chapel Hill. He is the author of many books, including *FDR Years: On Roosevelt and His Legacy*.

When . . . the murder of John Kennedy sent Johnson to the White House, commentators stressed that he was the first resident of a southern state to become President in a century—the first since another Johnson had taken power, also as the result of an assassination. Not a few white southerners rejoiced that the country at last had a President who spoke with a familiar accent. A limousine driver in Greensboro, North Carolina, said, "He sounds like one of us!" A Birmingham factory foreman remarked, "That was a rotten way for Kennedy to go, but I'll be frank with you, I think Johnson will be a big

Excerpted from William E. Leuchtenburg, "The Old Cowhand from Dixie," *The Atlantic Monthly*, December 1992. Reprinted by permission of the author.

improvement. He understands the South." Civil-rights advocates, on the other hand, especially blacks, expressed dismay.

White supremacists and civil-rights activists both misread Johnson. He had long since ceased to condone racism, and he was determined, as leader not of a section but of a nation, to reach out to a constituency above as well as below the Mason-Dixon line. "I'm going to be the best friend the Negro ever had," he told a member of the White House staff. "I've lived in the South a long time, and I know what hatred does to a man." Within a short time of his taking office, black leaders had a decidedly more favorable perception of him. After meeting with Johnson, Martin Luther King Jr. declared, "As a southerner, I am happy to know that a fellow southerner is in the White House who is concerned about civil rights."

The Civil Rights Act of 1964

Johnson sealed this impression by the vigor with which he pushed what became the Civil Rights Act of 1964. Shortly after succeeding Kennedy, according to one account, Johnson summoned his former mentor, Senator Russell, to the Oval Office and told him, "Dick, you've got to get out of my way. I'm going to run over you. I don't intend to cavil or compromise. I don't want to hurt you. But don't stand in my way." Russell continued to oppose the civil-rights bill, but he was increasingly aware that with his former ally committed to wielding all the authority of the White House against him, resistance was futile. Bill Moyers recalls, "Dick Russell would say to me, 'Now you tell Lyndon . . . that I've been expecting the rod for a long time, and I'm sorry that it's from his hand the rod must be wielded, but I'd rather it be his hand than anybody else's I know. Tell him to cry a little when he uses it.'"

As the bitter struggle over the civil-rights bill dragged on month after month in the first half of 1964—the southern filibuster lasted eighty-three days—southern disaffection with Johnson mounted; but, undeterred, he overcame his southern foes to drive it through. His victory at the end of such a nasty and protracted battle appeared to provide an occasion for celebration. On the night after he signed the bill into law, however, Johnson told Bill Moyers gloomily, "I think we just delivered the South to the Republican Party for a long time to come."

In the 1964 campaign the Republican Party fielded a presidential candidate who catered to the white supremacists: Arizona Senator Barry Goldwater, who had said bluntly, "We're not going to get the Negro vote as a bloc in 1964 or 1968, so we ought to go hunting where the ducks are." He did just that when, during the struggle over the civil-rights bill, he cast one of the few votes from outside the South against breaking the southern filibuster. In offering the electorate such a stark choice, Goldwater gave southern Democrats an opportunity to demonstrate their outrage at LBJ's leadership on race by crossing over to the Republicans.

Johnson's Southern Strategy

To hold the South for the Democratic Party, Johnson adopted two different personae. Often he gave a stock speech in which he asked for "a truly national party which is stranger to no region, . . . knows no North, no South, no East, no West." At other times, however, Johnson reminded southerners that he was one of them. When he spoke in Georgia in May of 1964, *The New York Times* reported that he "identified himself wholeheartedly as a Southerner with family roots in the red earth of Georgia."

Johnson made his boldest move when he sent his wife on an eight-state tour of the South, a trip she was eager to take. She told her aides, "I know the Civil Rights Act was right, and I don't mind saying so. But I'm tired of people making . . . snide jokes about the corn-pone and redneck. . . . I want to say to those people . . . that I love the South, I'm proud of the South. . . . And I want them to know that as far as *this* President and his wife are concerned, the South belongs to the United States."

At each stop before Lady Bird spoke, the train "commander," the loyal Louisiana congressman Hale Boggs, would warm up the crowd by asking, "How many of you-all know what red-eye gravy is?" After getting the expected hand waves of assent, he would respond, "Well, so do I. And so does Lyndon Johnson!" He would promise, "When Lyndon

Johnson is re-elected we're gonna have ham in every pot. We're gonna have ham and grits on every plate. We're gonna have ham with plenty of good ol' red-eye gravy." Having made this profound campaign pledge, he would continue, "You know what we had on this train this morning? Hominy grits. About noontime we're gonna start servin' turnip greens and black-eyed peas. Later on, farther south, we're gonna have some crawfish bisque, some red beans and rice, and some creole gumbo." His face wreathed in "a hush-puppy grin," in the words of a campaign worker, Boggs would then conclude, "Now, about this race. You're not gonna turn your back on the first southern-born President in a hundred years?" The crowd, laughing and smiling, would answer with a shout: "All the way with LBJ."

When the train pulled into Union Station in New Orleans, in Hale Boggs's home state, on the night of October 9, Lady Bird found the President there to greet her. Johnson had come with more in mind than being a dutiful husband. He knew he was being hard pressed in the Deep South by Goldwater, and few ambitions were dearer to him than his desire to sweep the South. Nonetheless, in a year of alarms about a vicious "white backlash," Johnson brushed aside counsel that he soft-pedal the race issue, and decided to make a major statement on behalf of civil rights, "not in New York or Chicago or Los Angeles," he later noted, "but in New Orleans—near home, in my own backyard."

The Speech

At a banquet in New Orleans that night, he told more than 2,000 people, "Whatever your views are, we have a Constitution and we have a Bill of Rights, and we have the law of the land, and two thirds of the Democrats in the Senate voted for [the civil-rights bill] and three fourths of the Republicans. I signed it, and I am going to enforce it, . . . and I think any man that is worthy of the high office of President is going to do the same thing. . . . I am not going to let them build up the hate and try to buy my people by appealing to their prejudice." "The applause," Johnson observed drily some years later, "was less than overwhelming."

Undismayed, he plunged ahead to tell the story of a great southern senator, near the end of his days, who had once spoken eloquently to the young Sam Rayburn, recently arrived in the House, about the critical economic needs of their section, and who had then added, "Sammy, I wish I felt a little better. . . . I would like to go back down there and make them one more Democratic speech. I just feel like I have one in me. The poor old state, they haven't heard a Democratic speech in thirty years." Bellowing, arms outstretched, Johnson gave his Louisiana listeners the ancient senator's final words: "All they ever hear at election time is *Nigra, Nigra, Nigra!*"

The audience let out a gasp. "This took the breath away from most of us," a Washington correspondent has written. "The crowded ballroom became strangely silent." Jack Valenti remembered, "Over that audience there flowed a consternation that could be felt everywhere in the auditorium. It was a physical thing, surprise, awe; ears heard what they plainly could not hear, a cataclysmic wave hit everyone there with stunning and irreversible force." Then the audience rose to its feet and the hall was "rocked by a thunderous cheer" that lasted fully five minutes.

Many of his most acerbic critics have affirmed that this was Johnson's finest hour. There was no way a northerner could have delivered that speech and had it carry the same meaning. He spoke, in the words of Theodore White, "in the presence of other Southerners as a Southerner who had come to wisdom." When Johnson "publicly chided Southerners for their treatment of blacks," George Reedy has written, he "drew applause that is still ringing in my ears. He could be superb!" The Texas progressive Bill Brammer has said, "The highlight of the 1964 campaign, a highlight any way you look at it, was the speech in New Orleans, what people call the 'nigra, nigra, nigra' speech. It galvanized me. I was ready to go out and kill. That's how great he was."

"We Shall Overcome"

The New Orleans crowd rewarded Johnson with a mighty ovation, but a month later Louisiana denied him its electoral votes—by registering a thumping 57 percent for Goldwater.

The Arizona senator also walloped Johnson in South Carolina, Alabama, and Georgia, and in Mississippi, where Republicans had long been anathema, Goldwater rolled over the President with an incredible 87 percent. Goldwater's success in capturing five Deep South states sometimes led observers to overlook Johnson's still greater achievement of winning six southern states, but the raw totals are deceptive, for they conceal evidence of dramatic slippage. Johnson ran better in rock-ribbed Maine and in Vermont than in any state of the former Confederacy. Even more significant, Goldwater captured a majority of the ballots cast by whites in every state of the former Confederacy save Texas.

Johnson learned how far the white South had departed from him when, in 1965, he demanded a voting-rights law in an address to Congress in which, identifying himself with the anthem of the civil-rights movement, he declared, "And we *shall* overcome"—words that infuriated southern senators. At breakfast the following morning Spessard Holland, of Florida, asked angrily, "Did you hear ol' Lyndon say 'we shall overcome'?" The moderate Lister Hill, of Alabama, turning to Richard Russell, asked, "Dick, tell me something. You trained that boy. . . . What happened to that boy?" The Georgia senator responded, "I just don't know, Lister. . . . He's a turncoat if there ever was one.". . .

In 1968 dissatisfaction with LBJ's reckless policies in Vietnam drove him from office, but it was the backlash in the South against his racial program that ended the party's hold on the White House. Congressman F. Edward Hebert recalled, "In Louisiana he was absolutely hated because they considered him a turncoat. They considered Lyndon Johnson the most horrible man that ever lived." In the November election the Democratic presidential candidate, Hubert Humphrey, paid the price for Johnson's advocacy of civil-rights laws when he lost every southern state save Texas. So thoroughly did the reaction against Johnson's championing of equality rewrite the nation's electoral maps that for the next quarter of a century, Democratic presidential candidates received fewer than one out of three white ballots cast in the South.

The End of the Civil Rights Coalition

Gerald Early

Martin Luther King Jr.'s leadership of the civil rights movement paid off with the Civil Rights Act of 1964 and the Voting Rights Act of 1965. But as he tried to steer the movement beyond these victories toward the goal of economic equality for blacks, he found less success.

In this article, Gerald Early describes King's efforts to form a broad coalition of black radicals and middle-class conservatives. King's tactics—using nonviolent direct action to dramatize the sin of racism underlying Jim Crow in the South—were inherently radical, as were his true views. As the radicalism and violence within American society grew during the 1960s, King's sympathies and beliefs turned more toward black nationalism. However, because of his earlier position as a moderate, he was not accepted as a leader among radicals. He therefore lost his position as the central figure in the civil rights movement.

Early is the director of the African American Studies Department at Washington University in St. Louis. He is the author or editor of a number of books, including *How the War in the Streets Is Won: Poems on the Quest of Love and Faith.*

That a black person must have something like an African memory, even if totally fictive, is something that no one questions much now. Martin Luther King found that concern irrelevant in the shaping of a radical politic. Ironically, King's radicalism grew from his insistent, even provincial belief in the utter sufficiency of Americanism and the utter sufficiency of the Social Gospel tradition and religious revivals.

From Gerald Early, "Martin Luther King and the Middle Way," *The Christian Century*, August 28, 1996. This article was excerpted from an essay in *Martyrs: Contemporary Writers on Modern Lives of Faith*, edited by Susan Bergman (San Francisco: HarperSanFrancisco, 1996) and is reprinted by permission of the author.

In short, King was forced to invent himself as he went along, and he grew with his job, remarkably creating a black radical political tradition, not only in what his positions ultimately became but in the criticism that his various positions generated. There would have been no Black Power movement of the vehemence that we had, no possibility for the emergence of a black leftist or socialist movement, and no black nationalist ideology as clearly defined as it became had not King achieved his remarkable stature and so magnetically pushed his own vision.

King Was a New Radical

King was not of age in the 1930s, so the Marxist decade of American history had no direct influence in shaping his mind. Moreover, King's childhood in the 1930s in Atlanta was a far more privileged one than that of most black children and a good many whites, since his father was a successful pastor of a large black church. King felt a degree of guilt about this his entire life. Perhaps this is why he was moved to become a social reformer in the first place: an intense dissatisfaction with the philistine, anti-intellectual nature of black middle-class life. King surely went out of his way in his life to appear neither philistine nor anti-intellectual. The sheer urgency with which he pursued his public career as reformer and the urgency that punctuated his message of freedom now for blacks seemed at least partly driven by a dislike for the apathetic, petty, contrived and materialistic diversions of the black middle class. Indeed, King would fit almost perfectly the new radical, as defined by Christopher Lasch in *The New Radicalism in America, 1889–1963*: a person who had never been poor who discovered the dispossessed and who also discovered intellectuals.

One of King's heroes was the great black socialist and union leader A. Philip Randolph, so indirectly, of course, King was influenced by the radical politics of the 1920s and 1930s. But King emerged in the post-World War II era, when the United States was engaged in all-out ideological war against radical politics in the form of communism and when liberalism in this country was particularly constrained, disavowing its leftist associations. Liberals such as Lionel Trilling, Arthur Schlesinger, Mary McCarthy, David Reisman and Daniel Bell were all trying to find the center, an absolutely centrist position of liberal anticommunism. Even one of King's liberal Protestant influences, Reinhold Niebuhr, who had Marxist sentiments, tried to do much the same in his tricky balancing of the individual and the community, the citizen and the state, which King copied nearly verbatim. Niebuhr, for instance, wrote in a 1945 article in *Commentary*:

> The consistent socialization of all economic power is no more adequate a solution for our problem than a consistent disavowal of political authority upon economic process. The latter leads to anarchy as the former leads to tyranny. The wisest nations experiment in order to find a *middle way* which will insure a maximum of freedom and security. [Emphasis mine.]

This position of balancing personal freedom and welfare-state security would be King's for his entire public career—the only position possible in a country that was now defining itself almost entirely through the prism of national security. Calling King a "conservative militant," a man who practices compromise and caution, much to the chagrin of more radical civil rights factions, August Meier wrote in 1965: "King occupies a position of strategic importance as the 'vital center' within the civil rights movement." King further emphasized his position as the middle man within the realm of black politics. In his "Letter from Birmingham Jail," he said that he stood

> in the middle of two opposing forces in the Negro community. One is the force of complacency made up of Negroes who, as a result of long years of oppression, have been so completely drained of self-respect and a sense of "somebodiness" that they have adjusted to segregation, and, of a few Negroes in the middle class who, because of a degree of academic and economic security, and because at points they profit by segregation, have unconsciously become insensitive to the problems of the masses. The other force is one of bit-

terness and hatred, and comes perilously close to advocating violence. It is expressed in the various black nationalist groups that are springing up over the nation.

Another way of seeing King's position as a bargaining agent for blacks was expressed in his *Playboy* interview, where he said: "I mean to say that a strong man must be militant as well as moderate. He must be a realist as well as an idealist." In short, King served as the center between black and white and as the center between black radicalism and black conservatism. It was convenient for King to label black nationalism as "bitter" and "hateful," yet he had to know, in truth, that it was a competing form of black hope that he was bound to disparage. King knew, indeed, that his exploitation of a nationalistic sense of black destiny—he never discouraged references to himself as Moses—was responsible for his success and legitimacy as a leader. What interested King was neither being a conformist nor being a nonconformist—he was both and neither simultaneously—but being able to manipulate the forces of conformity and nonconformity in both white and black politics for the greatest concessions—actual or symbolic—that he could gain.

The Dilemma of Black Americanization

King's own centrism was expressed in the search for the mainstream of American life into which the black American could integrate. King had been greatly influenced by Gunnar Myrdal's massive 1944 sociological study of race relations, *An American Dilemma*. King was a sociology major at Morehouse, which he attended from 1944 to 1948, and doubtless read at least a portion of this work. The book made clear for King the strategy that other African-American leaders played out with less success. If the problem in America was the disjuncture between the American creed of freedom and equality and the existence of blacks as a disenfranchised, pariah group, then the solution was to make the country uncomfortable, embarrassed, downright guilty, explosively tense, about this disjuncture and the hypocrisy it implied until whites where moved or forced to make the country live up to its creed by including blacks as full-fledged citizens.

This was King's version of black Americans' continued quest for absorption, to lose himself in an Americanism he was never permitted to enjoy in order to be himself, to realize himself. For King and the civil rights leaders, Americanization was the golden door that would open to political and economic power for blacks. The irony for the civil rights movement was that the Americanization of the Negro instead wound up calling into question both the process of Americanization and the presumed meaning of the African-American presence in American life. In the end, America did not validate black folk as much as black folk wound up validating American democracy.

At first, King may not have realized this implication in the movement, but it became clearer later as his philosophy of redemptive love developed and as his politics became more explicitly leftist or anticapitalist. The irony for Martin Luther King was that the man who started out as a bourgeois centrist became the major force behind the invention of the new popular front in the 1960s and the all-out ideological attack on Americanism as symbolized by—as this new popular front construed things—racism, militarism and corporate power.

The Popular Front for Civil Rights

King first tried to create a new popular front with the March on Washington in 1963, an event designed to pull together a coalition of liberal white intelligentsia, Jews, labor unions, liberal Catholics and Protestants, bohemians and Beats, old social justice radicals of the 1930s and, of course, blacks to form an antiracism, anti-right-wing political movement. Two hundred and fifty thousand people attended, and 60,000 of them were white. Here was a version of King's Beloved Community, as he called it, and to many it resembled nothing so much as a kind of leftist utopia. This coalition was to be buttressed on one side by the antiracist assaults of the new wave of sociology, slavery historiography, anthropology. On the second side, it was to be buttressed by the new innovations in popular music with rock-and-roll, the return of the radical folk music of the 1930s with Bob Dylan, Phil Ochs, Pete Seeger, Odetta, Joan Baez, Buffy Sainte-Marie, and politically self-conscious jazz, all of which extolled the romanticized, even sentimentalized virtues of miscegenation, ethnic consciousness, committed youth, the working-class life, and a bourgeois vision of the liberated artist. By 1965, black popular music, led by Motown Records, had so successfully crossed over that *Billboard* quit running its Rhythm and Blues and Black Music chart. On the third side, the new popular front was to be supported by an activist federal government, particularly activist executive and judicial branches with the Kennedy administration and the Warren court.

It should not seem odd that there was such a huge cultural component for King's new popular front. By the 1950s, black people had become a considerable cultural force in the United States. Indeed, King's fame through his leadership of the Montgomery bus boycott was made possible largely because of the cultural power, the cultural charisma of the Negro. It may be that blacks wielded very little political or economic power in the United States, but they were a significant cultural presence, and questions of politics in the U.S. had relentlessly, since the turn of the century, become more and more questions of culture to be played out in the cultural realm. Norman Mailer's influential 1957 essay "The White Negro" portrayed blacks in a stereotypical light, but it did in fact suggest that blacks were central in the radical transformation of American culture. As Mailer wrote about hipsterism as the transformation of American values: "And in this wedding of the white and the black it was the Negro who brought the *cultural* dowry" (emphasis mine).

The fact that King gave this new popular front a Christian mission was strategically of the utmost importance if the movement was ever to have legitimacy with mainstream liberals and moderates and carry blacks along as well. It was the genius of King that he was able to convince so many for so long, as the brilliant black theologian Howard Thurman observed, that racism was not simply un-American in some provincial sense of being against our creed of fair play but was, in fact, a sin against God and that it jeopardized America's special destiny as the new Israel. The major problem that was to dog King until his death in April 1968 was that he could never entirely shake being seen as something of an inadvertent sellout by the younger black radicals, in part because of the very Christian rhetoric that was needed to keep King's coalition alive and keep King vital and distinct on the civil rights scene.

The Kennedy assassination, the escalation of the war in Vietnam, the sex revolution, the illegal drug revolution, the emergence of black power, and the nihilistic violence of the black urban riots forced King to reinvent his position and to try to reinvent this new popular front when he gave his 1967 anti-Vietnam War speech at Riverside Church in New York. By this time, after failed campaigns in Albany, Georgia, and Chicago, a moderately successful but costly one in Birmingham, somewhat successful campaigns in Danville, Virginia, and St. Augustine, Florida, and a memorable march from Selma to Montgomery, King had come to the realization that the "vast majority of white Americans are racists." He also saw racism as connected to capitalism and both as the instruments of American neocolonialism. Most of this sort of thinking was stock leftist criticism of American foreign policy of the middle and late 1960s. Despite his continued rhetoric of centrism—that is, of redemptive love and nonviolent direct action (King, after all, was never seen by either the radical left or Black Power advocates as anything other than a bourgeois social reformer till his death)—it was clear to everyone that he was now obviously a democratic socialist and a fairly frustrated man.

His last campaign, meant to bring blacks and whites together, the Poor People's March, of which virtually no one at the Southern Christian Leadership Conference approved and which he did not live to see, was called by King "a class struggle." He did not have nearly the set of historical circumstances, let alone the moral and political authority, to make such a popular-front coalition work in 1967 as it had in 1963. Four years during this extremely accelerated period in American history changed the entire landscape in which

King operated, and although by 1967 he was still enormously useful to the new left, he was virtually useless to bourgeois liberals who opposed his stand against the war; also, his position was eroding in the black community, although, of course, because he was a clergyman and a man who sacrificed so much for his people, he still was held in high regard. King simply was unable, at this point, to make the rhetorical or symbolic linkage between American exceptionalism and black exceptionalism as he had in the past. Perhaps it was ego, as Carl Rowan suggested in 1967. King was the most influential black person in America at the time. Did he think that whites would really listen to him about the Vietnam War? I doubt if he necessarily thought they would, as they had not really listened to him about anything else.

For blacks, by 1967 King no longer was seen as the man with a realistic or compelling solution. Within a period of ten years, from the end of the Montgomery bus boycott in 1956 to the Selma march of 1965, nonviolent direct action and redemptive love had virtually run its course as a political tool for black people in the U.S. As Marcus Garvey wrote in October 1919, "No mercy, no respect, no justice will be shown the Negro until he forces all other men to respect him." And for many black people, it seemed impossible to think that any real respect or justice would be gained from nonviolence. Despite the fact that King's actions had produced the Civil Rights Act of 1964 and the Voting Rights Act of 1965, the virtual destruction of the most overt forms of discrimination, and a higher regard for black Americans in the world than they had ever before enjoyed as a result of this extraordinary protest movement, most blacks felt that they had seen few tangible results—drugs, rampant violence, joblessness, utter cultural isolation, single parenthood, and police brutality wracked most northern ghettos—and the white backlash against the gains of the civil rights movement was considerable and vehement. King hardly seemed like a man who was in control of the forces he had set loose. Indeed, King had set loose forces from both the left and the right over which he had no control whatsoever—and which made any seeming centrism for him impossible if he was to retain any sense of trust from the black community.

"We'll meet on edges soon," folksinger Bob Dylan sang, and that is precisely what King did: he forced various elements of American society to meet on edges, on the very edges of sanity, on the very edges of the new frontier, the urban street. It was in the streets of the cities, north and south, where King through his demonstrations and the energy they set loose had the citizens of the United States committing violence, enacting political repression, venting self-destructive rage on the one hand and praying to God for endurance, mercy, forgiveness and transcendence on the other. We enacted before the entire world, as both catharsis and salvation, a tragedy and a farce, and in doing so completely unraveled Americanism as a legitimate cultural or moral force. King, magnificently and inadvertently, defeated and discredited the very ideology that he wished to legitimate by having Negroes walk through the sunlit passageway of American bourgeois life. He was the only black in American history who was created and defeated by the very set of forces that he ultimately unhinged. . . .

"In America," James Baldwin wrote, "life seems to move faster than anywhere else on the globe and each generation is promised more than it will get: which creates, in each generation, a furious, bewildered rage, the rage of people who cannot find solid ground beneath their feet." King's failure, like that of the other integrationists, was that he promised more than he could deliver to a new generation of blacks. Like other American prophets, he also promised more than God would deliver in this world—neither complete fulfillment nor utter destruction. King did do something no other black leader had done, no other American leader had really done. He gave a younger generation of blacks a sense of honor, for no other African-American generation would be so tempered by the chiliastic possibilities inherent in war. No other African-American generation would be so shaped by the chiliastic possibilities of its own American fate. No other American generation, bereft of its belief in piety, would be, alas, so disillusioned by the cost of our uneasy racial peace.

The Chicago Freedom Movement

James R. Ralph Jr.

By 1966, the civil rights movement had gained sweeping successes in the fight to overturn legal segregation in the South. Leaders then turned attention to fighting discrimination in the North. But northern and southern activists had always differed on tactics and goals.

James R. Ralph Jr. describes in the following article the failure of the Southern Christian Leadership Conference to adapt its tactics of civil disobedience and peaceful demonstrations to the fight for fair housing in the North. The Chicago Freedom Movement therefore failed to redirect the energies of the nonviolent movement. The SCLC's plan failed to spur federal intervention in the situation and also failed to alleviate housing inequities. However, Ralph argues, the demonstrations inspired a number of activists who fought for economic parity over the years.

Ralph is the author of *Northern Protest: Martin Luther King, Jr., Chicago, and the Civil Rights Movement.*

On Friday evening, August 5, 1966, Martin Luther King Jr. was tired and torn by competing emotions. He had stripped off the jacket of his gray suit and removed his red and gray tie and was now sitting—recovering—on an old couch in a home on Chicago's South Side. Just hours earlier he had witnessed thousands of angry whites from heavily ethnic, middle-income neighborhoods heckle, jeer and assault his Chicago Freedom Movement followers, despite police protection, on a march protesting housing discrimination on Chicago's southwest side. King himself had been felled by a

Reprinted from James R. Ralph Jr., "Home Truths: Dr. King and the Chicago Freedom Movement," *American Visions*, August/September 1994, by permission of *American Visions*, 1101 Pennsylvania Ave. NW, Suite 820, Washington, DC 20004.

rock that struck his head. "Frankly, I have never seen as much hatred and hostility on the part of so many people," he said slowly. "To my mind those people represent the most tragic expression of man's inhumanity to man."

The SCLC in Chicago

While King lamented the racial intolerance that suffused Chicago's white neighborhoods, he also sensed—with much relief—that the Chicago crusade was beginning to reach its potential. Since the fall of 1965, King's Southern Christian Leadership Conference (SCLC) lieutenants and field staffers, in league with their Chicago allies, had searched for a strategy to end racial injustice in the Windy City. Early in the campaign, they focused on developing community organizations, especially in the newer black ghetto on Chicago's West Side. Jesse Jackson, meanwhile, had brought local clergy together to form a chapter of Operation Breadbasket with the mission to advance economic opportunities for black Chicagoans.

Throughout the fall and winter, the Chicago Freedom Movement claimed modest victories, but the North was foreign terrain for the SCLC, which had toiled for nearly a decade on Southern soil. The obstacles to successful insurgency in this huge, sprawling and complex city were formidable, and the spark for a truly electrifying campaign remained elusive.

Although King and his allies sought to recruit a "coalition of conscience" to support a program of democratic and social renewal, many influential Chicagoans were skeptical—and even critical—of that effort. The Rev. Joseph H. Jackson, the famed pastor of the historic Olivet Baptist Church on Chicago's South Side and the president of the National Baptist Convention, the largest African-American religious association, was one of the sharpest detractors. The older Jackson (who was not related to Jesse Jackson) had already squared off against King and other activist ministers. For years, he had warned against the inevitable harmful repercussions of civil disobedience, and now he lamented that King had brought his crusade to Chicago, Jackson's hometown.

In the summer of 1966, Jackson even debated King in a

rare encounter between the two prominent clergymen on a local television program. While Jackson acknowledged that Chicago was not a paradise for blacks, he refused to label it an immoral society and doubted whether protests—"a continuous dramatization"—of the city's failings would "help us solve" its problems.

The Rev. Jackson of Olivet was not the only important black Chicagoan who was cool toward the Chicago Freedom Movement. Six of the city's African-American aldermen, who represented wards on both the South and the West sides, wanted no part of this campaign. They had prospered under the current rules, and they—like some black Chicagoans—preferred familiar ways to radical change. Indeed, when news broke that King and the SCLC had targeted Chicago as the site of its first Northern campaign, Ralph Metcalfe, the former Olympic sprinter and a leading black alderman, stated, "We have competent leadership in Chicago and all things necessary to work out our city's own destiny."

Metcalfe's words endorsed the view of Chicago's chief politician, Mayor Richard J. Daley. Hailed as America's most powerful mayor and known as a confidant of Democratic presidents, Daley presided over a potent political apparatus, which virtually controlled the black wards, and he simply loathed the arrival of outsiders who were certain, in his mind, to stir up trouble within his city. Daley himself had praised King for his successes in the South, but he saw no reason for the Nobel Peace Prize winner to ally himself with Chicago civil rights agitators who for months now had displayed no respect for the efforts of his regime to make Chicago a better home for its citizens.

The Need for a Movement in the North

King and his supporters, however, were convinced of the necessity of nonviolent protests. There was a need, asserted Al Raby, a Chicago schoolteacher and the co-leader of the Chicago Freedom Movement, for "a constant pricking of the conscience." And as King told the Rev. Joseph Jackson, social change did not result from "sitting around having nice conversations."

Their sense of urgency heightened with the rise of the black power impulse after the shooting of James Meredith in Mississippi in June 1966 and with the eruption of a riot on Chicago's West Side one month later. It seemed to King and his lieutenants that the most basic assumptions of their crusade—nonviolence and interracialism—were being challenged in the African-American community. The nonviolent civil rights movement needed to prove its relevance in this new era, especially to Northern blacks.

Responding to this pressure, the Chicago Freedom Movement decided to focus on housing segregation, one of the culprits behind the ghetto conditions that plagued so many black Chicagoans. Although some in the community doubted that living among whites was a critical issue, real estate discrimination offered an attractive target for some important reasons: It was neither as subtle nor as elusive as most forms of Northern discrimination. Indeed, it was much like the lunch counter discrimination that had been so triumphantly eliminated by the Southern black protest movement. Specific culprits could easily be fingered. Chicago realtors were the Northern George Wallaces, as one activist put it, standing "in the doorway of thousands of homes being offered for sale or rent" and preventing "Negroes and other minorities from choosing freely where they may live."

And so, in July 1966, Chicago activists, led by veterans of Southern demonstrations, began testing real estate firms for discriminatory practices. After their suspicions had proved correct, they mounted marches into white neighborhoods to protest unfair black exclusion and to spur corrective measures. By early August, King could legitimately claim that there was "a good nonviolent fight in Chicago."

The demonstrations persisted through the month of August as insurgents, black and white, warded off hostile whites during forays into Chicago's southwest and northwest sides and into nearby suburbs. The zeal for social justice was intense. "We march," one activist noted, "we return home emotionally drained, from some inner reservoirs replenish our strength, and go back."

The discipline of the marchers was impressive. Even gang

members, who often served as march marshals, toed the non-violent line. "I saw their noses being broken and blood flowing from their wounds; and I saw them continue and not retaliate, not one of them, with violence," King later marveled.

The Supposed Failure of the Chicago Movement

In the end, this most important sustained episode of Northern civil rights protest of the 1960s led to a series of meetings between city officials, including Mayor Daley, civil rights activists, real estate agents, and business and religious leaders that produced a program to promote equal housing opportunity. King hailed this development as the "most significant and far-reaching victory that has ever come about in a Northern community on the whole question of open housing."

Most observers, however, have not been so generous in their assessment of the Chicago Freedom Movement. In a little-known but remarkable book, *Unholy Shadows and Freedom's Holy Light*, the Rev. Joseph Jackson claimed that it was "most fortunate for Chicago and for the United States of America that the campaign of 1966 . . . failed in Chicago." Otherwise, Jackson argued, "the rule of law would have ended in this city, and the headquarters would have been shifted from City Hall to private offices, hotel rooms and streets or wherever the visiting diplomats elected to assemble."

As an old King opponent, Jackson overstated the case, but many historians agreed with his premise that King's campaign had failed. In the mid-1970s, one commentator, Godfrey Hodgson, in his influential history of modern America, dismissed the Chicago campaign as a rout. More recently, historian Adam Fairclough labeled the Chicago initiative a "defeat" for King and the civil rights movement.

Evidence abounds to support such an interpretation. The Chicago campaign did not give the nonviolent movement the lift that King and his supporters had hoped. Unlike the Selma, Ala., protests a year earlier, the Chicago marches did not inspire sweeping federal legislation. Indeed, in September 1966 Congress failed to endorse a civil rights bill, which included a fair-housing measure, for the first time during the Second Reconstruction.

And in Chicago, even some participants in the open-housing marches denounced the final "Summit Agreement" as a "sellout." Under the leadership of Robert Lucas, the head of the Chicago chapter of the Congress of Racial Equality (CORE), they staged in early September 1966 their own protest march—not sanctioned by King or his lieutenants—into nearby Cicero, known as a bastion of white hostility toward African Americans. The Cicero demonstration was yet another indication that the coalition that had dismantled the Jim Crow regime in the South was now unraveling. For the last months of his life, King would endure greater criticism from black militants than ever before.

And the Chicago Freedom Movement failed to keep its promise to "end slums." The distress of black Chicagoans still confined today to the West Side and South Side ghettos, including some of the most impoverished places in America, dramatically attests to this failure. Years after the Chicago campaign, one West Side resident admitted, "I'm sure that wasn't [King's] dream—the way things are now." Then she lamented, "Nothing really happened."

Moreover, there has always been some debate within the African-American community about the importance of residential integration. During the summer of 1966, some black Chicagoans—even some of those sympathetic to the movement—wondered whether open-housing marches highlighted "a fundamental issue." As one activist remarked, housing discrimination "was more of a middle-class issue."

Variations on such sentiments can be found today. "I want to live in a black neighborhood," one Chicago alderman recently declared, "and if banks would give us money to fix up the houses we live in, nobody would have to move."

The Successes of the Movement

But should the final judgment of the Chicago Freedom Movement be so negative? This campaign, after all, catapulted Jesse Jackson to the forefront of the civil rights movement. As a college student in the early 1960s, he had been a leader of the protests in Greensboro, N.C., and then had joined the Selma protests; but until SCLC came to Chicago, where he was then a seminarian, Jackson was but one more young black activist. His energy and dynamism soon made him indispensable to the Chicago Freedom Movement, and when the marches stopped he remained in Chicago, nurturing Operation Breadbasket. In the early 1970s, Operation Breadbasket, which had been under SCLC's auspices, became Operation PUSH, a Jackson vehicle and the eventual launch pad of Jackson's political career.

The Chicago Freedom Movement also gave birth to the Leadership Council for Metropolitan Open Communities. A product of the Summit Agreement in August 1966, the Leadership Council has retained the support of Chicago business leaders and, through litigation and aggressive tactics, has pioneered attacks on housing discrimination. In the words of two housing experts, Douglas Massey and Nancy Denton, "probably no fair housing group in the country has been more energetic or successful in promoting equal housing opportunities."

Despite these efforts, residential segregation remains formidable in Chicago, which now ranks as the third-most segregated city in America. Today, nearly 86 percent of metropolitan Chicago's black population would have to be moved in order for each of Chicago's neighborhoods to reflect the city's overall racial makeup.

The Chicago Freedom Movement was the most publicized effort in the nation's history to spotlight the curse of housing barriers. While its legacy must not be overstated, it did expose, as Bernard LaFayette Jr., one of the campaign's chief strategists, noted in late 1966, the myth "that a Negro can live where he wants to in the North," and it did prove that "large numbers of people in a Northern city can be mobilized for nonviolent direct action in the face of mass violence." This is not a meager message for a country still divided by housing segregation and often seemingly lacking faith that citizens themselves, acting together, can organize for change.

The Anti-War Movement

Herbert Shapiro

Passage of the Gulf of Tonkin resolution in August 1964 marked the beginning of America's deep involvement in the Vietnam War. Many of the churchmembers and students who had been active in the civil rights movement joined the growing protests against the war. But black civil rights leaders were conflicted, torn between patriotism and the principles of nonviolence.

Major civil rights leaders consistently opposed American involvement in wars in Third World countries, Herbert Shapiro states in this article. They believed that overseas wars diverted attention from the cause of social justice for blacks at home. Activists also perceived a similarity between America's imperialist policies toward Third World citizens and white supremacists' attitudes toward black Americans. Shapiro argues that the coalition of black and white activists in the anti–Vietnam War movement was a natural outgrowth of the civil rights movement.

Shapiro is a professor of history at the University of Cincinnati, Ohio.

In retrospect, it was quite to be expected that the issues of opposition to the Vietnam War and the status of Black Americans, the antiwar movement and the civil rights movement, would become linked. American involvement in Southeast Asia, beginning with the effort to restore French colonial rule, had long exhibited a disdain for rights of self-determination, a matter of concern to those interested in equal rights at home. The escalation of the United States' role in the war came quickly on the heels of the decisive victories in the struggle against overt segregation, just when it appeared that federal

Excerpted from Herbert Shapiro, "The Vietnam War and the American Civil Rights Movement," *Journal of Ethnic Studies*, Winter 1989. Reprinted by permission of the publisher. (Endnotes in the original have been omitted in the reprint.)

authorities were placing the elimination of poverty and racism at the top of the national agenda. The Johnson administration's turning away from the promises made during the 1964 election campaign appropriately engendered a sense of betrayal. What was happening appeared to be another instance in a long history of justice deferred. As Vincent Harding writes, "a vicious, racist and imperialist war was being fought against another nonwhite people in Vietnam" at the same time as "intransigent hearts and minds were digging in at new battle lines of whiteness, in jobs, in communities, in schools, in spirits." The American nation chose "to betray again its own initial, spasmodic, frightened movements forward towards new black-white life." In place of a crusade for democracy at home the administration opted for a war that would be fought with unprecedented cruelty against Asian civilians, persons reduced in the battlefront argot to the dehumanized status of "gooks." This was the war as it appeared to civil rights activists who already had learned in the cauldron of Southern struggle that federal power most often alternated between stances of unreliable friendship and outright hostility. It could be questioned which was the true image of federal power, Lyndon Johnson invoking the words "we shall overcome," or J. Edgar Hoover's observation that his bureau was not in the business of protecting the lives of civil rights workers. Civil rights activists were not likely to accept Lyndon Johnson's rhetoric on faith, especially when it could reasonably be wondered if this escalation, this embrace of Goldwater's militarism, had not secretly been planned all along. Senator Fulbright caught the tragic irony of the situation: "Abroad we are engaged in a savage and unsuccessful war against poor people in a small and backward nation. At home—largely because of the neglect resulting from twenty-five years of preoccupation with foreign involvements—our cities are exploding in violent protest against generations of social injustice."

Blacks and the War

The logic of the situation was reinforced by the realities that draft calls impinged heavily on civil rights workers, and it soon became obvious that Blacks were suffering a disproportionate share of the casualties. The impact of the draft was keenly felt by volunteers of the Student Nonviolent Coordinating Committee (SNCC). "SNCC workers," Clayborne Carson writes, "resented the military draft for it threatened to deprive the organization of many of its male personnel. SNCC workers generally lacked the deferments available to college students, and they could expect little sympathy from their draft boards, most of which were in the South." Movement activist Mary King remembers what she saw in Mississippi: "I had observed at dusty crossroads and at Mississippi train platforms the aluminum coffins bearing bodies arriving from southeast Asia. I noticed that, at least where I was, they were overwhelmingly met by black families."

David Halberstam recalls that, upon his 1964 return from Vietnam, "a bearded young integration worker in Mississippi" told him: "I enjoyed your coverage of America's other colonial war." Already at the time of the Mississippi Freedom Summer, volunteers in training at Oxford, Ohio asked Justice Department representative John Doar: "How is it that the government can protect the Vietnamese from the Viet Cong and the same government will not accept the moral responsibility of protecting the people in Mississippi?" The questioner was not then questioning American intentions in Vietnam, but was calling into doubt the moral integrity of government policy. The question received only the bland reply: "I would rather confine myself to Mississippi." At the August 1964 service for three civil rights workers murdered in Mississippi, SNCC's Robert Moses held up a newspaper with the headline "LBJ Says 'Shoot to Kill' in The Gulf of Tonkin." Moses was linking the readiness to inflict violence in Vietnam with the lack of will to enforce human rights at home. In 1965 Mississippi activists again returned to the theme of the contradiction between American policy abroad and official actions at home. The McComb branch of the Mississippi Freedom Democratic Party declared: "1. No Mississippi Negroes should be fighting in Vietnam for the White Man's freedom until all the Negro people are free in Mississippi. . . . 2. No one has a right to ask us to risk our lives and kill other colored people in Santo Domingo and Vietnam, so that the white American can get richer. . . . We don't know anything about Communism, Socialism, and all that, but we do know that Negroes have caught hell right here under this American Democracy."

The Nonviolent Movement

In 1964 Bayard Rustin, coordinator of the 1963 March on Washington, was one of several prominent pacifists who drafted a "Declaration of Conscience" that proclaimed a conscientious refusal to cooperate with the United States' government in the prosecution of the war in Vietnam. The signers' view was that "we shall encourage the development of other nonviolent acts, including acts which involve civil disobedience, in order to stop the flow of American soldiers and munitions to Vietnam." John Lewis, James Bevel, Robert Moses, A. Philip Randolph, all prominently identified with the civil rights movement, were among the additional signers. Earlier, on Easter Sunday 1962, Rustin had spoken to a peace assemblage gathered at the United Nations at which some of the marchers carried signs protesting growing United States' involvement in Vietnam. On December 19, 1964, A. Philip Randolph was one of the speakers at a New York City demonstration of one thousand calling for an end to the Vietnamese war. All of this indicates that the participation by known and respected civil rights leaders in criticizing official Vietnam policy was an existing reality before the major escalations of 1965.

That those identified with the cause of civil rights would sometimes speak out on questions of American foreign policy was not something new. Moorfield Storey, the pioneer civil rights activist, was consistently antiwar and staunchly anti-imperialist. Speaking of the acquisition of the Philippines Storey declared that "this great land has now turned oppressor, and the guilt must be shared by every citizen who by word or silence consents." In 1899 Bishop Alexander Walters of the A.M.E. Zion Church told the Afro-American Council: "I do not think that America is prepared to carry on expansion at this time, especially if it be among the dark races of the earth. The white man of America is impregnated with color-phobia. He has been taught for centuries that the black man, no matter where he dwells, has no rights which the white man is bound to respect, hence he is not prepared to grant dark skinned people the most favorable opportunities for development." Blacks saw a relationship between foreign policy and the American racial situation. As Willard Gatewood observes, "For some Negroes the insurrection in the Philippines was an aspect of the larger struggle of darker races throughout the world to combat oppression by white men." In the 1920s Storey warmly supported the effort by the NAACP, led by James Weldon Johnson, to end American occupation of Haiti. Contemporary with the issue of American policy in Southeast Asia, the NAACP criticized American policy with regard to South Africa, particularly calling attention to calls by American naval vessels at South African ports. The notion that Black leadership should refrain from articulating its own views regarding foreign policy matters finds little support in the traditions of Afro-America.

Yet, it must be noted that the involvement of leaders and supporters of the civil rights movement in the antiwar cause surpassed anything previously seen in American history, affecting the consciousness of millions of Americans, Black and White. A basic consideration here is that the civil rights movement itself symbolized the coming together in struggle of Black and White Americans. It expressed the vision of an integrated society that was a key goal of those seeking the dismantling of segregation. As civil rights workers took up the peace issue, they brought with them a commitment to Whites and Blacks working together for common ends.

Chapter 4

The Fight for Rights Continues

Turning Points
IN WORLD HISTORY

Integration or Anti-Discrimination?

Denton L. Watson

A long-standing debate exists between blacks who believe in integration and those who favor self-segregation as a path to social equality for blacks. The NAACP adopted integration as its goal. It was successful in striking down the laws that enshrined segregation in the South, but it was less successful in promoting programs of integration and in breaking patterns of discrimination in the North, according to Denton L. Watson.

In the following viewpoint, he argues that the failure of integration made racial self-segregation a more attractive option. The NAACP should adopt a new legal strategy to fight discrimination and enforce civil rights laws.

Watson, a former official of the NAACP, is a journalist. He is the author of *Lion in the Lobby*.

The advent of Black History Month in February will bring the usual spurt of debates about civil rights. The problem with such reflection, however, is that, while it may be entertaining and useful for venting steam—like President Clinton's advisory panel on civil rights—it is unable to provide any comprehensive recommendations for solving worsening problems. The impasse lies with the National Association for the Advancement of Colored People. As it celebrates its eighty-eighth birthday on February 12, the NAACP remains a shadow of what was once an organization on the cutting edge of the movement.

The question prompting the current identity crisis is the same one that dichotomized the organization decades ago:

Excerpted from Denton L. Watson, "The NAACP at the Crossroads," *The Humanist*, January/February 1998. Reprinted by permission of the author.

how valid is integration as a civil rights goal? Frustrated by the intense attacks on civil rights by right-wing reactionaries, a growing number of the NAACP's leaders have recently expressed strong doubts about pursuing the goal. Like Booker T. Washington at the turn of the century and W. E. B. Du Bois in the 1930s, these African Americans have been drawing the wagons around themselves, feeling that the best strategy for survival in a racist society is self-segregation.

The Rejection of Self-Segregation

When the NAACP rejected self-segregation decades ago in a bitter battle that further defined the organization, Du Bois, one of its founders, was forced to resign as editor of the *Crisis*, its journal. So for the organization to today imply any doubt in its founding strategy is further indication of how severely it has been damaged by years of weak leadership and infighting.

This is the same NAACP which led the nineteen-year school desegregation movement that in 1954 won the unanimous Supreme Court decision in *Brown v. Board of Education*. The landmark case overturned the "separate but equal" doctrine established by the High Court in 1896, which relegated African Americans to second-class citizenship or worse. *Brown* cleared the way for the passage of the most comprehensive civil rights laws in the nation's history and for subsequent court orders to enforce and expand the decision.

Despite violent white opposition, the NAACP pressed for integration. Not even when African Americans themselves began questioning the busing of their children into hostile white areas of cities like Boston and Detroit did the organization waver in its course. For the NAACP knew, as one white woman spat, "it's not the bus but the niggers" that was the problem.

The extent of the NAACP's debate over integration today is best demonstrated by the differing positions of Dennis C. Hayes, the organization's general counsel, and his assistant Willie Abrams. Hayes believes the problem is caused by confusing *integration* with *assimilation*—a concept he firmly rejects because it is "built upon a philosophy of white supremacy." All versions of assimilation, Hayes insists, "operate under the implicit assumption that there is something wrong with the racial otherness of black folk." When discussing those blacks who want to segregate themselves, Hayes states:

> While, theoretically, we might imagine that a racial minority group might for positive reasons want to segregate themselves even though there exists complete openness from the dominant society, this is not the reality of racial politics in this country. Indeed, when Booker T. Washington called for segregation—in part because he accepted the position that blacks were unfit and must prove themselves to whites before segregation could end—the reality was that many African Americans adopted segregation as an accommodation to, and protection from, white racism. While this is understandable from a self-survival point of view, it has been the NAACP's considered wisdom over eighty-eight years that such an accommodation to white racists . . . does nothing to destabilize white hierarchy; and it does nothing to destabilize the philosophy of white supremacy.

Hayes maintains that true integration

> creates and maintains a more inclusive society where individuals and groups have opportunities to participate equally in their communities. Inclusion then gives us tools to build a democratic society, the ability to approach complex issues from many perspectives . . . and that's why we are for it.

Abrams, however, embraces a "plural but equal" concept, which he insists is different from "separate but equal." For him, "plural but equal" represents a voluntary separation of blacks in schools and communities. He says this is different from traditional forms of segregation because it will not "run out the white family that moves in." Neither, he maintains, will the white community run out blacks who enter. He thus believes that identifiable racial or ethnic communities are entitled to neighborhood schools because the "history of school integration really demonstrates that, in order to have viable schools, we must have some community" with parental input into them.

Like white segregationists, Abrams maintains that busing children long distances to schools outside their neighborhoods has been the real enemy to improving education for African Americans because it "destroys the main ingredient that is really needed to have good schools." He argues that a few children will indeed do well in any environment, as they did even in slavery. So, according to Abrams, "In situations where you have children being bussed out of their communities, you're going to find a few kids who are going to do well in those [integrated schools]." But by and large, he insists, the majority of children in these programs fail "because they are cut off from the parental and community support they need."

Integration in Practice

The relevance of the school integration debate was underscored last spring by a study conducted by Gary Orfield of Harvard University. It showed that, despite a generation of school desegregation progress in the eleven states of the Old Confederacy and six border states, resegregation in this region is rapidly increasing. Throughout the North, meanwhile, widespread demographic changes, reflected in the growth of the white suburban ring around black and Hispanic inner-city populations, have worsened segregation.

The profound social implications of these changes are evident in the almost total failure of many predominantly black school districts to properly educate their student populations; the chronic presence of guns, drugs, and related crime; the preponderance of blacks and Hispanics in prisons; and the further intensification of housing segregation. The resulting social pathology is worsened by the overseas flight of the types of factory and decent-paying unskilled jobs that once gave earlier poor white populations hope for a better future.

The trend was ensured when the Reagan administration destroyed the remnants of school desegregation programs. In the 1980s, the Justice Department opposed many pending cases that had been brought by the NAACP and its offspring, the NAACP Legal Defense and Educational Fund. This opposition prompted Congress to end the federal desegregation assistance program in the 1981 Omnibus Budget Reconciliation Act. The Bush administration remained committed to the reversal. And even though President Clinton has vowed to work toward racial and ethnic reconciliation, his administration has felt no meaningful pressure from the NAACP to correct the previous twelve years of reversal on school desegregation. . . .

The Focus Needed

In 1974, Clarence Mitchell Jr., the late director of the NAACP Washington Bureau, recognized the urgent need for the organization to revamp its programs and shift its focus from the South to the North in order to address new types of civil rights problems that resulted from systemic or institutional discrimination. Despite his legendary status on Capitol Hill that won him the popular moniker "101st senator," he encountered bitter opposition from some of those who earlier had been his strongest allies.

The root of the problem was that, as the strategy for the school desegregation campaign developed and the NAACP concentrated its legal resources on attacking the "separate but equal" doctrine, focus shifted overridingly to the goal of integration. With the *Brown* victory, integration became the NAACP's grail, and the term became synonymous with full political and social equality because its achievement was regarded as being the most expedient way to implement the organization's egalitarian philosophy. The idea was also very attractive because, as Michael Sussman, a former member of the NAACP's legal staff who handled the organization's recent school desegregation case in Yonkers, New York, argues, "Integration is the best indication [of] what kind of society we aspire [to for our children] and what kinds of values we want to transmit [to them]."

Indeed, *integration was the only appropriate, and thus the most effective, response to the South's state-imposed Jim Crow system.* It destroyed a system that had imprisoned not only the oppressed blacks but also the whites in the region. It broke down the color line and gave southern blacks a sense of social freedom they never had. Its achievement was intended to eradicate all sense of racial inferiority, which was inherent in segregation. And where the courts closely monitored the implementation of its orders, integration worked.

Yet, initially the NAACP and other black leader's did not realize the extent to which discrimination still could be practiced under integration. That was the reason Robert H. Johnson, president of the Bergen County (New Jersey) NAACP Branch, gave for opposing a school desegregation plan there. Like Willie Abrams, he insisted that "racial balance is not the important factor here; equal and quality education is."

Johnson pointed to studies that "show that an integrated school does not necessarily provide quality education." That has been because of the common practices of tracking black students in avowedly integrated schools or placing them in special education programs, thus segregating them from whites in order to provide them with inferior education. Another example is the pervasive glass ceiling in the workplace that limits the advancement of minorities and women to higher-level jobs.

By shifting its emphasis overridingly to integration, the NAACP overlooked the extent to which northerners as well as southerners were determined to continue racial discrimination at any cost and, thus, to perpetuate in the victims of racism the feelings of inferiority. This is the problem that bothers blacks like Abrams.

Why Integration Undermines Equality

At times, the resolute quest for integration undermined the NAACP's founding philosophy by confusing appearances of social acceptance for full political and social equality—the type that the NAACP sought to reaffirm under the Fourteenth and Fifteenth Amendments. Enforcement of the Fourteenth Amendment's equal protection clause should not have been tantamount to simple race mixing. To be equal there has to be mutual respect for each group's heritage and culture.

But neither could the NAACP alter its historical quest for an integrated society without destroying its own *raison d'etre*. In readjusting its programs to meet new needs, it should have been mindful that integration is a social concept while equality under the law is grounded in the Constitution. Consequently, without obtaining additional resources to support meaningful integration—that is, the transformation of institutions and social attitudes—the goal could be counterproductive, such as spurring white flight.

In many instances, therefore, the confusion of the goal of integration with the broader goal of equality opened up the opportunity for the NAACP's enemies to severely undercut its legal and political strategies by simply changing the rules. President Nixon, for one, with his southern strategy, whiplashed the NAACP mercilessly in the early 1970s around the busing issue. But as Nixon aide John Ehrlichman acknowledged some time ago, Nixon's design was not to take back all of the civil rights gains, only some. Ehrlichman's explanation was intended to distance the Nixon administration from that of President Reagan. Reagan, Ehrlichman noted, was determined to destroy all civil rights progress. So was President Bush.

The reason the Nixon, Reagan, and Bush administrations succeeded in attacking civil rights to the extent they did was due in large measure to the NAACP not stressing enough that integration was simply a *tool* for achieving equality. Thus, there is merit in Abrams' argument that African Americans do need to protect and strengthen their institutions. However, they cannot do so in a manner that undermines the equal protection foundations of *Brown*.

The Overturning of Gains

In the 1972 battle to bar the use of federal funds for school busing, Mitchell sensed the problem but was unable to adjust his strategy because he was locked into the integration policy. For him to have attempted to shift strategies then would have played into his enemies' hands. In Congress, the battle was led by Representative Edith S. Green (Democrat—Oregon), one of Mitchell's foremost allies during the struggle for passage of the 1964 Civil Rights Act with its Title VI, to facilitate school desegregation, and Title VII, barring discrimination in employment.

At the very outset, Green supported school integration. She was angered, however, that the NAACP was pressing for integration before using the civil rights laws to improve all-black or predominantly black schools as *a route to* school desegregation. Consequently, she and other former allies from the North led the battle to weaken some of the laws they themselves had helped to pass. The result was that the NAACP suffered its first decisive defeat since the 1950s.

Similarly, California's recent Proposition 209 and other intense attacks on affirmative action are determined attempts to cripple Title VII. Because Titles VI and VII were firmly undergirded by the Fourteenth Amendment, however, they are still effective in many cases when enforced. The problem today, nevertheless, is that the nation has no coherent civil rights program, and African Americans are confused because the NAACP is confused over strategy.

After the decisive defeat, Mitchell proposed a new, comprehensive program for the NAACP in 1973 that would have combatted the systemic causes of discrimination. However, an exhausted Roy Wilkins, then executive director, ignored the proposal, preferring instead to create day care, prison, and other superficial programs. Mitchell's program, rooted in the law, would have shifted the organization back to the goal of seeking equality by, for example, utilizing the rapidly increasing strength of the black vote and the increasing number of black elected officials to address the civil rights problems of the North. His program also would have aided blacks in developing businesses, as well as creating other economic benefits.

The Challenge

The challenge for the NAACP therefore is to develop a comprehensive program that is firmly rooted in the organization's founding egalitarian philosophy and within the context of its demonstrated legal and political strategies. It has to rebuild its legal department and reinvest in the general counsel the required autonomy that made the organization a giant of social change, as well as adopt elements of Mitchell's proposals which are still relevant. Furthermore, it should:

- Develop new legal programs for combatting systemic discrimination, which is practiced through residential redlining and other forms of housing segregation.
- Get Congress to address the abysmal state of urban education by creating an urban Marshall Plan that is based on the magnet school concept and provides decent-paying jobs in the inner cities for residents there.
- Eliminate the genocidal use of the criminal justice system against African Americans, especially young males.
- Fully enforce the civil rights laws, including reasserting the original mission of the U.S. Civil Rights Commission and the Equal Employment Opportunity Commission.
- Launch a national program to include the teaching of civil rights history as a standard requirement in public schools to ensure that all Americans understand the intrinsic value of the struggle for equality.

The NAACP has a moral responsibility to play a potent, effective role in redefining America in the new millennium. President Clinton is providing the leadership on civil rights that Mitchell and other leaders had sought throughout the NAACP's history by creating the civil rights advisory panel, headed by the distinguished historian John Hope Franklin. Unless the NAACP resumes its flagship role in this mission, those aspirations "to find ways to celebrate our differences" will be doomed to compromise. That is a tragedy America cannot afford.

Equal Economic Opportunity

Herb Boyd

Under the Civil Rights Act of 1964 and subsequent executive orders, businesses and universities that receive contracts or public funds from the federal government are asked to take affirmative action to hire minorities and women from the pool of qualified applicants. This policy was put in place by presidents Johnson and Nixon, but it has been narrowed under other administrations.

In the following selection, Herb Boyd, a contributing writer for the NAACP publication *Crisis*, outlines the original intent of affirmative action and traces the roots of opposition to the policy. Many people seek to dismantle the program, claiming it is a failure. But white women have benefited from affirmative action, even while blacks have been consistently denied opportunities. Blacks must pressure the government to make good on the promise of equal economic opportunity.

It seems no matter where you turn nowadays from small businesses in Akron, Ohio to the federal government, affirmative action is the topic of discussion. Whether affirmative action, which extends special economic and educational privileges on the basis of race to compensate for past discrimination, will continue is the question of the hour, and it may well be a critical issue in the 1996 presidential campaign.

It may be best to define what is meant by affirmative action before examining the contending positions. Put in a concise, encyclopedic framework, affirmative action is a formal effort to provide increased employment opportunities for women and ethnic minorities for past and present patterns of discrimination. In his 1965 Howard University

Excerpted from Herb Boyd, "Dismantling Affirmative Action: The Broken Promise to Black America," *Crisis*, May/June 1995. Greenhaven Press wishes to thank The Crisis Publishing Co., Inc., the publisher of the magazine of the National Association for the Advancement of Colored People, for authorizing the use of this work.

speech that became the basis for affirmative action, President Lyndon Johnson asserted, "You do not take a person who, for years, has been hobbled by chains and liberate him, bring him to the starting line and then say, 'You are free to compete with all others' and still justly believe you have been completely fair." Under the Equal Opportunity Act of 1972, most federal contractors and subcontractors, all state governments and institutions (including universities), and most local governments must initiate plans to increase the proportions of their female and minority employees until they are equal to the proportions existing in the available labor market.

Affirmative Action and Quotas

In this definition there is no mention of quotas, a concept that the law's detractors view as tantamount to "reverse discrimination." The origin of this assertion can be traced to the Bakke case in 1978 when a white applicant to the University of California-Davis Medical School claimed he was denied an admission though he scored higher than several minority students who obtained admission through 16 of 100 seats set aside for them. The Supreme Court ruled in his favor, declaring that affirmative action plans that establish racial quotas are unconstitutional.

"Affirmative action," writes Reverend Calvin Butts of Harlem's Abyssinian Baptist Church and Rabbi Douglas E. Krantz of Armonk, N.Y., "is not based on timetables with predesigned quota systems that must be fulfilled by those who are unqualified. That is a setup, and it is unfair. It will not work for anybody. Affirmative means that there are two equally qualified candidates for admission to a university, for a promotion in a job or for a bank loan, then the equally qualified candidate from the minority group receives the promotion, the admission or the loan."

Nor does affirmative action have much impact in the private sector, unless the company has a contract with the federal government. Moreover, nothing is said about employers actively seeking minorities or women; and the provision has no power to determine the hiring outcome when two employees of equal status but of different races qualify for a job.

And above all the law does not empower women or minorities to dislodge whites to make room for minorities. All these are common misconceptions, and like the proverbial nine blind men who explain what an elephant is, based on the different parts of its anatomy in their grasp, affirmative action means different things to different people.

Personal Stories

For Mildred Greene, a black woman who runs her own travel agency in Manhattan, affirmative action turned her life around. "If it had not been for affirmative action," she says, "I would have never been hired by American Airlines. The plan helped me fulfill my dream." Greene was hired by the airline after it launched an affirmative action initiative in 1969. She worked at the airline for 15 years, first as a key-punch operator and then at several other jobs.

"But when it came time for promotions the company reneged on its promise," Greene relates. "Like most of the blacks, I was confined to a menial job with little chance to rise any higher. I think when I took the job a code was fixed by my name and that determined my destiny with them."

Seeing no future with American Airlines, Greene established her travel agency ten years ago, and while she has a large clientele, she would like to expand her operations. But getting a loan to upgrade her business has been repeatedly denied. "I tried the local banks but I ran into redlining and was blocked by loan officers who said my credit was a problem, which was not the case. Then I tried to get a small business loan from the federal government but I was turned down because I didn't employ enough people," she explains. "Well, if I were able to employ the number of people they required, I wouldn't need a loan."

One of the benefits of operating your own business is that you don't have to worry about the rejection and indifference of personnel officers or wonder whether you will be seriously considered for a job or for advancement up the corporate ladder. Aziz Gueye Adetimirin, a native of Nigeria, was frustrated with his job at United Airlines and left after becoming mired in the same position.

"They promised me a lot of good things," Adetimirin recalls, "but it was all a lot of talk." Two years ago, he started his
own weekly newspaper, *The Network Journal*, in Brooklyn.
There are five full-time employees, the paper is doing rather
well, but Adetimirin would like to expand his business to meet
the changing demands of the market place. "Getting support
from your own people and being independent is very reward-
ing, even if the income is not exactly what I would like to
have," he says. He supports affirmative action but believes
that black people are not getting much out of it. "If anyone is
getting anything out of affirmative action, it's been white
women. There is even a newspaper here in Brooklyn that tar-
gets blacks from the Caribbean run by white women," he says.

White Women vs. Minorities

Many observers of affirmative action feel that the moment
white women were paired with minorities, the impact of the
act was lessened considerably. There have been a number of
public debates in which black men are seen arguing with white
women about the relative merits of affirmative action. These
white women insist that their gains were not the result of any
governmental edict, but they are mistaken, says Jesse Jackson.
"Since passage of civil rights laws 30 years ago," Jackson
writes in a recent op-ed article, "affirmative action has been
working. Republicans focus on race and not on women, but in
reality a majority of Americans benefit from affirmative action—women and their families the most, with employment
obstacles being lifted as millions entered the job market."

Writer Bernice Powell Jackson addresses the problem and
some of its more salient ramifications. ". . . The inclusion of
white women in the work force through affirmative action
has benefited white families directly by increasing their
earning and standard of living. Since most white women are
married to white men, white men, too, have benefited from
affirmative action."

Two prominent women's organizations voiced their support for affirmative action. "We will not be eliminated from
this debate," declared Eleanor Smeal of the Feminist Majority. Patricia Ireland, president of the National Organization

for Women said she was deeply disturbed that the Clinton Administration has not issued a firm statement supporting affirmative action. Senator Carol Moseley-Braun recently told a gathering of the American Association of University Women that they must continue to fight for their rights. "The glass ceiling is all too real," she said. "And there are efforts underway to put cement on it. We will not stand by and allow that to happen."

Lack of Political Support

Meanwhile, President Clinton's position on this matter has been typically centrist, ordering a review of federal affirmative action programs. He has reportedly asked his staff to identify the programs that work and those that might be unfair. "I'm against discrimination," he told a group of college journalists in late March. "I'm against giving people opportunities who are unqualified." Clinton recently promised to sign a bill that would end tax breaks designed to boost minority ownership of broadcast properties, an indication perhaps of his slide away from affirmative action.

For a while it appeared that Clinton's likely opponent in his presidential bid next year, Senate Majority Leader Bob Dole, was also caught in a dilemma, since he had once voted to set aside some federal contracts for minorities and women. But he quickly let it be known where he stood on the issue. "My past record on civil rights does not and should not disqualify me from raising legitimate questions about the continuing effectiveness of affirmative action," Dole said. Wade Henderson, head of the NAACP's Washington Bureau and the association's chief national lobbyist, says he is disturbed by Dole's reversal. "Senator Dole's apparent change of heart on the need for affirmative action programs is troubling. . . . Surely the senator who gave the nation the Glass Ceiling Commission would not now turn a blind eye to the evidence that suggests affirmative action is still necessary."

An Index of Inequality

And it certainly is, if the statistics supplied by the NAACP are any indication. African Americans, who constitute 11 percent of the total work force, are less than 4 percent of the following occupations as of 1993: lawyers and judges (2.7%), dentists (1.9%), doctors (3.7%), industrial engineers (3.4%), engineers (3.7%), managers in marketing, advertising and public relations (3.1%). A Korn Kerry International survey in 1991, reports Earl Ofari Hutchinson, found that less than 1 percent of the top corporate executives were black. Moreover, average earnings of black workers, as a percentage of white workers' earnings, fell from 75.1 percent to 73.1 percent between 1980 and 1990. In 1993, African Americans received fewer than 3 percent of U.S. doctorates awarded, and many of them are denied this opportunity because of the scarcity of loans and scholarships. And if Newt Gingrich gets his way, these few educational assistance programs will be scrapped. It is sadly ironic that students of color are prohibited preferential treatment consideration while universities routinely bend the rules to admit children of alumni. . . .

"I do believe the private sector will be a powerful force to correct those inequities on its own," said Hugh L. McColl, Jr., chairman and C.E.O. of NationsBank in Charlotte, N.C., and an advocate of affirmative action. "I am greatly encouraged by the spread of voluntary diversity programs across corporate America. Business reasons for these initiatives go beyond compliance with affirmative action regulation." In other words, McColl continued, "businesses understand they must have a more diverse employee base to serve today's diverse customer base. The danger is that diversity programs digress into shallow, meaningless publicity efforts, rather than sharpened, business-driven strategies to increase the value and effectiveness of the company."

And if the so-called self-correcting mechanism in business and the government fails, there are those who have pressured for demonstrations and hearings. This was the tack recently taken in Detroit, when the city's branch of the NAACP convened a special hearing on the attacks on affirmative action and state and federal budget cuts.

"The hearings on affirmative action mark a continuous step in a series of strategies that will help mobilize the people." asserted Reverend Wendell Anthony, pastor of Fellowship Chapel and president of the Detroit chapter of the NAACP. "Diverse groups must apply pressure on elected officials and policy makers on their commitment and responsibility to the people."

Angry White Males

That the legions of "angry white males" and the Republican right are willing to place this debate in the hands of the people is a cynical move, given the time, energy and money they have spent brainwashing the masses to accept their agenda. What the white Americans need to understand is that black Americans are not the enemy. Our opportunity does not translate into their deprivation. A recent report prepared by Alfred Blumrosen, a law professor at Rutgers University, revealed that there was scant evidence of employment discrimination against white men, and that many claims of "reverse discrimination" were without merit. And those who doubt this report might follow *New York Times* columnist Bob Herbert's suggestion to "pair up a white guy with a black guy and send them off in search of the same job." You know what the result will be.

It seems that as soon as the economy takes a downturn and jobs become scarce, many whites translate their job security anxieties into racism. Whenever a person of color succeeds, whites often refuse to recognize that race was more likely an obstacle to their success than an asset.

"Equal opportunity is the promise; discrimination is the problem," Jesse Jackson has said. "Affirmative action is just a conservative way to redress the problem and redeem the promise."

And that promise grows dimmer with each day.

Black Voting in Mississippi

Bell Gale Chevigny

In 1964, hundreds of black and white students went to Mississippi to participate in a voter registration drive. In 1994, a Mississippi voter education project invited the Freedom Summer participants to a reunion.

According to Bell Gale Chevigny, although the Freedom Summer effort failed to overthrow Mississippi's discriminatory system in 1964, blacks had secured electoral power by 1994. A few individuals—inspired during Freedom Summer—fought to create black majority voting districts. This enabled hundreds of blacks to be elected to political office. But it has not resulted in improvements in economic prospects for blacks, and only a few young blacks choose not to move away for better employment opportunities.

Chevigny teaches literature at the State University of New York, Purchase. She is the editor of *The Woman and the Myth: Margaret Fuller's Life and Writings*.

Listening to black people in Mississippi as they talked about whether things had changed for the better in the thirty years since Freedom Summer was like hearing every kind of music that's come from this part of America. "Yes and no," they said, and the "No" was as various as the blues.

"No jobs!" was the harsh refrain from a class of students working toward high school equivalency certificates at a community center in Tutwiler. State statistics bear them out: From 1960 to 1990 joblessness among African-Americans went from 7.9 percent to 15.9 percent; over the same period there has been an exodus of blacks from the state, reducing their share of the population from 42 percent to 35.6 percent.

Excerpted from Bell Gale Chevigny, "Still It's a Fight for Power," *The Nation*, August 22, 1994. Reprinted by permission of *The Nation*.

Others lamented the "straying" of children, the loss of family and community strength. They blamed the influx of drugs, a falling away from the church or loss of "spiritual backbone," the persistence of racism and the divisive effects of integration.

The Loss of Community

Some sang a sweeter "back in the sixties" blues about how the community and the civil rights movement used to be one and the same, how people took care of one another. In Mc-Comb, Linda Taylor, a product of the Freedom School and now co-chair of a race relations committee established by the Chamber of Commerce, said it best when describing the influence of her women neighbors as she was coming up: "I could do nothing *but* succeed because these people would not *let* me do anything else." Aurelia Taylor (no relation), who directs a health center in Clarksdale, told me she'd fled the dead-end life of the Delta, swearing she'd never come back, but then she fell in love with the idea of community health. "Besides," she said, "my mother was an activist and always told me to give back to the movement." The movement gave those it touched a sense of obligation and history—but where is it now?

Part of the answer lies with those in Mississippi who said, yes, things had changed for the good in these thirty years. More often than not that "Yes" was like a movement shout: "We got the vote!" I heard people cry in Jackson, in Philadelphia and Kosciusko to the northeast, in McComb to the south and in the towns and hamlets of the Delta northwest—Greenville, Cleveland, Clarksdale, Indianola, Tutwiler and Webb. "We have forty-two black state legislators; that's almost a quarter of them, twenty elected just in 1992!" They fumbled for the latest total of black elected officials throughout the state—700? 800? "Eight hundred ninety," said Constance Slaughter-Harvey, Assistant Secretary of State for Elections, updating her count for this story. These include ninety members of county boards of supervisors, eight sheriffs, forty mayors, 405 municipal council members, 101 school board members and forty judges.

Electoral Challenges

Such an outcome was not dreamed of at the grim end of Freedom Summer. It was to register voters that Bob Moses of the Student Nonviolent Coordinating Committee (SNCC) first came to Mississippi from the North in 1961, breaching the wall that had excluded the state's African-Americans from political life. By 1964, when SNCC invited Northern volunteers for the summer, fewer than 4 percent of blacks had been registered. SNCC shifted strategies and began registering people in an integrated Mississippi Freedom Democratic Party. Excluded from participation by the regular all-white state Democratic Party, the M.F.D.P. argued that they alone had adhered to the rules and demanded their delegation be seated instead of the regulars at the convention in Atlantic City that August. When their delegation was denied seating and given only two at-large places, the civil rights workers walked away in disgust, delegate Fannie Lou Hamer saying memorably, "We didn't come all this way for no two seats!"

How then did the electoral triumphs that people speak of today come to pass? And what kind of social change, if any, have they brought with them? What is the state of community organizing? And to what extent can it bind the community together?

Overturning the electoral process was painstaking work. The M.F.D.P.'s refusal to compromise taught blacks they could defy powerful whites on a matter of principle and not be destroyed. Leslie McLemore, a historian of the Mississippi Freedom Democrats and a professor of political science at Jackson State, said it also made the Democratic Party integrate its process. But when the 1965 Voting Rights Act eased blacks' ability to vote, the state lashed back with vigorous racial gerrymandering. A series of lawsuits, requiring nine trips to the U.S. Supreme Court, preceded the drawing of "electable black districts."

A dynamo in the redistricting process has been the 84-year-old Henry Kirksey. Kirksey's penchant for life-threatening enterprise was clear in 1964 when he ran the Mississippi Free Press and turned over his rented offices to the Freedom Summer project. For this he had to face down the owner's gun between his eyes. "You damn son of a bitch, I ought to blow your head off" is what Kirksey remembers the white man saying. To which he replied, "Why don't you just go on and pull the trigger instead of putting on a show for these people?" The man put down the gun and a few days later ran after Kirksey apologizing, "You made me feel so damn little."

Electoral Successes

Experience with maps in the Army field artillery fitted Kirksey to become the mapmaker for new black districts. He has served as a demographic expert and often a plaintiff in redistricting cases. In his house in Tougaloo, he showed me baroque designs representing his latest effort, the carving of a second electable black Congressional district out of the state. Among those working with him is Bennie Thompson, a movement activist elected to Congress last year after Mike Espy, an African-American who supported the interests of the white planters, was made Secretary of Agriculture.

Kirksey knows firsthand the frustrations of being black and alone in the arenas of white politics. From 1980 to 1988 he served as the first black State Senator since Reconstruction. Then he quit. "I couldn't stand it anymore. There was no chance—there were only two blacks out of fifty-two—of impacting on any of the bills that came through. It was a waste of my time." When people said he shouldn't let go of that job, he said, "Job, hell! I thought it was a *responsibility*! Show you how stupid *I* am!" Yet, always the maverick, he is not above criticizing the fruits of his own labor in drawing up districts meant to redress the skewed black-white ratios. Some current black politicians, he feels, are "coalescing with their fellows" more than fighting tough issues. He told of how some older black legislators resisted the redistricting that resulted in the election of twenty more. "Slave culture is still with us."

Discussion Questions

Chapter 1: The Fight for Rights Begins

1. Denton L. Watson assesses the litigation strategy of the National Association for the Advancement of Colored People during the first half of the twentieth century. What was Martin Luther King Jr.'s strategy? What was the primary difference between the NAACP's strategy and King's later strategy?

2. Martin Luther King Jr. defines the strategy of nonviolence in the civil rights movement. According to King, why was nonviolence necessary in the struggle against segregation?

3. James H. Cone describes the life and philosophy of Malcolm X. Why was Malcolm called a racist during his lifetime? Why did Malcolm reject integration and redemptive love of whites (the strategy of nonviolence)?

4. Forrest R. White details the tactics of southern states in defying desegregation orders. According to White, why was discrimination in northern cities unaffected by the *Brown* decision?

5. John Doar recollects the efforts of the Civil Rights Division to litigate voting rights abuses in southern counties. Why did this strategy achieve only limited success in striking down segregation? In Doar's opinion, what was the chief misfortune of the division's efforts?

Chapter 2: Peaceful Demonstrations and Radical Tactics

1. Ronald Walters outlines the strategy of the sit-in protests conducted by students. Why did adults and established civil rights organizations oppose sit-ins? According to Walters, why was this tactic necessary?

2. David B. Oppenheimer argues that Martin Luther King Jr. lost an important legal opportunity during the protests in Birmingham. What legal strategy did King forgo? Why was the protest march more important to King?

3. James Findlay discusses the involvement of church members in the Freedom Summer voter registration drive. What lessons did these participants learn? In Nicolaus Mills's assessment,

why was the involvement of whites important to the civil rights movement?

4. Mike Miller relates the story of the Mississippi Freedom Democratic Party at the Democratic National Convention of 1964. Why did the MFDP's claim to legitimacy fail at the convention? Why did this produce such disillusionment within the movement?

5. Jan Howard examines closely the strategy of nonviolence. Why was it important for demonstrations to provoke violence by segregationists? Why were demonstrations considered failures if they could not provoke violence?

Chapter 3: From Protest to Politics

1. David J. Garrow compares the Voting Rights Act of 1965 with the Civil Rights Act of 1964. Why was the Voting Rights Act needed after passage of the Civil Rights Act? Why was the Voting Rights Act more important, in Garrow's opinion?

2. William E. Leuchtenburg explores the causes of the southern white backlash against the Democratic Party. In what ways did George McGovern appeal to southern whites to vote Republican? What were Lyndon B. Johnson's reasons for supporting civil rights?

3. Gerald Early describes Martin Luther King Jr.'s efforts to be the moderating figure in the civil rights coalition. Why was King's philosophy of nonviolence inherently radical, according to Early? Why was King rejected as a leader by radicals?

4. James R. Ralph Jr. gives an account of the Chicago movement and the protests for fair housing. What strategy did local Chicago activists favor for the movement? Why did the Southern Christian Leadership Conference's tactics of nonviolent protest fail, in Ralph's estimation?

Chapter 4: The Fight for Rights Continues

1. Denton L. Watson argues that the NAACP should refocus on litigation to fight discrimination. When did the NAACP begin to focus on integration as a goal? Why was this strategy unsuccessful, in Watson's view?

2. Herb Boyd defines affirmative action and outlines the reasons for maintaining it as a federal policy. What was the original goal

of affirmative action? Why is it no longer needed, according to some people? How has it been successful, according to Boyd?

3. Bell Gale Chevigny describes changes in Mississippi since Freedom Summer 1964. What does she identify as positive changes? What changes are still needed? What is the outlook for achieving these changes, in Chevigny's opinion?

Appendix of Documents

Document 1: The Supreme Court Strikes Down White Primaries

In the 1944 case of Smith v. *Allwright,* Texas argued that its state Democratic Party was a private organization that could limit participation in the selection of candidates for political office. The Supreme Court struck down the Texas voting statute, recognizing that it unconstitutionally denied blacks the ballot. The ruling was an important one in the string of decisions striking down segregationist voting practices in southern states.

The United States is a constitutional democracy. Its organic law grants to all citizens a right to participate in the choice of elected officials without restriction by any state because of race. This grant to the people of the opportunity for choice is not to be nullified by a state through casting its electoral process in a form which permits a private organization to practice racial discrimination in the election. Constitutional rights would be of little value if they could be thus indirectly denied. *Lane* v. *Wilson,* 307 U.S. 268, 275.

The privilege of membership in a party may be, as this Court said in *Grovey* v. *Townsend,* 295 U.S. 45, 55, no concern of a state. But when, as here, that privilege is also the essential qualification for voting in a primary to select nominees for a general election, the state makes the action . . . of the party the action of the state. In reaching this conclusion, we are not unmindful of the desirability of continuity of decision in constitutional questions. However, when convinced of former error, this Court has never felt constrained to follow precedent. In constitutional questions, where correction depends upon amendment, and not upon legislative action, this Court throughout its history has freely exercised its power to reexamine the basis of its constitutional decisions. This has long been accepted practice, and this practice has continued to this day. This is particularly true when the decision believed erroneous is the application of a constitutional principle, rather . . . than an interpretation of the Constitution to extract the principle itself. Here, we are applying, contrary to the recent decision in

Grovey v. *Townsend,* the well established principle of the Fifteenth Amendment, forbidding the abridgement by a state of a citizen's right to vote. *Grovey* v. *Townsend* is overruled.

Stanley Forman Reed, *Smith* v. *Allwright* 321 U.S. 649 (1944). Cornell Law Library Legal Information Institute, http://www2.law.cornell.edu.

Document 2: The Supreme Court Strikes Down Segregated Education

In the decision of Brown *v.* Board of Education of Topeka, Kansas, *the Supreme Court reversed its 1896 ruling in the case of* Plessy *v.* Ferguson. *The* Plessy *decision had stated that separate but equal accommodations for blacks and whites were constitutional, thus recognizing the legality of segregation. The* Brown *decision stated that separate educational facilities for whites and blacks were inherently unequal and therefore unconstitutional.*

Today, education is perhaps the most important function of state and local governments. Compulsory school attendance laws and the great expenditures for education both demonstrate our recognition of the importance of education to our democratic society. It is required in the performance of our most basic public responsibilities, even service in the armed forces. It is the very foundation of good citizenship. Today it is a principal instrument in awakening the child to cultural values, in preparing him for later professional training, and in helping him to adjust normally to his environment. In these days, it is doubtful that any child may reasonably be expected to succeed in life if he is denied the opportunity of an education. Such an opportunity, where the state has undertaken to provide it, is a right which must be made available to all on equal terms.

We come then to the question presented: Does segregation of children in public schools solely on the basis of race, even though the physical facilities and other "tangible" factors may be equal, deprive the children of the minority group of equal educational opportunities? We believe that it does.

In *Sweatt* v. *Painter, supra,* in finding that a segregated law school for Negroes could not provide them equal educational opportunities, this Court relied in large part on "those qualities which are incapable of objective measurement but which make for greatness in a law school." In *McLaurin* v. *Oklahoma State Regents, supra,* the Court, in requiring that a Negro admitted to a white graduate school be treated like all other students, again resorted to intangible considerations: ". . . his ability to study, to engage in discussions and exchange views with other students, and, in general, to learn his profession.". . . . Such considerations apply with added force to children in grade and high schools. To separate them from others of similar age and qualifications solely because of their race generates a feeling of inferiority as to their status in the community that may affect their hearts and minds in a way unlikely ever to be undone. The effect of this separation on their educational opportunities was well stated by a finding in the Kansas case by a court which nevertheless felt compelled to rule against the Negro plaintiffs:

Segregation of white and colored children in public schools has a detrimental effect upon the colored children. The impact is greater when it has the sanction of the law, for the policy of separating the races is usually interpreted as denoting the inferiority of the Negro group. A sense of inferiority affects the motivation of a child to learn. Segregation with the sanction of law, therefore, has a tendency to [retard] the educational and mental development of Negro children and to deprive them of some of the benefits they would receive in a racial[ly] integrated school system.

Whatever may have been the extent of psychological knowledge at the time of *Plessy* v. *Ferguson*, this finding is amply supported by modern authority. Any language . . . in *Plessy* v. *Ferguson* contrary to this finding is rejected.

We conclude that, in the field of public education, the doctrine of "separate but equal" has no place. Separate educational facilities are inherently unequal. Therefore, we hold that the plaintiffs and others similarly situated for whom the actions have been brought are, by reason of the segregation complained of, deprived of the equal protection of the laws guaranteed by the Fourteenth Amendment. This disposition makes unnecessary any discussion whether such segregation also violates the Due Process Clause of the Fourteenth Amendment.

Earl Warren, *Brown* v. *Board of Education of Topeka, Kansas* 347 U.S. 483 (1954). Cornell Law Library Legal Information Institute, http://www2.law.cornell.edu.

Document 3: The Supreme Court Decrees Enforcement of Desegregation

One year after its landmark Brown *v.* Board of Education *ruling, the Supreme Court ordered southern school districts to end enforced segregation "with all deliberate speed." Many southern states defied the decree. Not until 1969 did the Supreme Court order immediate compliance with the desegregation ruling.*

While giving weight to these public and private considerations, the courts will require that the defendants make a prompt and reasonable start toward full compliance with our May 17, 1954, ruling. Once such a start has been made, the courts may find that additional time is necessary to carry out the ruling in an effective manner. The burden rests upon the defendants to establish that such time is necessary in the public interest and is consistent with good faith compliance at the earliest practicable date. To that end, the courts may consider problems related to administration, arising from the physical condition of the school plant, the school transportation system, personnel, revision of school districts and attendance areas into compact units to achieve a system of determining admission to the public schools . . . on a nonracial basis, and revision of local laws and regulations which may be necessary in solving the foregoing problems. They will also consider the adequacy of any plans the defendants may propose to meet these problems and to effectuate a transition to a racially nondiscriminatory school system. During this period of transition, the courts will retain jurisdiction of these cases.

The judgments below, except that, in the Delaware case, are accordingly reversed, and the cases are remanded to the District Courts to take such proceedings and enter such orders and decrees consistent with this opinion as are necessary and proper to admit to public schools on a racially nondiscriminatory basis with all deliberate speed the parties to these cases. The judgment in the Delaware case—ordering the immediate admission of the plaintiffs to schools previously attended only by white children—is affirmed on the basis of the principles stated in our May 17, 1954, opinion, but the case is remanded to the Supreme Court of Delaware for such further proceedings as that Court may deem necessary in light of this opinion.

It is so ordered.

Brown v. Board of Education of Topeka, Kansas 349 U.S. 294 (1955). Cornell Law Library Legal Information Institute, http://www2.law.cornell.edu.

Document 4: The Southern Manifesto

In response to the Supreme Court order to desegregate schools, southern politicians took a defiant stand. In Congress a group of southern senators protested the overturning of the Plessy v. Ferguson *ruling and the violation of states' rights.*

In the case of *Plessy* v. *Ferguson* in 1896 the Supreme Court expressly declared that under the 14th amendment no person was denied any of his rights if the States provided separate but equal public facilities. This decision has been followed in many other cases. It is notable that the Supreme Court, speaking through Chief Justice Taft, a former President of the United States, unanimously declared in 1927 in *Lum v. Rice* that the "separate but equal" principle is "within the discretion of the State in regulating its public schools and does not conflict with the 14th amendment."

This interpretation, restated time and again, became a part of the life of the people of many of the States and confirmed their habits, customs, traditions, and way of life. It is founded on elemental humanity and commonsense, for parents should not be deprived by Government of the right to direct the lives and education of their own children.

Though there has been no constitutional amendment or act of Congress changing this established legal principle almost a century old, the Supreme Court of the United States, with no legal basis for such action, undertook to exercise their naked judicial power and substituted their personal political and social ideas for the established law of the land.

This unwarranted exercise of power by the Court, contrary to the Constitution, is creating chaos and confusion in the States principally affected. It is destroying the amicable relations between the white and Negro races that have been created through 90 years of patient effort by the good people of both races. It has planted hatred and suspicion where there has been heretofore friendship and understanding.

Without regard to the consent of the governed, outside agitators are threatening immediate and revolutionary changes in our public-school systems. If done, this is certain to destroy the system of public education in some of the States.

With the gravest concern for the explosive and dangerous condition created by this decision and inflamed by outside meddlers:

We reaffirm our reliance on the Constitution as the fundamental law of the land.

We decry the Supreme Court's encroachments on rights reserved to the States and to the people, contrary to established law, and to the Constitution.

We commend the motives of those States which have declared the intention to resist forced integration by any lawful means.

We appeal to the States and people who are not directly affected by these decisions to consider the constitutional principles involved against the time when they too, on issues vital to them, may be the victims of judicial encroachment.

Even though we constitute a minority in the present Congress, we have full faith that a majority of the American people believe in the dual system of government which has enabled us to achieve our greatness and will in time demand that the reserved rights of the States and of the people be made secure against judicial usurpation.

We pledge ourselves to use all lawful means to bring about a reversal of this decision which is contrary to the Constitution and to prevent the use of force in its implementation.

In this trying period, as we all seek to right this wrong, we appeal to our people not to be provoked by the agitators and troublemakers invading our States and to scrupulously refrain from disorder and lawless acts.

"The Decision of the Supreme Court in the School Cases—Declaration of Constitutional Principles," United States of America Congressional Record, Proceedings and Debates of the 84th Congress, Second Session, vol. 102, part 4, March 11, 1956.

Document 5: The Montgomery Bus Boycott Comes to a Close

Nearly one year after it began, the effort to end discrimination on buses in Montgomery, Alabama, indirectly triumphed. The boycott failed to persuade the bus lines and city leaders to implement a less discriminatory system of seating black and white passengers, but the court appeal filed on behalf of Rosa Parks and others succeeded in striking down Alabama's segregation statute.

For the past year the eyes of the world have been on the Negroes of Montgomery, Alabama, as against great odds they have continued their courageous, stubborn boycott of the city's bus lines, dramatizing their struggle to win equal rights as riders. All the while, in the background, a legal case filed by four Negro women in the city has been quietly making its way up through the courts, challenging the Alabama state laws and the Montgomery city statutes requiring segregation on public buses. By fall it had reached the Supreme Court. On November 13 that court surprised those who predicted it might let the issue simmer for a while by handing down its decision forthwith. It affirmed a lower court ruling that the challenged statutes are invalid because they "violate the due process and equal protection clauses of the 14th Amendment to the Constitution of the United States." Its ruling, of course, applies to all states, all cities. The decision followed those in every other such segregation case that has been brought before the highest court in the land: interstate transportation, public schools, golf courses, parks. As in those cases, it brought denunciation throughout the south, as state officials threatened to enforce segregation on local bus lines no matter what the court decrees. But the decisions will stand; each such test makes their foundations more secure, eventual compliance more certain. As the court spoke, the effectiveness of the boycott in Montgomery was being attested by an action which at the same time sounded its death knell: filing of a petition by the city to halt operation of the car pool organized as an alternative to public transportation. At word of the decision in Washington, Montgomery's Negroes rejoiced ("Now we've won justice !") and predicted that their organized protest, its reason for existence removed, would come to an end. And all around the world, people of color were once again assured that isolated sputterings do not set national policy, that the United States is officially set on a course—undulating perhaps, but undeviating—leading to complete justice and equal justice for *all* its people.

From "Segregation on Intrastate Buses Ruled Illegal," editorial, ©1956 Christian Century Foundation. Reprinted by permission from the November 28, 1956, issue of *The Christian Century.*

Document 6: Why Blacks Can't Wait for Equality

In a February 1961 article, Martin Luther King Jr. urged newly elected President John F. Kennedy to use executive orders, political persuasion, and the influence of his office to fight for civil rights. In a subsequent secret meeting at the White House, Kennedy informed King that he would not pursue civil rights as a primary agenda.

To coordinate the widespread activities on the civil rights front, the President should appoint a Secretary of Integration. The appointee should be of the highest qualifications, free from partisan political obligations, imbued with the conviction that the government of the most powerful nation on earth cannot lack the capacity to accomplish the rapid and complete solution to the problem of racial equality.

These proposals for federal action do not obviate the necessity for the people themselves to act, of course. An Administration of good faith can be strengthened immeasurably by determined popular action. This is the great value of the non-violent direct-action movement that has engulfed the South. On the one hand, it gives large numbers of people a method of securing moral ends through moral means. On the other hand, it gives support and stimulation to all those agencies which have the power to bring about meaningful change. Thousands of courageous students, sitting peacefully at lunch counters, can do more to arouse the Administration to positive action than all of the verbal and written commentaries on governmental laxity put together.

When our government determines to ally itself with those of its citizens who are crusading for their freedom within our borders, and lends the might of its resources creatively and unhesitatingly to the struggle, the blight of discrimination will begin rapidly to fade.

History has thrust upon the present Administration an indescribably important destiny—to complete a process of democratization which our nation has taken far too long to develop, but which is our most powerful weapon for earning world respect and emulation. How we deal with this crucial problem of racial discrimination will determine our moral health as individuals, our political health as a nation, our prestige as a leader of the free world. I can think of few better words for the guidance of the new Administration than those which concluded the 1946 report of the President's Commission on Civil Rights: "The United States is not so strong, the final triumph of the democratic ideal not so inevitable that we can ignore what the world thinks of us or our record." These words are even more apt today than on the day they were written.

Martin Luther King Jr., "Equality Now," *Nation*, February 4, 1961.

Document 7: The Freedom Rides Provoke Violence

The Freedom Rides of 1961 were organized to test southern compliance with the Supreme Court's Boynton v. Virginia decision, which ordered desegregation of interstate transportation accommodations. James Farmer, director of the Congress of Racial Equality, called off the demonstrations when one bus was burned and riders were shot at and beaten outside Montgomery, Alabama. The Student Nonviolent Coordinating Committee then continued the rides all the way to New Orleans, facing more riots and violence.

In 1960 the Supreme Court issued a ruling, in the Boynton case, banning segregation in the terminal facilities used by interstate passengers. Yet, in the months that followed, reports continued to pour into our office indicating that the South was defying the Supreme Court's edict, just as some of the Southern states have defied the Court's school desegregation rulings. It was to close this gap between the interpretation and the implementation of the law that the Freedom Riders rode.

Who were the Freedom Riders? By what right did we seek to "meddle in the South's business"? Ever since the election of Rutherford B. Hayes to the Presidency in 1876, and the bargain with the South which it entailed, the Southern states have maintained that what they do with the Negro is their own business, and "outsiders" have no right to interfere. The Freedom Riders rejected this essentially states' right doctrine of race relations. None of us, in the North or in the South, can afford the moral luxury of unconcern about injustice. Further, the states' rights doctrine is just as outmoded on the domestic scene as Nineteenth Century isolationism is on the international. Today, how can we think of outsiders keeping hands off injustice in Alabama, when outsiders all over the world can be threatened with destruction by events in a far away place like Laos? How would the dead of Korea view Mississippi's claim that only Mississippians have a right to concern themselves with injustice in that state?

So we came from all over the country, from both races and of all ages, to test compliance with the law, to exercise the right of all Americans to use all transportation facilities with the dignity of equality, to shake Americans out of their apathy on this issue and expose the real character of segregation to the pitiless scrutiny of a nation's conscience.

Outsiders? As Americans, from whatever state, all of us are Mississippians and Minnesotans, Carolinians and Californians, Alabamans and Arizonans. No American can afford to ignore the burning bus and the bloody heads of the mob's victims. Who can fail to be stirred by the new convicts for conscience, black and white, who walked with pride into Southern jails, especially in Mississippi, surrendering their own personal freedom in the struggle for a greater freedom for everyone? . . .

Mississippians, born into segregation, are human too. The Freedom Riders' aim is not only to stop the practice of segregation, but somehow to reach the common humanity of our fellow men and bring it to the surface where they can act on it themselves. This is a basic motive behind the Freedom Rides, and nonviolence is the key to its realization.

It is not only that Southerners and other Americans have been shaken in their unjust racial practices, or out of their lethargy. Now, as a result of the Freedom Rides, the world at large, and especially the developing nations of Africa and Asia, have been offered the opportunity of viewing a new, more constructive approach to America's racial dilemma. If the world looks now it will see that many dedicated and conscientious Americans of both races, rather than sweeping the dirt of discrimination under the rug, are striving, at any cost, to remove the dirt from their house. If Africans witnessed our national shame in the necessity for the Freedom Rides, they saw our nation's hope and promise in the fact that there were so many Americans willing to risk their freedom and even their lives to erase that shame.

The world and America saw also the Freedom Riders' challenge to the traditions and fears which have immobilized so many Negroes in Dixie. In terminals in the South, and on the buses, many Negro passengers took the Freedom Riders' cue and dared to sit and ride "first class." This was another purpose of the Rides themselves: to break down the voluntary submission of Negroes to racial injustice, a submission created by generations of suppression with the rope and with fire and with economic reprisal. As I entered the white waiting room in one terminal in the South, a Negro woman passenger from the same bus caught my eye and anxiously beckoned me to follow her into the dingy but safe colored section. Moments later, when she saw me served at the lunch counter in the white section, she joined me for a cup of coffee.

Excerpted from James Farmer, "I Will Save My Soul," *The Progressive*, November 1961, by permission of *The Progressive*, 409 E. Main St., Madison, WI 53703.

Document 8: Civil Disobedience Begins in Birmingham

In defiance of a district court order banning protest demonstrations, black civil rights leaders in Birmingham, Alabama, staged marches on city hall, demanding the right to register to vote. The protests lasted through April and May 1963 and gained national media attention.

The patience of an oppressed people cannot endure forever. The Negro citizens of Birmingham for the last several years have hoped in vain for some evidence of good faith resolution of our just grievances.

Birmingham is part of the United States and we are *bona fide* citizens. Yet the history of Birmingham reveals that very little of the democratic process touches the life of the Negro in Birmingham. We have been segregated racially, exploited economically, and dominated politically. Under the leadership of the Alabama Christian Movement for Human Rights, we sought relief by petition for the repeal of city ordinances requiring segregation and the institution of a merit hiring policy in city employment. We were rebuffed. We then turned to the system of the courts. We weathered set-back after set-back, with all of its costliness, finally winning the terminal, bus, parks and airport cases. The bus decision has been implemented begrudgingly and the parks decision prompted the closing of all municipally-owned recreational facilities with the exception of the zoo and Legion Field. The airport case has been a slightly better experience with the experience of hotel accommodations and the subtle discrimination that continues in the limousine service.

We have always been a peaceful people, bearing our oppression with super-human effort. Yet we have been the victims of repeated violence, not only that inflicted by the hoodlum element but also that inflicted by the blatant misuse of police power. Our memories are seared with painful mob experience of Mother's Day 1961 during the Freedom Rides. For years, while our homes and churches were being bombed, we heard nothing but the rantings and ravings of racist city officials.

The Negro protest for equality and justice has been a voice crying in the wilderness. Most of Birmingham has remained silent, probably out of fear. In the meanwhile, our city has acquired the dubious reputation of being the worst big city in race relations in the United States.

Fred L. Shuttlesworth, "The Birmingham Manifesto," *Freedomways*, vol. 4, no. 1, Winter 1964.

Document 9: Hundreds Are Arrested and Beaten in Birmingham

During the protests in Birmingham, hundreds of blacks marched on city hall, staged sit-ins, and picketed downtown stores to protest continued defiance of desegregation orders. Police attempted to disperse the crowds by turning fire hoses and unleashing dogs on demonstrators. Hundreds of protesters were arrested, filling the jails beyond capacity. King wrote the following letter to urge white clergy and the federal government to take action in the situation.

Oppressed people cannot remain oppressed forever. The yearning for freedom eventually manifests itself, and that is what has happened to the American Negro. Something within has reminded him of his birthright of freedom, and something without has reminded him that it can be gained. Consciously or unconsciously, he has been caught up by the *Zeitgeist*, and with his black brothers of Africa and his brown and yellow brothers of Asia, South America and the Caribbean, the U.S. Negro is moving with a sense of great urgency toward the promised land of racial justice. If one recognizes this vital urge that has engulfed the Negro community, he should readily understand why public demonstrations are taking place. The Negro has many pent-up resentments and latent frustrations, and he must release them. So let him march; let him make prayer pilgrimages to the city hall; let him go on freedom rides—and try to understand why he must do so. If his repressed emotions are not released in nonviolent ways, they will seek expression through violence; this is not a threat but a fact of history. I have not said to my people, "Get rid of your discontent." Rather, I have tried to say that this normal and healthy discontent can be channeled into the creative outlet of nonviolent direct action. And now this approach is being termed extremist.

But though I was initially disappointed at being categorized as an extremist, as I continued to think about the matter I gradually gained a measure of satisfaction from the label. Was not Jesus an extremist for love: "Love your enemies, bless them that curse you, do good to them that hate you, and pray for them which despitefully use you, and persecute you." Was not Amos an extremist for justice: "Let justice roll down like waters and righteousness like an everflowing stream." Was not Paul an extremist for the Christian gospel: "I bear in my body the marks of the Lord Jesus." Was not Martin Luther an extremist: "Here I stand; I can do no other so help me God." And John Bunyan: "I will stay in jail to the end of my days before I make a butchery of my conscience." And Abraham Lincoln: "This nation cannot survive half slave and half free." And Thomas Jefferson: "We hold these truths to be self-evident, that all men are created equal. . . ." So the question is not whether we will be extremists but what kind of extremists we will be. Will we be extremists for hate or for love? Will we be extremists for the preservation of injustice or for the extension of justice? Perhaps the south, the nation and the world are in dire need of creative extremists.

I had hoped that the white moderate would see this need. Perhaps I was too optimistic; perhaps I expected too much. I suppose I should have realized that few members of the oppressor race can understand the deep groans and passionate yearnings of the oppressed race, and still fewer have the vision to see that injustice must be rooted out by strong, persistent and determined action. I am thankful, however, that some of our white brothers have grasped the meaning of this social revolution and committed themselves to it. They are still all too few in quantity, but they are big in quality. Some—such as Ralph McGill, Lillian Smith, Harry

Golden and James McBride Dabbs—have written about our struggle in eloquent and prophetic terms. Others have marched with us down nameless streets of the south. They have languished in filthy, roach-infested jails, suffering the abuse and brutality of policemen who view them as "dirty nigger lovers." Unlike so many of their moderate brothers and sisters, they have recognized the urgency of the moment and sensed the need for powerful "action" antidotes to combat the disease of segregation.

Martin Luther King Jr., "Letter from Birmingham Jail," *Christian Century*, June 12, 1963.

Document 10: Governor Wallace Blocks Integration at the University of Alabama

Under a federal district court order, two black students—James Hood and Vivian Malone—gained admittance to the University of Alabama at Tuscaloosa. Governor George Wallace protested the desegregation order with a defiant statement.

I stand here today, as Governor of this sovereign state, and refuse to willingly submit to illegal usurpation of power by the Central Government. I claim today for all the people of the state of Alabama those rights reserved to them under the Constitution of the United States. Among those powers so reserved and claimed is the right of state authority in the operation of the public schools, colleges and universities. My action does not constitute disobedience to legislative and constitutional provisions. It is not defiance for defiance sake, but for the purpose of raising basic and fundamental constitutional questions. My action is a call for strict adherence to the Constitution of the United States as it was written—for cessation of usurpation and abuses. My action seeks to avoid having state sovereignty sacrificed on the altar of political expediency.

Further, as the Governor of the State of Alabama, I hold the supreme executive power of this state, and it is my duty to see that the laws are faithfully executed. The illegal and unwarranted actions of the Central Government on this day, contrary to the laws, customs and traditions of this state, is calculated to disturb the peace.

I stand before you today in place of thousands of other Alabamians whose presence would have confronted you had I been derelict and neglected to fulfill the responsibilities of my office. It is the right of every citizen, however humble he may be, through his chosen officials of representative government to stand courageously against whatever he believes to be the exercise of power beyond the constitutional rights conferred upon our Federal Government. It is this right which I assert for the people of Alabama by my presence here today.

Again I state—this is the exercise of the heritage of freedom and liberty under the law—coupled with responsible government.

Now, therefore, in consideration of the promises, and in my official capacity as Governor of the State of Alabama, I do hereby make the following solemn proclamation:

Whereas, the Constitution of Alabama vests the supreme executive powers of the state in the Governor as the chief magistrate, and said Constitution requires of the Governor that he take care that the laws be faithfully executed; and,

Whereas, the Constitution of the United States, Amendment 10, reserves to the states respectively or to the people, those powers not delegated to the United States, nor prohibited to the states; and,

Whereas, the operation of the public school system is a power reserved to the State of Alabama under the Constitution of the United States and Amendment 10 thereof; and,

Whereas, it is the duty of the Governor of the State of Alabama to preserve the peace under the circumstances now existing, which power is one reserved to the State of Alabama and the people thereof under the Constitution of the United States and Amendment 10 thereof:

Now, therefore, I, George C. Wallace, as Governor of the State of Alabama, have by my action raised issues between the Central Government and the sovereign State of Alabama, which said issues should be adjudicated in the manner prescribed by the Constitution of the United States; and now being mindful of my duties and responsibilities under the Constitution of the United States, the Constitution of the State of Alabama, and seeking to preserve and maintain the peace and dignity of this state, and the individual freedoms of the citizens thereof, do hereby denounce and forbid this illegal and unwarranted action by the Central Government.

GEORGE C. WALLACE,
Governor of Alabama

"Text of Proclamation by Gov. Wallace," *New York Times*, June 12, 1963.

Document 11: President Kennedy Calls Out the Alabama National Guard

The admittance of two black students to the University of Alabama at Tuscaloosa provoked threats of violence from segregationists. President

John F. Kennedy ordered the Alabama National Guard to preserve the peace and to escort the students onto the campus.

This afternoon, following a series of threats and defiant statements, the presence of Alabama National Guardsmen was required on the University of Alabama to carry out the final and unequivocal order of the United States District Court of the Northern District of Alabama.

That order called for the admission of two clearly qualified young Alabama residents who happened to have been born Negro.

That they were admitted peacefully on the campus is due in good measure to the conduct of the students of the University of Alabama who met their responsibilities in a constructive way.

I hope that every American, regardless of where he lives, will stop and examine his conscience about this and other related incidents.

This nation was founded by men of many nations and backgrounds. It was founded on the principle that all men are created equal, and that the rights of every man are diminished when the rights of one man are threatened.

Today we are committed to a worldwide struggle to promote and protect the rights of all who wish to be free. And when Americans are sent to Vietnam or West Berlin we do not ask for whites only.

It ought to be possible, therefore, for American students of any color to attend any public institution they select without having to be backed up by troops. It ought to be possible for American consumers of any color to receive equal service in places of public accommodation, such as hotels and restaurants, and theaters and retail stores, without being forced to resort to demonstrations in the street. . . .

And it ought to be possible for American citizens of any color to register and to vote in a free election without interference or fear of reprisal.

It ought to be possible, in short, for every American to enjoy the privileges of being American without regard to his race or his color.

Outlines Negroes' Plight

In short, every American ought to have the right to be treated as he would wish to be treated, as one would wish his children to be treated. But this is not the case.

"Transcript of the President's Address," *New York Times*, June 12, 1963.

Document 12: John Lewis Gives a Radical Speech at the March on Washington

At the March on Washington in August 1963, John Lewis, president of the Student Nonviolent Coordinating Committee, planned to give the following speech denouncing as too timid the civil rights legislation pending in Congress. Other participants in the march forced Lewis to tone down the speech.

We march today for jobs and freedom, but we have nothing to be proud of, for hundreds and thousands of our brothers are not here. They have no money for their transportation, for they are receiving starvation wages, or no wages at all.

In good conscience, we cannot support wholeheartedly the administration's civil rights bill, for it is too little and too late. There's not one thing in the bill that will protect our people from police brutality.

This bill will not protect young children and old women from police dogs and fire hoses, for engaging in peaceful demonstrations. This bill will not protect the citizens in Danville, Virginia, who must live in constant fear in a police state. This bill will not protect the hundreds of people who have been arrested on trumped-up charges. What about the three young men in Americus, Georgia, who face the death penalty for engaging in peaceful protest?

The voting section of this bill will not help thousands of black citizens who want to vote. It will not help the citizens of Mississippi, of Alabama and Georgia, who are qualified to vote but lack a sixth-grade education. "ONE MAN, ONE VOTE" is the African cry. It is ours, too. It must be ours.

People have been forced to leave their homes because they dared to exercise their right to register to vote. What is there in this bill to ensure the equality of a maid who earns $5 a week in the home of a family whose income is $100,000 a year?

For the first time in one hundred years this nation is being awakened to the fact that segregation is evil and that it must be destroyed in all forms. Your presence today proves that you have been aroused to the point of action.

We are now involved in a serious revolution. This nation is still a place of cheap political leaders who build their careers on immoral compromises and ally themselves with open forms of political, economic and social exploitation. What political leader here can stand up and say, "My party is the party of principles?" The party of Kennedy is also the party of Eastland. The party of Javits is also the party of Goldwater. Where is *our* party?

In some parts of the South we work in the fields from sunup to sundown for $12 a week. In Albany, Georgia, nine of our leaders have been indicted not by Dixiecrats but by the federal government for peaceful protest. But what did the federal government do when Albany's deputy sheriff beat attorney C.B. King and left him half dead? What did the federal government do when local police officials kicked and assaulted the pregnant wife of Slater King, and she lost her baby?

It seems to me that the Albany indictment is part of a conspiracy on the part of the federal government and local politicians in the interest of expediency.

I want to know, which side is the federal government on?

John Lewis with Michael D'Orso, *Walking with the Wind: A Memoir of the Movement.* New York: Simon & Schuster, 1998.

Document 13: Martin Luther King Jr.'s Speech at the March on Washington

Martin Luther King Jr., president of the Southern Christian Leadership Conference, was the keynote speaker at the March on Washington and the most recognizable figure in the civil rights movement. His speech drew lukewarm response until he began to extemporize about his dream of integration.

So I say to you, my friends, that even though we must face the difficulties of today and tomorrow, I still have a dream. It is a dream deeply rooted in the American dream that one day this nation will rise up and live out the true meaning of its creed—we hold these truths to be self evident, that all men are created equal.

I have a dream that one day on the red hills of Georgia, sons of former slaves and sons of former slave-owners will be able to sit down together at the table of brotherhood.

I have a dream that one day, even the state of Mississippi, a state sweltering with the heat of injustice, sweltering with the heat of oppression, will be transformed into an oasis of freedom and justice.

I have a dream my four little children will one day live in a nation where they will not be judged by the color of their skin but by content of their character. I have a dream today!

I have a dream that one day, down in Alabama, with its vicious racists, with its governor having his lips dripping with the words of interposition and nullification, that one day, right there in Alabama, little black boys and black girls will be able to join hands with little white boys and white girls as sisters and brothers. I have a dream today!

I have a dream that one day every valley shall be exalted, every hill and mountain shall be made low, the rough places shall be made plain, and the crooked places shall be made straight and the glory of the Lord will be revealed and all flesh shall see it together.

This is our hope. This is the faith that I go back to the South with.

With this faith we will be able to hear out of the mountain of despair a stone of hope. With this faith we will be able to transform the jangling discords of our nation into a beautiful symphony of brotherhood.

With this faith we will be able to work together to pray together, to struggle together, to go to jail together, to stand up for freedom together, knowing that we will be free one day. This will be the day when all of God's children will be able to sing with new meaning—"my country 'tis of thee; sweet land of liberty; of thee I sing; land where my fathers died, land of the pilgrim's pride; from every mountain side, let freedom ring"—and if America is to be a great nation, this must become true.

So let freedom ring from the prodigious hilltops of New Hampshire.

Let freedom ring from the mighty mountains of New York.

Let freedom ring from the heightening Alleghenies of Pennsylvania.

Let freedom ring from the snow-capped Rockies of Colorado.

Let freedom ring from the curvaceous slopes of California.

But not only that.

Let freedom ring from Stone Mountain of Georgia.

Let freedom ring from Lookout Mountain of Tennessee.

Let freedom ring from every hill and molehill of Mississippi, from every mountainside, let freedom ring.

And when we allow freedom to ring, when we let it ring from every village and hamlet, from every state and city, we will be able to speed up that day when all of God's children—black men and white men, Jews and Gentiles, Catholics and Protestants—will be able to join hands and to sing in the words of the old Negro spiritual. "Free at last, free at last; thank God Almighty, we are free at last."

Document 14: Fannie Lou Hamer Speaks at the Democratic National Convention

At the Democratic National Convention in Atlantic City, New Jersey, in June 1964, the Mississippi Freedom Democratic Party argued that it should be seated as the legitimate delegation from Mississippi because the regular party had unconstitutionally excluded blacks from voting. Fannie Lou Hamer, an elected representative of the MFDP, told how she had been punished for registering to vote.

Mr. Chairman, and the Credentials Committee, my name is Mrs. Fannie Lou Hamer, and I live at 626 East Lafayette Street, Ruleville, Mississippi, Sunflower County, the home of Senator James O. Eastland, and Senator Stennis.

It was the 31st of August in 1962 that eighteen of us traveled twenty-six miles to the county courthouse in Indianola to try to register to try to become first-class citizens. We was met in Indianola by Mississippi men, highway patrolmens, and they only allowed two of us in to take the literacy test at the time. After we had taken this test and started back to Ruleville, we was held up by the City Police and the State Highway Patrolmen and carried back to Indianola, where the bus driver was charged that day with driving a bus the wrong color.

After we paid the fine among us, we continued on to Ruleville, and Reverend Jeff Sunny carried me four miles in the rural area where I had worked as a timekeeper and sharecropper for eighteen years. I was met there by my children, who told me the plantation owner was angry because I had gone down to try to register. After they told me, my husband came, and said the plantation owner was raising cain because I had tried to register, and before he quit talking the plantation owner came, and said, "Fannie Lou, do you know—did Pap tell you what I said?"

I said, "Yes, sir."

He said, "I mean that," he said. "If you don't go down and withdraw your registration, you will have to leave," said, "Then if you go down and withdraw," he said. "You will—you might have to go because we are not ready for that in Mississippi."

And I addressed him and told him and said, "I didn't try to register for you. I tried to register for myself." I had to leave that same night.

On the 10th of September, 1962, sixteen bullets was fired into the home of Mr. and Mrs. Robert Tucker for me. That same night two girls were shot in Ruleville, Mississippi. Also Mr. Joe McDonald's house was shot in.

And in June, the 9th, 1963, I had attended a voter-registration workshop, was returning back to Mississippi. Ten of us was traveling by the Continental Trailway bus. When we got to Winona, Mississippi, which is Montgomery County, four of the people got off to use the washroom, and two of the people—to use the restaurant—two of the people wanted to use the washroom. The four people that had gone in to use the restaurant was ordered out. During this time I was on the bus. But when I looked through the window and saw they had rushed out, I got off of the bus to see what had happened, and one of the ladies said, "It was a state highway patrolman and a chief of police ordered us out."

I got back on the bus and one of the persons had used the washroom got back on the bus, too. As soon as I was seated on the bus, I saw when they began to get the four people in a highway patrolman's car. I stepped off the bus to see what was happening and somebody screamed from the car that the four workers was in and said, "Get that one there," and when I went to get in the car, when the man told me I was under arrest, he kicked me.

I was carried to the county jail, and put in the booking room. They left some of the people in the booking room and began to place us in cells. I was placed in a cell with a young woman called Miss Euvester Simpson. After I was placed in the cell I began to hear sounds of licks and screams. I could hear the sounds of licks and horrible screams, and I could hear somebody say, "Can you say, yes sir, nigger? Can you say yes, sir?"

And they would say other horrible names. She would say, "Yes, I can say yes, sir."

"So say it."

She says, "I don't know you well enough."

They beat her, I don't know how long, and after a while she began to pray, and asked God to have mercy on those people.

And it wasn't too long before three white men came to my cell. One of these men was a State Highway Patrolman and he asked me where I was from, and I told him Ruleville. He said, "We are going to check this." And they left my cell and it wasn't too long before they came back. He said, "You are from Ruleville all right," and he used a curse word, and he said, "We are going to make you wish you was dead."

I was carried out of that cell into another cell where they had two Negro prisoners. The State Highway Patrolman ordered the first Negro to take the blackjack. The first Negro prisoner ordered me, by orders from the State Highway Patrolman for me, to lay down on a bunk bed on my face, and I laid on my face. The first Negro began to beat, and I was beat by the first Negro until he was exhausted, and I was holding my hands behind me at that time on my left side because I suffered from polio when I was six years old. After the first Negro had beat until he was exhausted, the State Highway Patrolman ordered the second Negro to take the blackjack.

The second Negro began to beat and I began to work my feet, and the State Highway Patrolman ordered the first Negro who had beat to set on my feet to keep me from working my feet. I began to scream and one white man got up and began to beat me in my head and tell me to hush. One white man—my dress had worked up high, he walked over and pulled my dress down—and he pulled my dress back, back up.

I was in jail when Medgar Evers was murdered. . . .

All of this is on account we want to register, to become first-class citizens, and if the Freedom Democratic Party is not seated now, I question America, is this America, the land of the free and the home of the brave where we have to sleep with our telephones off the hooks because our lives be threatened daily because we want to live as decent human beings, in America?

"Thank you."

Quoted in Kay Mills, *This Little Light of Mine: The Life of Fannie Lou Hamer.* New York: E.P. Dutton, 1993.

Document 15: Malcolm X Leaves the Nation of Islam

From the mid-1950s to the end of 1963, black nationalist Malcolm X was the principal spokesman for the Nation of Islam. Suspended from that position in December 1963—reportedly for saying that the assassination of President Kennedy was a case of "the chickens coming home to roost"—Malcolm left the movement in March 1964.

I am going to organize and head a new mosque in New York City, known as the Muslim Mosque, Inc. This gives us a religious base, and the spiritual force necessary to rid our people of the vices that destroy the moral fiber of our community.

Our political philosophy will be black nationalism. Our economic and social philosophy will be black nationalism. Our cultural emphasis will be black nationalism.

Many of our people aren't religiously inclined, so the Muslim Mosque, Inc., will be organized in such manner to provide for the active participation of all Negroes in our political, economic, and social programs, despite their religious or non-religious beliefs.

The political philosophy of black nationalism means: we must control the politics and the politicians of our community. They must no longer take orders from outside forces. We will organize, and sweep out of office all Negro politicians who are puppets for the outside forces.

Our accent will be upon youth: we need new ideas, new methods, new approaches. We will call upon young students of political science throughout the nation to help us. We will encourage these young students to launch their own independent study, and then give us their analysis and their suggestions. We are completely disenchanted with the old, adult, established politicians. We want to see some new faces—more militant faces.

Concerning the 1964 elections: we will keep our plans on this a secret until a later date—but we don't intend for our people to be the victims of a political sellout again in 1964.

The Muslim Mosque, Inc., will remain wide open for ideas and financial aid from all quarters. Whites can help us, but they can't join us. There can be no black-white unity until there is first some black unity. There can be no workers' solidarity until there is first some racial solidarity. We cannot think of uniting with others, until after we have first united among ourselves. We cannot think of being acceptable to others until we have first proven acceptable to ourselves. One can't unite bananas with scattered leaves.

Concerning nonviolence: it is criminal to teach a man not to defend himself when he is the constant victim of brutal attacks. It is legal and lawful to own a shotgun or a rifle. We believe in obeying the law.

In areas where our people are the constant victims of brutality, and the government seems unable or unwilling to protect them, we should form rifle clubs that can be used to defend our lives and our property in times of emergency, such as happened last year in Birmingham; Plaquemine, Louisiana; Cambridge, Maryland; and Danville, Virginia. When our people are being bitten by dogs, they are within their rights to kill those dogs.

We should be peaceful, law-abiding—but the time has come for the American Negro to fight back in self-defense whenever and wherever he is being unjustly and unlawfully attacked.

If the government thinks I am wrong for saying this, then let the government start doing its job.

Excerpted from *Malcolm X Speaks*, edited by George Breitman (New York: Pathfinder Press, 1993). Copyright ©1965, 1989 by Betty Shabazz and Pathfinder Press. Reprinted by permission.

Document 16: The SCLC's Strategy After the Civil Rights Act of 1964

After achieving the goal of effective civil rights legislation, the Southern Christian Leadership Conference faced the challenge of consolidating its gains and translating them into political power for blacks. Bayard Rustin, one of the founders and the chief strategist of the SCLC, outlined the prospects for the civil rights movement.

Such speculations aside, it is clear that Negro needs cannot be satisfied unless we go beyond what has so far been placed on the agenda. How are these radical objectives to be achieved? The answer is simple, deceptively so: *through political power.*

There is a strong moralistic strain in the civil rights movement which would remind us that power corrupts, forgetting that the absence of power also corrupts. But this is not the view I want to debate here, for it is waning. Our problem is posed by those who accept the need for political power but do not understand the nature of the object and therefore lack sound strategies for achieving it; they tend to confuse political institutions with lunch counters.

A handful of Negroes, acting alone, could integrate a lunch counter by strategically locating their bodies so as *directly* to interrupt the operation of the proprietor's will; their numbers were relatively unimportant. In politics, however, such a confrontation is difficult because the interests involved are merely *represented.* In the execution of a political decision a direct confrontation may ensue (as when federal marshals escorted James Meredith into the University of Mississippi—to turn from an example of non-violent coercion to one of force backed up with the threat of violence). But in arriving at a political decision, numbers and organizations are crucial, especially for the economically disenfranchised. (Needless to say, I am assuming that the forms of political democracy exist in America, however imperfectly, that they are valued, and that elitist or putschist conceptions of exercising power are beyond the pale of discussion for the civil rights movement.)

Neither that movement nor the country's twenty million black people can win political power alone. We need allies. The future of the Negro struggle depends on whether the contradictions of this society can be resolved by a coalition of progressive forces which becomes the *effective* political majority in the United States. I speak of the coalition which staged the March on Washington, passed the Civil Rights Act, and laid the basis for the Johnson landslide—Negroes, trade unionists, liberals, and religious groups.

Bayard Rustin, "From Protest to Politics: The Future of the Civil Rights Movement," *Commentary*, February 1965.

Document 17: King Points Out the Need for the Voting Rights Act of 1965

The Civil Rights Act of 1964 and the reelection of Lyndon B. Johnson were significant victories for the civil rights movement because they ensured the federal government's commitment to the movement's goals. But Martin Luther King Jr. saw that further steps were needed to secure rights for blacks.

The Civil Rights Act was expected by many to suffer the fate of the Supreme Court decisions on school desegregation. In particular, it was thought that the issue of public accommodations would encounter massive defiance. But this pessimism overlooked a factor of supreme importance. The legislation was not a product of charity of white America for a supine black America, nor was it the result of enlightened leadership by the judiciary. This legislation was first written in the streets. The epic thrust of the millions of Negroes who demonstrated in 1963 in hundreds of cities won strong white allies to the cause. Together, they created a "coalition of conscience" which awoke a hitherto somnolent Congress. The legislation was polished and refined in the marble halls of Congress, but the vivid marks of its origins in the turmoil of mass meetings and marches were on it, and the vigor and momentum of its turbulent birth carried past the voting and insured substantial compliance.

Apart from its own provisions, the new law stimulated and focused attention on economic needs. An assault on poverty was planned in 1964, and given preliminary and experimental shape.

The fusing of economic measures with civil rights needs; the boldness to penetrate every region of the Old South; the undergirding of the whole by the massive Negro vote, both North and South, all place the freedom struggle on a new elevated level.

The old tasks of awakening the Negro to motion while educating America to the miseries of Negro poverty and humiliation in their manifold forms have substantially been accomplished. Demonstrations may be limited in the future, but contrary to some belief, they will not be abandoned. Demonstrations educate the onlooker as well as the participant, and education requires repetition. That is one reason why they have not outlived their usefulness. Furthermore, it would be false optimism to expect ready compliance to the new law everywhere. The Negro's weapon of non-violent direct action is his only serviceable tool against injustice. He may be willing to sheath that sword but he has learned the wisdom of keeping it sharp.

Yet new times call for new policies. Negro leadership, long attuned to agitation, must now perfect the art of organization. The movement needs stable and responsible institutions in the communities to utilize the new strength of Negroes in altering social customs. In their furious combat to level walls of segregation and discrimination, Negroes gave primary emphasis to their deprivation of dignity and personality. Having gained a measure of success they are now revealed to be clothed, by comparison with other Americans, in rags. They are housed in decaying ghettos and provided with a ghetto education to eke out a ghetto life. Thus, they are automatically enlisted in the war on poverty as the most eligible combatants. Only when they are in full possession of their civil rights everywhere, and afforded equal economic opportunity, will the haunting race question finally be laid to rest.

What are the key guides to the future? It would not be overoptimistic to eliminate one of the vain hopes of the segregationists—the white backlash. It had a certain reality in 1964, but far less than the segregationists needed. For the most part it was powered by petulance rather than principle. Therefore, when the American people saw before them a clear choice between a future of progress with racial justice or stagnation with ancient privilege, they voted in landslide proportions for justice. President Johnson made a creative contribution by declining to mute this issue in the campaign.

The election of President Johnson, whatever else it might have been, was also an alliance of Negro and white for common interests. Perceptive Negro leadership understands that each of the major accomplishments in 1964 was the product of Negro militancy *on a level that could mobilize and maintain white support*. Negroes acting alone and in a hostile posture toward all whites will do nothing more than demonstrate that their conditions of life are unendurable and that they are unbearably angry. But this has already been widely dramatized. On the other hand, whites who insist upon exclusively determining the time schedule of change will also fail, however wise and generous they feel themselves to be. A genuine Negro-white unity is the tactical foundation upon which past and future progress depends.

Martin Luther King Jr., "'Let Justice Roll Down,'" *Nation*, March 15, 1965.

Document 18: Integration Is an Illusion

Many southern whites held a nostalgic view of the relations between whites and blacks during slavery. They pointed to the ghetto riots taking place in

*northern cities as an indication that blacks enjoyed a happier (though un-
equal) position in southern society than elsewhere in the country.*

It was not until after World War I that many of us began to look
at these matters with a new and suddenly perceptive eye. Little by
little, we are comprehending the injustice inherent in certain ancient customs. Where once we accepted segregation in public
transportation as a simple way of life, now such a practice is widely
viewed as simply absurd. In my own city of Richmond, whites and
Negroes sit indifferently on the buses, where they please, and no
one pays the slightest attention. Most of us were raised to the custom of segregated libraries. The Negroes had branches of their
own. Now the idea of a segregated library seems grotesque. In the
same fashion, we have become accustomed to Negro police,
Negro firemen, Negro clerks, Negro operators of construction
equipment. And all of these changes have been grafted solidly onto
a body of some three hundred years of history.

At the same time we have also comprehended what so many of
our liberal friends refuse to comprehend, that in terms of the
whites' social and cultural values, the Negro people, as a people, are
in truth today not equal to the white people, as a people, and that
overnight "integration," predicated upon imagined equality, is the
cruelest illusion of all. In most rural Southern communities, massive integration of public schools would mean massive calamity.
Where white persons constitute a political minority, as they do in
140 Southern counties, the wholesale extension of the franchise
overnight would mean disruption of order. No law, and no court
decree, in and of itself, can produce "equality." Excluding all arguments about heredity, nothing but time can produce the home en-
vironments that contribute to excellence in education. Today's Negroes are three hundred years from African jungles; but the whites,
by God's grace, are two thousand years from Greece and Rome.

This is, of course, the American dilemma, and the South's
dilemma. As Garry Wills has remarked in *National Review*, the
problem is to acquire the patience "of the bewildered parent who
recognizes himself in the odd behavior of his growing son, and not
expect invariably adult composure from people only now being allowed to exercise some of their legitimate adult rights." The point
is that, by and large, the Negro has not reached social adulthood.
We compound error by pretending that he has; and we should understand that the process of growth and maturity cannot be hur-
ried by artificial stimulations.

James Jackson Kilpatrick, "A Conservative Prophecy: Peace Below, Tumult Above," *Harper's
Magazine*, April 1965.

Document 19: The Need for Affirmative Action

President Lyndon B. Johnson dedicated the federal government to ensuring civil rights for blacks, but he recognized that it would take additional action to help blacks achieve social equality.

Nothing is of greater significance to the welfare and vitality of this nation than the movement to secure equal rights for Negro Americans.

This Administration is dedicated to that movement. It is also dedicated to helping Negro Americans grasp the opportunities that equal rights make possible.

Much has been done—within government and without—to secure equal rights. Much remains to be done if a people enslaved by centuries of bigotry and want are to realize the opportunities of American life.

In June of this year I spoke to the graduating class of Howard University about the condition of most Negroes in America. Before me were those for whom the future was illuminated with hope. My thoughts were of the others—those for whom equality is now but an abstraction.

I said, "You do not take a person who for years has been hobbled by chains and liberate him, bring him up to the starting line of a race, and say, 'you are free to compete with all the others,' and still justly believe that you have been completely fair.

"Thus it is not enough to open the gates of opportunity. All our citizens must have the ability to walk through those gates.

"This is the next and more profound stage of the battle for civil rights . . . the task is to give 20 million Negroes the same choice as every other American to learn and work and share in society, to develop their abilities—physical, mental, and spiritual—and to pursue their individual happiness.". . .

It will not be enough to provide better schools for Negro children, to inspire them to excel in their studies, if there are no decent jobs waiting for them after graduation. It will not be enough to open up job opportunities, if the Negro must remain trapped in a jungle of tenements and shanties. If we are to have peace at home, if we are to speak with one honest voice in the world—indeed, if our country is to live with its conscience—we must affect every dimension of the Negro's life for the better.

We have begun to do that—sometimes haltingly and in great trepidation, sometimes boldly and with a high heart. The will of government and of the people has been committed to resolving the long, bitter trial of the Negro American in the only way that was ever really possible: by including him in our society.

Lyndon B. Johnson, "Foreword to the Issue," *Daedalus*, vol. 94, no. 4, Fall 1965.

Document 20: Black Power

In 1966 the Student Nonviolent Coordinating Committee voted to exclude whites and to abandon the path of nonviolence as defined by Martin Luther King Jr. Stokely Carmichael, an early advocate of militant black power, became the organization's new president.

Black power can be clearly defined for those who do not attach the fears of white America to their questions about it. We should begin with the basic fact that black Americans have two problems: they are poor and they are black. All other problems arise from this two-sided reality: lack of education, the so-called apathy of black men. Any program to end racism must address itself to that double reality.

Almost from its beginning, SNCC sought to address itself to both conditions with a program aimed at winning political power for impoverished Southern blacks. We had to begin with politics because black Americans are a propertyless people in a country where property is valued above all. We had to work for power, because this country does not function by morality, love, and nonviolence, but by power. Thus we determined to win political power, with the idea of moving on from there into activity that would have economic effects. With power, the masses could *make or participate in making* the decisions which govern their destinies, and thus create basic change in their day-to-day lives.

But if political power seemed to be the key to self-determination, it was also obvious that the key had been thrown down a deep well many years earlier. Disenfranchisement, maintained by racist terror, makes it impossible to talk about organizing for political power in 1960. The right to vote had to be won, and SNCC workers devoted their energies to this from 1961 to 1965. They set up voter registration drives in the Deep South. They created pressure for the vote by holding mock elections in Mississippi in 1963 and by helping to establish the Mississippi Freedom Democratic Party (MFDP) in 1964. That struggle was eased, though not won, with the passage of the 1965 Voting Rights Act. SNCC workers could then address themselves to the question: "Who can we vote for, to have our needs met—how do we make our vote meaningful?"

SNCC had already gone to Atlantic City for recognition of the

Mississippi Freedom Democratic Party by the Democratic convention and been rejected; it had gone with the MFDP to Washington for recognition by Congress and been rejected. In Arkansas, SNCC helped thirty Negroes to run for School Board elections; all but one were defeated, and there was evidence of fraud and intimidation sufficient to cause their defeat. In Atlanta, Julian Bond ran for the state legislature and was elected—twice—and unseated—twice. In several states, black farmers ran in elections for agricultural committees which make crucial decisions concerning land use, loans, etc. Although they won places on a number of committees, they never gained the majorities needed to control them.

All of the efforts were attempts to win black power. Then, in Alabama, the opportunity came to see how blacks could be organized on an independent party basis. An unusual Alabama law provides that any group of citizens can nominate candidates for county office and, if they win 20 per cent of the vote, may be recognized as a county political party. The same then applies on a state level. SNCC went to organize in several counties such as Lowndes, where black people—who form 80 per cent of the population and have an average annual income of $943—felt they could accomplish nothing within the framework of the Alabama Democratic Party because of its racism and because the qualifying fee for this year's elections was raised from $50 to $500 in order to prevent most Negroes from becoming candidates. On May 3, five new county "freedom organizations" convened and nominated candidates for the offices of sheriff, tax assessor, members of the school boards. These men and women are up for election in November—if they live until then. Their ballot symbol is the black panther: a bold, beautiful animal, representing the strength and dignity of black demands today. A man needs a black panther on his side when he and his family must endure—as hundreds of Alabamians have endured—loss of job, eviction, starvation, and sometimes death, for political activity. He may also need a gun and SNCC reaffirms the right of black men everywhere to defend themselves when threatened or attacked. As for initiating the use of violence, we hope that such programs as ours will make that unnecessary; but it is not for us to tell black communities whether they can or cannot use any particular form of action to resolve their problems. Responsibility for the use of violence by black men, whether in self defense or initiated by them, lies with the white community.

Excerpted from Stokely Carmichael, "What We Want," *New York Review of Books*, September 22, 1966.

Document 21: The Death of Martin Luther King Jr.

Martin Luther King Jr. was assassinated on April 4, 1968, in Memphis, Tennessee, where he was leading a protest in conjunction with a strike by black garbage workers. Morehouse College president emeritus Benjamin E. Mays published the following eulogy.

Although there are some who rejoice in his death, there are millions across the length and breadth of this world who are smitten with grief that this friend of mankind—all mankind—has been cut down in the flower of his youth. . . .

Let it be thoroughly understood that our deceased brother did not embrace non-violence out of fear or cowardice. Moral courage was one of his noblest virtues. As Mahatma Gandhi challenged the British Empire without a sword and won, Martin Luther King Jr. challenged the interracial wrongs of his country without a gun. And he had faith to believe that he would win the battle for social justice. I make bold to assert that it took more courage for King to practice nonviolence than it took his assassin to fire the fatal shot.

He was severely criticized for his opposition to the war in Vietnam. It must be said, however, that one could hardly expect a prophet of Dr. King's commitments to advocate nonviolence at home and violence in Vietnam. Nonviolence to King was total commitment not only in solving the problems of race in the United States, but in solving the problems of the world. . . .

We all pray that the assassin will be apprehended and brought to justice. But make no mistake, the American people are in part responsible for Martin Luther King Jr.'s death. The Memphis officials must bear some of the guilt for Martin Luther's assassination. The strike should have been settled several weeks ago.

If we love Martin Luther King Jr., and respect him, as this crowd testifies, let us see to it that he did not die in vain; let us see to it that we do not dishonor his name by trying to solve our problems through rioting in the streets.

But let us see to it also that the conditions that cause riots are promptly removed, as the President of the United States is trying to get us to do. Let black and white alike search their hearts; and if there be any prejudice in our hearts against any racial or ethnic group, let us exterminate it and let us pray, as Martin Luther King Jr. would pray if he could: "Father, forgive them for they know not what they do."

If we do this, Martin Luther King Jr. will have died a redemptive death from which all mankind will benefit. . . .

I close by saying to you what Martin Luther King Jr. believed, that if physical death was the price he had to pay to rid America of prejudice and injustice, nothing could be more redemptive. To paraphrase the words of the immortal John Fitzgerald Kennedy, permit me to say that Martin Luther King Jr.'s unfinished work on earth must truly be our own.

Excerpted from the *Negro History Bulletin*, vol. 31, no. 5, May 1968. Used by permission of the Moorland Spingarn Research Center, Washington, D.C.

Document 22: Desegregation of the Armed Forces

During World War II, President Harry S Truman ordered the creation of some integrated units within the armed services. In 1948, he ordered the total desegregation of all the armed services.

EXECUTIVE ORDER 9981
Establishing the President's Committee on Equality of Treatment and Opportunity in the Armed Services

Whereas it is essential that there be maintained in the armed services of the United States the highest standards of democracy, with equality of treatment and opportunity for all those who serve in our country's defense:

Now therefore, by virtue of the authority vested in me as President of the United States, by the Constitution and the statutes of the United States, and as Commander in Chief of the armed services, it is hereby ordered as follows:

1. It is hereby declared to be the policy of the President that there shall be equality of treatment and opportunity for all persons in the armed services without regard to race, color, religion or national origin. This policy shall be put into effect as rapidly as possible, having due regard to the time required to effectuate any necessary changes without impairing efficiency or morale.

2. There shall be created in the National Military Establishment an advisory committee to be known as the President's Committee on Equality of Treatment and Opportunity in the Armed Services, which shall be composed of seven members to be designated by the President.

3. The Committee is authorized on behalf of the President to examine into the rules, procedures and practices of the armed services in order to determine in what respect such rules, procedures and practices may be altered or improved with a view to carrying out the policy of this order. The Committee shall confer and advise with the Secretary of the Air Force, and shall make such recommendations to the President and to said Secretaries as in the

judgement of the Committee will effectuate the policy hereof.

4. All executive departments and agencies of the Federal Government are authorized and directed to cooperate with the Committee in its work, and to furnish the Committee such information or the services of such persons as the Committee may require in the performance of its duties.

5. When requested by the Committee to do so, persons in the armed services or in any of the executive departments and agencies of the Federal Government shall testify before the Committee and shall make available for the use of the Committee such documents and other information as the Committee may require.

6. The Committee shall continue to exist until such time as the President shall terminate its existence by Executive Order.

Harry S. Truman

Source: Fed. Register 13 (1948): 4313.

President Harry S. Truman, Executive Order 9981 (1948), Federal Register 13 (1948): 4313. Published on Civnet: http://www.civnet.org/resources/teach/basic/part6/35.htm.

Document 23: The Civil Rights Act of 1964

After the assassination of John F. Kennedy, President Lyndon B. Johnson vowed to pass strong civil rights legislation to memorialize the ideals of the slain civil rights champion. Title II of the new legislation barred discrimination in public accommodations.

CIVIL RIGHTS ACT
Title II

Sec. 201. (a) All persons shall be entitled to the full and equal enjoyment of the goods, services, facilities, privileges, advantages, and accommodations of any place of public accommodation, as defined in this section, without discrimination or segregation on the ground of race, color, religion, or national origin.

(b) Each of the following establishments which serves the public is a place of public accommodation within the meaning of this title if its operations affect commerce, or if discrimination or segregation by it is supported by State action:

(1) any inn, hotel, motel, or other establishment which provides lodging to transient guests, other than an establishment located within a building which contains not more than five rooms for rent or hire and which is actually occupied by the proprietor of such establishment as his residence;

(2) any restaurant, cafeteria, lunchroom, lunch counter, soda fountain, or other facility principally engaged in selling food for consumption on the premises, including, but not limited to, any

such facility located on the premises of any retail establishment; or any gasoline station;

(3) any motion picture house, theater, concert hall, sports arena, stadium or other place of exhibition or entertainment; and

(4) any establishment (a)(i) which is physically located within the premises of any establishment otherwise covered by this subsection, or (ii) within the premises of which is physically located any such covered establishment, and (b) which holds itself out as serving patrons of such covered establishment.

(c) The operations of an establishment affect commerce within the meaning of this title if (1) it is one of the establishments described in paragraph (1) of subsection (b); (2) in the case of an establishment described in paragraph (2) of subsection (b), it serves or offers to serve interstate travelers or a substantial portion of the food which it serves, or gasoline or other products which it sells, has moved in commerce; (3) in the case of an establishment described in paragraph (3) of subsection (b), it customarily presents films, performances, athletic teams, exhibitions, or other sources of entertainment which move in commerce; and (4) in the case of an establishment described in paragraph (4) of subsection (b), it is physically located within the premises of, or there is physically located within its premises, an establishment the operations of which affect commerce within the meaning of this subsection. For purposes of this section, "commerce" means travel, trade, traffic, commerce, transportation, or communication among the several States, or between the District of Columbia and any State, or between any foreign country or any territory or possession and any State or the District of Columbia, or between points in the same State but through any other State or the District of Columbia or a foreign country.

(d) Discrimination or segregation by an establishment is supported by State action within the meaning of this title if such discrimination or segregation (1) is carried on under color of any law, statute, ordinance, or regulation; or (2) is carried on under color of any custom or usage required or enforced by officials of the State or political subdivision thereof; or (3) is required by action of the State or political subdivision thereof. . . .

(e) The provisions of this title shall not apply to a private club or other establishment not in fact open to the public, except to the extent that the facilities of such establishment are made available to the customers or patrons of an establishment within the scope of subsection (b).

Sec. 202. All persons shall be entitled to be free, at any establishment or place, from discrimination or segregation of any kind on the ground of race, color, religion, or national origin, if such discrimination or segregation is or purports to be required by any law, statute, ordinance, regulation, rule, or order of a State or any agency or political subdivision thereof.

Sec. 203. No person shall (a) withhold, deny, or attempt to withhold or deny, or deprive or attempt to deprive, any person of any right or privilege secured by section 201 or 202, or (b) intimidate, threaten, or coerce, or attempt to intimidate, threaten, or coerce any person with purpose of interfering with any right or privilege secured by section 201 or 202, or (c) punish or attempt to punish any person for exercising or attempting to exercise any right or privilege secured by section 201 or 202.

Source: U.S. Statutes at Large 78 (1964): 241.

Civil Rights Act (1964), Title II. U.S. Statutes at Large 78 (1964): 241. Published on Civnet: http://www.civnet.org/resources/teach/basic/part6/39.htm.

Chronology

December 1946
President Harry S. Truman creates the President's Committee on Civil Rights, which issues the report *To Secure These Rights.*

July 1948
President Truman establishes the Fair Employment Practices Commission to ensure fair hiring practices for blacks in civil service positions; Truman also orders desegregation of the armed services.

June 1950
In *McLaurin* v. *Oklahoma State Regents* and *Sweatt* v. *Painter,* the Supreme Court strikes down classroom and social segregation in graduate education programs, ruling that they violate the Fourteenth Amendment's equal protection clause.

May 1954
Ruling in *Brown* v. *Board of Education of Topeka, Kansas,* and associated cases, the Supreme Court overturns state-enforced segregation in schools. It reverses the 1896 decision of *Plessy* v. *Ferguson* and the doctrine of "separate but equal" in public accommodations.

July 1954
The first White Citizens Council is established in Indianola, Mississippi, to organize white supremacist opposition to desegregation.

May 1955
After hearing further arguments in the *Brown* v. *Board of Education* cases, the Supreme Court orders southern states to implement desegregation with "all deliberate speed."

October 1955
The Supreme Court orders the University of Alabama to admit Autherine Lucy, a young black woman. After rioting by white students, the university expels Lucy.

December 1955
Rosa Parks is arrested on a Montgomery, Alabama, bus after she refuses to vacate her seat for white passengers. Black community leaders quickly organize the Montgomery Improvement Associa-

tion to direct a boycott of the city's buses. The boycott lasts more than a year, during which time the homes of Martin Luther King Jr., Fred Shuttlesworth, and other leaders are bombed by the Ku Klux Klan.

March 1956
Southern congressmen sign the Declaration of Principles—the "Southern Manifesto"—which urges resistance to federal desegregation orders.

January 1957
The Southern Christian Leadership Conference (SCLC) is organized to lead the civil rights movement in the South.

September 1957
Congress passes the Civil Rights Act of 1957, which creates the Civil Rights Division within the Justice Department.

September 24, 1957
President Dwight D. Eisenhower sends federal troops to escort nine black students into Little Rock Central High School. On September 4, Governor Orval Faubus had called out the Arkansas National Guard to block the students' entrance.

February 1960
Four black college students stage a sit-in at the Woolworth's lunch counter in Greensboro, North Carolina. The demonstration gains national media attention, and sit-in protests spread throughout the South.

February 1960
In *Gomillion* v. *Lightfoot*, the Supreme Court rules that redistricting in Tuskegee, Alabama, is unconstitutional because it excludes black voters.

April 1960
The Student Nonviolent Coordinating Committee (SNCC) is organized with Marion Barry as chairman.

May 1960
President Eisenhower signs the Civil Rights Act of 1960, which authorizes federal judges to appoint referees to oversee black voter registration in southern counties.

October 1960
Martin Luther King Jr. and others are arrested in Atlanta during a sit-in. Robert Kennedy secures King's release from the Georgia State Prison.

December 1960
In *Boynton v. Virginia*, the Supreme Court strikes down segregation in interstate bus and railroad facilities.

March 1961
President John F. Kennedy orders the establishment of the federal Equal Employment Opportunities Commission to enforce fair hiring practices.

May 1961
James Farmer, executive director of the Congress of Racial Equality, organizes Freedom Rides from Washington, D.C., to New Orleans to test southern states' compliance with the *Boynton* decision. When the riders are violently attacked and one bus is burned near Montgomery, Alabama, Farmer disbands the rides. SNCC volunteers take over, but they—along with an assistant attorney general from the Civil Rights Division—are beaten by a white mob in Birmingham, Alabama, as police stand by and watch.

November 1961
Civil rights activists in Albany, Georgia, organize the Albany movement to agitate for voting rights and desegregation. Despite numerous nonviolent demonstrations and marches, the movement ends the following August without achieving its goals.

August 1962
SNCC opens voter registration schools in Mississippi to teach blacks to pass voter registration tests.

October 1962
James Meredith becomes the first black student admitted to the University of Mississippi, leading to the most violent campus riot of the decade. President Kennedy places the Mississippi National Guard under federal jurisdiction to quell the violence.

April–May 1963
In Birmingham, Alabama, hundreds of demonstrators march on city hall, picket stores, and stage sit-ins to protest continued segregation.

Police chief Eugene "Bull" Connor disperses the demonstrators with police dogs and fire hoses. Birmingham's jails are filled with arrested marchers, including hundreds of children and Martin Luther King Jr. King publishes "Letter from Birmingham Jail," prodding white churches and the federal government to take action.

June 1963

Governor George Wallace stands in the doorway of a University of Alabama building to symbolically block the admission of two black students. President Kennedy orders the Alabama National Guard to clear the way.

June 12, 1963

Medgar Evers, field secretary of the NAACP, is murdered in Jackson, Mississippi.

August 28, 1963

The March on Washington for Jobs and Freedom draws a quarter million marchers to the Lincoln Memorial to demand federal civil rights legislation. King delivers his "I Have a Dream" speech.

November 22, 1963

President John F. Kennedy is assassinated in Dallas, Texas.

April 1964

SNCC workers—frustrated with the slow progress of voter registration efforts—found the Mississippi Freedom Democratic Party.

June 1964

James Chaney—a young black activist—and Andrew Goodman and Michael Schwerner—two white students—are murdered in Philadelphia, Mississippi, at the beginning of the Freedom Summer voter registration drive.

July 1964

The Civil Rights Act of 1964 bars discrimination in public accommodations and in hiring. Race riots erupt in Harlem and Brooklyn.

July 22–27, 1964

The Mississippi Freedom Democratic Party challenges the legitimacy of the all-white Mississippi delegation at the Democratic National Convention in Atlantic City.

February 21, 1965
Malcolm X is assassinated in New York.

March 7, 1965
Civil rights demonstrators are attacked and beaten by state troopers on the Edmund Pettus Bridge outside Selma, Alabama, as they begin a march to Montgomery to demand the right to register and vote. Later in the month, they are permitted to complete the march under federal military protection. Several demonstrators are murdered by the Klan.

August 1965
The largest race riot ever occurs in the Watts neighborhood of Los Angeles.

January 1966
The SCLC organizes marches as part of the Chicago movement for fair housing. The protests are unsuccessful. SNCC becomes the first civil rights organization to state formal opposition to the war in Vietnam.

May 1966
Stokely Carmichael becomes chairman of SNCC, which adopts the Black Power creed and later in the year expels white members.

July 1967
Thurgood Marshall becomes the first black Supreme Court justice.

April 4, 1968
Martin Luther King Jr. is assassinated in Memphis, Tennessee.

April 1968
Congress passes the Civil Rights Act of 1968, which bars discrimination in housing.

August 1969
President Richard M. Nixon orders federal agencies to implement affirmative action programs.

October 1969
In *Alexander v. Holmes*, the Supreme Court orders southern school districts to desegregate "at once."

For Further Research

Books

Ralph D. Abernathy, *And the Walls Came Tumbling Down: An Autobiography.* San Francisco: HarperCollins, 1989.

Jervis Anderson, *Bayard Rustin: Troubles I've Seen: A Biography.* San Francisco: HarperCollins, 1997.

Harry S. Ashmore, *Civil Rights and Wrongs: A Memoir of Race and Politics.* New York: Pantheon, 1994.

Taylor Branch, *Pillar of Fire: America in the King Years, 1963–1965.* New York: Simon & Schuster, 1998.

Clarice T. Campbell, *Civil Rights Chronicle: Letters from the South.* Jackson: University Press of Mississippi, 1997.

Clayborne Carson, ed., *The Movement, 1964–1970.* New York: Greenwood, 1993.

David L. Chappell, *Inside Agitators: White Southerners in the Civil Rights Movement.* Baltimore: Johns Hopkins University Press, 1994.

E. Culpepper Clark, *The Schoolhouse Door: Segregation's Last Stand at the University of Alabama.* New York: Oxford University Press, 1993.

Townsend Davis, *Weary Feet, Rested Souls: A Guided History Through the Civil Rights Movement.* New York: W.W. Norton, 1998.

Tom Dent, *Southern Journey: My Return to the Civil Rights Movement.* New York: William Morrow, 1997.

John Dittmer, *Local People: The Struggle for Civil Rights in Mississippi.* Champaign: University of Illinois Press, 1994.

John Egerton, *Speak Now Against the Day: The Generation Before the Civil Rights Movement in the South.* New York: Knopf, 1994.

Charles Evers, *Have No Fear: The Charles Evers Story.* New York: John Wiley & Sons, 1996.

James Findlay, *Church People in the Struggle: The National Council of Churches and the Black Freedom Movement, 1950–1970.* New York: Oxford University Press, 1993.

David Halberstam, *The Children.* New York: Knopf, 1998.

Martin Luther King Jr., *Papers of Martin Luther King, Jr.* Ed. Clayborne Carson. Berkeley and Los Angeles: University of California Press, 1997.

John Lewis and Michael D'Orso, *Walking with the Wind: A Memoir of the Movement.* New York: Simon & Schuster Trade, 1998.

Thurgood Marshall, *Dream Makers, Dream Breakers: The World of Justice.* Boston: Little, Brown, 1993.

Douglas McAdam, *Freedom Summer.* New York: Oxford University Press, 1990.

Kay Mills, *This Little Light of Mine: The Life of Fannie Lou Hamer.* New York: NAL Dutton, 1993.

Nicolaus Mills, *Like a Holy Crusade: Mississippi, 1964—The Turning of the Civil Rights Movement in America.* New York: Ivan R. Dee, 1992.

James Ralph, *Northern Protest: Martin Luther King, Jr., Chicago, and the Civil Rights Movement.* Cambridge, MA: Harvard University Press, 1993.

John A. Salmond, *My Mind Set on Freedom: A History of the Civil Rights Movement, 1954–1968.* New York: Ivan R. Dee, 1997.

Harvard Sitkoff, *The Struggle for Black Equality, 1954–1992.* Ed. Eric Foner. New York: Hill & Wang, 1993.

Robert Weisbrot, *Freedom Bound.* New York: W.W. Norton, 1989.

Andrew J. Young, *An Easy Burden: The Civil Rights Movement and the Transformation of America.* San Francisco: HarperCollins, 1996.

Periodicals

Marie Brenner, "Judge Motley's Verdict," *New Yorker,* May 16, 1994.

John Cloud, "The KGB of Mississippi," *Time,* March 30, 1998.

Richard Conniff, "Frederick Douglass Always Knew He Was Meant to Be Free," *Smithsonian,* February 1995.

Ellis Cose, "The Voting Rights Act: A Troubled Past," *Newsweek,* June 14, 1993.

Marshall Frady, "The Children of Malcolm," *New Yorker,* October 12, 1992.

David J. Garrow, "Marshall, Hoover, and the NAACP," *Newsweek,* December 16, 1996.

James N. Giglio, "Kennedy," *American Visions*, February/March 1995.

David Halberstam, "And Now, Live from Little Rock," *Newsweek*, September 29, 1997.

Benjamin T. Harrison, "Impact of the Vietnam War and the Civil Rights Movement in the Midsixties," *Studies in Conflict and Terrorism*, July–September 1996.

Kristen L. Hays, "Topeka Comes Full Circle," *Modern Maturity*, April/May 1994.

John R. Howard, "The Making of a Black Muslim," *Society*, January/ February 1998.

Murray Kempton, "The High Cost of Victory," *New York Review of Books*, June 27, 1991.

Joe Klein, "The Legacy of Summerton," *Newsweek*, May 16, 1994.

Michael S. Mayer, "Ike in Office," *American Visions*, February/ March 1995.

Keith Weldon Medley, "The Sad Story of How 'Separate but Equal' Was Born," *Smithsonian*, February 1994.

James Meredith, "A Challenge to Change," *Newsweek*, October 6, 1997.

Lamar P. Miller, "A Brown-Out Since 1954?" *Education Digest*, April 1996.

Charles Edwards O'Neill, "Separate but Never Equal," *America*, April 1, 1995.

Michael Riley, "Confessions of a Former Segregationist," *Time*, March 2, 1992.

James Traub, "Separate and Equal," *Atlantic Monthly*, September 1991.

Tim Unsworth, "Murder in Black and White," *U.S. Catholic*, March 1998.

Bernard A. Weisberger, "Dreams Deferred," *American Heritage*, March 1990.

Sean Wilentz, "The Last Integrationist: John Lewis's American Odyssey," *New Republic*, July 1, 1996.

Charles Reagan Wilson, "Church Burnings and Christian Community," *Christian Century*, September 25–October 2, 1996.

Index

Aaron, Henry, 133
Abernathy, Ralph, 57
Abrams, Willie, 214–15, 218
Adetimirin, Aziz Gueye, 224–25
affirmative action
  defined, 222–23
  and economic inequality, 226–27
  lack of political support for, 226
  personal stories on, 224–25
  and quotas, 223
  whites and, 228
  white women and, 225–26
African Americans
  Americanization of, 194–95
  and "black power," 152–53
  bonding with white church
    members, 143–44
  drafted for Vietnam War, 208–209
  excluded from voting, 175–76
  on housing discrimination, 205
  inequality and, 226–27
  integration with whites, 139–40,
    145–47
  and Jim Crow system, 14–16
  Malcolm X's influence on, 62–63,
    69
  in Mississippi, 229
  murder of, 31, 82, 95–97, 179
  nationalism of, 65–67, 194
  opposition to Vietnam War,
    209–11
  opposition to whites in Freedom
    Summer, 132–37
  in popular culture, 196
  self-segregation by, 215
  struggle for freedom, 58–59
  turning away from King, 198–99
  white ministers' respect for,
    144–46
  see also civil rights movement;
    segregation
Alabama
  civil disobedience in, 119–21
  segregation in, 118
  voter qualifications in, 91
  voter registration in, 102–103
  voter rights enforced in, 92–93, 94

after Voting Rights Bill, 105–106
  see also Birmingham movement;
    Selma march
Alabama Christian Movement for
  Human Rights, 119
Alabama National Guard, 29
Albany, Georgia, 28
Allen, Louis, 96–97
American Airlines, 224
American Dilemma, An (Myrdal), 18,
  194
American Federation of Labor, 18,
  39
Anthony, Wendell, 227–28

Baez, Joan, 196
Baker, Wilson, 105, 106
Baldwin, James, 168, 199
Barnett, Ross, 29, 86
Barrett, St. John, 91
Barton, Billy, 83–84
Beckwith, Byron De La, 82
Bell, Daniel, 193
Bell, Griffin, 97, 98
Bethune, Mary McLeod, 41
Bevel, James, 122, 210
Bilbo, Gilmore, 42
Birmingham movement, 28–29,
  119–21
  children of, 122–23
  success of, 123–24
Black Legion, 63
Black Panther Party, 34
"black power," 34, 152–53
Blair, Ezell, 116
Blake, Eugene Carson, 129–30
Bloody Sunday, 33
Blumrosen, Aldred, 228
Boggs, Hale, 187–88
Bolling, Spottswood, 20
Bolling v. Sharpe, 20
bombings, 23, 30
  and Montgomery bus boycott,
    54–55
boycotts
  of Birmingham businesses, 119,
    124

278